THE ELEMENTS OF BANKRUPTCY

FOURTH EDITION

DOUGLAS G. BAIRD

HARRY A. BIGELOW DISTINGUISHED SERVICE PROFESSOR
THE UNIVERSITY OF CHICAGO

NEW YORK, NEW YORK
FOUNDATION PRESS
2006

Cover Design: Keith Stout

Cover Art: Paul Klee, "Composition With Triangles"

Foundation Press, of Thomson/West, has created this publication to provide you with accurate and authoritative information concerning the subject matter covered. However, this publication was not necessarily prepared by persons licensed to practice law in a particular jurisdiction. Foundation Press is not engaged in rendering legal or other professional advice, and this publication is not a substitute for the advice of an attorney. If you require legal or other expert advice, you should seek the services of a competent attorney or other professional.

        395 Hudson Street
        New York, NY 10014
        Phone Toll Free 1–877–888–1330
        Fax (212) 367–6799
        fdpress.com
Printed in the United States of America

ISBN–13: 978–1–59941–062–3
ISBN–10: 1–59941–062–1

TEXT IS PRINTED ON 10% POST CONSUMER RECYCLED PAPER

For Walter J. Blum

Contents

Introduction

Modern bankruptcy law is a domain with identifiable and coherent boundaries. In *The Elements of Bankruptcy* I offer an introduction to this world for lawyers and others who want to understand bankruptcy's fundamental rules and principles. My ambition is to show that modern bankruptcy law is at once rich, interesting, and accessible. This edition reflects the state of the law as of October 2005 with the changes brought about by the Bankruptcy Abuse Prevention and Consumer Protection Act of 2005.

The first three chapters chart the landscape. Chapter 1 explores both the substantive provisions of the Bankruptcy Code and the procedural rules that govern bankruptcy cases. Chapter 2 looks at the rights of the individual debtor in bankruptcy. Bankruptcy law gives the individual a fresh start: the "honest but unfortunate" debtor overwhelmed by debt can file a bankruptcy petition and walk away with the right to enjoy future income free from past debt. Ensuring that such individuals enjoy a fresh start while preventing those able to repay their debts from abusing the system introduces considerable complexity into the law.

Chapter 3 examines the absolute priority rule, the basic principle of corporate reorganizations. Corporations enter into bankruptcy for reasons different from those of individuals. Corporations already have limited liability under state law: when a corporation fails, its shareholders are not liable to the corporation or its creditors. By reorganizing under Chapter 11 of the Bankruptcy Code, an ailing but otherwise strong business replaces its existing capital structure with a sensible one that better reflects the condition in which it finds itself. The corporation, like the individual, discharges old debts through bankruptcy, but the reasons for doing so have nothing to do with protecting flesh-and-blood human beings from their creditors.

The different legal problems of financially troubled individuals and corporations are adjudicated in the same place—bankruptcy court—not only for historical reasons but also because they present similar administrative difficulties. In both situations, one needs to hold creditors at bay while sorting through the debtor's affairs, gathering the assets, ascertaining the liabilities, determining wrongdoing (if any), and authoritatively establishing who gets what. The remaining chapters in this book focus on the way in which this process works.

Chapter 4 examines how rights originating outside of bankruptcy are treated inside of bankruptcy. For the most part, a creditor's claim in bankruptcy turns on what the creditor had outside bankruptcy. Chapter 5 shows how the Bankruptcy Code ensures that the debtor's assets available to creditors outside of bankruptcy are available to them inside of bankruptcy as well. Chapter 6 completes our examination of the basic rights and obligations of the debtor and those with whom it has dealt by examining *executory contracts*. An executory contract is one in which each party owes obligations to the other. Hence, it is at once a liability and an asset.

A debtor may not transfer assets while insolvent unless it receives reasonably equivalent value in return, nor may it engage in other activities whose principal effect is to thwart creditors' ability to be repaid. This basic principle of fraudulent conveyance law, thus stated, is uncontroversial, but its effects are far reaching and are essential to police the abuses seen in Enron and other recent cases. It and the related issues of equitable subordination and substantive consolidation are the subject of chapter 7. Chapter 8 examines the law of voidable preferences. When bankruptcy is on the horizon, a debtor is no longer free to choose which creditors to pay. Existing preference law implements this idea through a complicated mixture of rules and standards.

When a bankruptcy petition is filed, creditors must cease their efforts to collect payment, but the debtor must continue to deal with the rest of the world as before. The Bankruptcy Code tries to achieve both ends through the automatic stay, which is the subject of chapter 9. Chapter 10 explores the dynamic of small and large Chapter 11 cases. Most Chapter 11 petitions are filed by small corporations; the challenge in these cases is not to preserve an ongoing business but to facilitate an entrepreneur's transition from one business to another. The corporation is the entity that formally files the petition, but the entrepreneur who owns it is the central focus. Large Chapter 11 cases, in contrast, are few in number but contain the vast bulk of the total assets in bankruptcy. In these cases, the business has an identity distinct from those who run it, and Chapter 11 allows the financially distressed company to obtain a new capital structure in a process akin to a merger or acquisition outside of bankruptcy. The book's final chapter looks at the process of creating and confirming a plan of reorganization.

This idea for this book grew out of my long and fruitful collaboration with Thomas Jackson, who introduced me to bankruptcy law when I was a student. The first edition took shape while I was giving a series of seminars at the law firm of Sonnenschein, Nath, and Rosenthal in the early 1990s. I have continued to learn from long conversations with many splendid judges and lawyers, including Frank Easterbrook, Russell Eisenberg, Richard Levin, Harvey Miller, Ronald Trost, and Eugene Wedoff. Work with a number of colleagues, especially Barry Adler, Donald Bernstein, Edward Morrison, and Robert Rasmussen, has helped me with this, the fourth edition. The careful eye and deft pen of my editor, Leslie Keros, put the manuscript in final form once again. Finally, I am grateful for the research support of the Russell Baker Scholar's Fund, the Lynde and Harry Bradley Foundation, the John M. Olin Foundation, and the Sarah Scaife Foundation.

Chapter One

A Road Map to Bankruptcy Law

The Structure of the Bankruptcy Code

The word *bankruptcy* derives from the medieval Italian custom of breaking the benches of a banker or merchant who absconded and left creditors unpaid. As the roots of the word suggest, the first English bankruptcy statutes were directed at merchant debtors, and they were viciously punitive. Indeed, their harsh character prompted one delegate to the Constitutional Convention in Philadelphia in 1787 to oppose granting Congress the power to enact uniform bankruptcy laws. Under English law, uncooperative bankrupts were hanged, and the Convention delegate feared that Congress might follow suit. For modern lawyers, the very incongruity of bankruptcy and the death penalty suggests, correctly, that bankruptcy law not be linked too closely with its seventeenth- and eighteenth-century English counterparts. We will do better by focusing on the law as it is today and turning to the history of bankruptcy law when appropriate.

The Bankruptcy Code is embodied in Title 11 of the United States Code. Although easily located, bankruptcy law remains a common law discipline in which a lawyer must reason by analogy and constantly be aware of general principles. Bankruptcy law is neither mechanical in its application nor narrow in the range of problems it confronts. A client in bankruptcy can face every legal problem that a person can face outside of bankruptcy.

Bankruptcy law is built on nonbankruptcy law; as a result, the bankruptcy lawyer must understand both the applicable nonbankruptcy law and the ways in which bankruptcy law may change it. An example will help to illustrate this point.

Suppose you represent a computer hardware manufacturer that has a patented process for making computer chips. Your client discovers that a competitor is using its process and that the competitor has also filed a bankruptcy petition. You need to know how the patent would be enforced outside of bankruptcy, and then look at how bankruptcy changes both the underlying right and the manner in which it can be vindicated.

This task is not as formidable as it might seem. Bankruptcy law changes nonbankruptcy law only when the purposes of bankruptcy require it. Ensuring flesh-and-blood individuals a fresh start requires such a change, but surprisingly little else does. In the absence of a specific bankruptcy provision to the contrary, bankruptcy takes nonbankruptcy rights as it finds them. Only the procedures change, and these change only to solve the particular problems bankruptcy is designed to address. The Bankruptcy Code thus works against the background of nonbankruptcy law. A general mandate, reinforced by 28 U.S.C. §959, requires that the trustee act in accordance with applicable nonbankruptcy law. A trustee enjoys the right to use property under §363, but the trustee must act consistently with applicable nonbankruptcy law. The trustee cannot use the debtor's chemistry laboratory to manufacture cocaine, nor may the trustee dump toxic waste on the debtor's property, not because of anything in the Bankruptcy Code but simply because these activities are illegal outside of bankruptcy.

The Supreme Court set forth this principle in *Butner v. United States*:

> Congress has generally left the determination of property rights in the assets of a bankrupt's estate to state law. Property interests are created and defined by state law. Unless some federal interest requires a different result, there is no reason why such interests should be analyzed differently simply because an interested party is involved in a bankruptcy proceeding.[1]

---

[1] Butner v. United States, 440 U.S. 48, 55 (1979).

Butner thus allows us to draw from a complicated statute a single organizing principle. Knowing the outcome under non-bankruptcy law can go a long way toward understanding the problem in bankruptcy. When a litigant seeks an outcome different from the one that would hold outside of bankruptcy, the bankruptcy judge will likely ask the litigant to identify the part of the Bankruptcy Code that compels the departure.

We can begin with a sketch of the basic structure of the Bankruptcy Code. The 1978 Bankruptcy Reform Act restructured the bankruptcy courts and bankruptcy procedure. The substantive provisions of the 1978 Act put in place the Bankruptcy Code, which constitutes Title 11 of the United States Code. It has been amended periodically. The most sweeping change, enacted in 2005, added considerable complexity to the Bankruptcy Code, but its basic structure and principles remain intact. Like other titles of the United States Code, Title 11 is divided into chapters. Chapters 1, 3, and 5 contain provisions that generally apply to all bankruptcy cases. The remaining chapters set out different procedures for distinct kinds of bankruptcy cases. Chapter 15 sets out the principles needed to facilitate cross-border insolvencies, the rules needed when a debtor in the United States has assets in another country or when a foreign debtor has assets here.

The United States Trustee is responsible for overseeing the administration of bankruptcy cases. The United States Trustee should ensure that cases do not languish in bankruptcy court, a fate not uncommon when the stakes are small and no single creditor has the incentive to investigate the debtor. This job is important not only to protect the general creditors but also to ferret out fraud, which often contributes to business failure.

Chapter 1 provides definitions (§101), tells us which parts of the Code apply to which kinds of cases (§103), and sets out eligibility requirements for each kind of bankruptcy case (§109). Chapter 1 also contains what appears to be a broad grant of power to the bankruptcy judge. Bankruptcy was originally in the province of the Chancellor, and §105 reflects these equitable origins. It grants the bankruptcy judge the power to "issue any order, process or judgment that is necessary or appropriate to carry out the provisions" of the Bankruptcy Code. But the section confers no independent powers on the judge. The power that a judge enjoys under §105 must derive ultimately from some other provision of the Bankruptcy Code.[2] Lawyers who advance an argument that relies solely on §105 should expect to lose. As Richard Posner put it, "The fact that a proceeding is equitable does not give the judge a free-floating discretion to redistribute rights in accordance with his personal views of justice and fairness, however enlightened those views may be."[3]

The heart of any code lies in its definitional section, and the definitions in §101 are the focal point of many disputes. The definitions of *creditor* and *claim*, for example, will play a central role in the bankruptcy of a business that faces mass tort liability. Suppose a business sells a product that causes harm many years later. Whether the business can deal with its tort liability in bankruptcy turns on whether these future victims are considered creditors and whether they have claims within the meaning of §101.

Section 101 also introduces us to the language of modern bankruptcy practice. It tells us, for instance, that the person whom a bankruptcy case concerns is a *debtor*. A person or a corporation in bankruptcy is no longer called a *bankrupt*. Although that word retains some currency among lay people, among bankruptcy lawyers it sounds old-fashioned and precious. Section 101 defines most of the terms that apply throughout the Bankruptcy Code, but not all. One of the most important definitions in the Bankruptcy Code, that of *notice and a hearing*, is found in §102, which nominally deals with rules of construction.

---

[2] See In re Kmart Corp., 359 F.3d 866, 871 (7th Cir. 2004); Gillman v. Continental Airlines, 203 F.3d 203 (3d Cir. 2000); Barbieri v. RAJ Acquisition Corp., 199 F.3d 616, 621 (2d Cir. 1999).

[3] In re Chicago, Milwaukee, St. Paul & Pacific Railroad, 791 F.2d 524 (7th Cir. 1986).

Many provisions in the Bankruptcy Code allow actions to take place after notice and a hearing. One should not, however, assume that everyone must receive actual notice or that a hearing is required in every instance. Section 102 tells us that we need to give only "such notice as is appropriate in the particular circumstances." Moreover, if no party requests a hearing or if a court finds there is insufficient time to have one, an actual hearing is not necessary. Over the years, a body of learning has developed around who needs to be notified at each stage and the consequences that follow if they are not.[4] As in many other contexts, the basic principles in bankruptcy track those outside. Most analyses begin with the observation of the Supreme Court in *Mullane v. Central Hanover Bank & Trust Company*:[5]

> An elementary and fundamental requirement of due process in any proceeding which is to be accorded finality is notice reasonably calculated, under all the circumstances, to apprise interested parties of the pendency of the action and afford them an opportunity to present their objections.

One section that is easy to miss is §104, which provides for indexing of many of the dollar thresholds elsewhere in the Bankruptcy Code. These thresholds are changed every three years through administrative regulation to reflect the consumer price index. Under §109, for instance, individuals wishing to file under Chapter 13 can have no more than a specified amount in unsecured claims. Section 109 also sets out who can take advantage of various chapters of the Bankruptcy Code.

Section 109 is as good a place as any to see how the Bankruptcy Code works. To know whether a limited liability company may be a debtor under Chapter 11, one looks first to §109(d). It states that to be a debtor under Chapter 11, one must qualify as a debtor under Chapter 7. Section 109(b) excludes some "persons" from Chapter 7, but does not mention limited liability companies. This brings us to §109(a), which tells us that

---

[4] See, e.g., Fogel v. Zell, 221 F.3d 955 (7th Cir. 2000).
[5] 339 U.S. 306, 314 (1950).

a debtor can enjoy the benefits of bankruptcy only if it is a person. Hence, a corporation is eligible for bankruptcy if it is a person. Section 101 tells us that *person* as used in the Bankruptcy Code includes a corporation. Section 101 goes on to define a corporation. It extends considerably beyond entities that are formally corporations under state law, and its language is broad enough to include a limited liability company. Hence, a limited liability company can file for bankruptcy. It is a "corporation," and a corporation is a "person," and persons, unless specifically excluded, can file bankruptcy petitions.

There is no explicit requirement that a debtor be in financial distress or insolvent before filing for bankruptcy. Section 101 of the Bankruptcy Code defines insolvency as the condition that exists when a debtor's liabilities fairly discounted exceed its assets, but insolvency itself is not a prerequisite for bankruptcy for individuals or for corporations. Indeed, §109(c) specifies that a municipality must be insolvent to file a Chapter 9 petition. The absence of any mention of insolvency in other parts of §109 creates the negative inference that other debtors need not be insolvent to be eligible for bankruptcy.

The absence of such an explicit requirement makes sense. Suppose a corporation has assets of $100, ordinary debt of $49, and a 50–50 chance of losing a lawsuit that would expose it to an additional $100 of liability. It is technically solvent: it has liabilities, fairly discounted, of $99 and assets of $100. Nevertheless, its ordinary creditors may recognize that there is a 50–50 chance they will not be paid. Hence, they will be restless and may trigger the kind of destructive race to assets that a bankruptcy proceeding can prevent.[6]

Moreover, insolvency may not be easy to measure at the outset of the case. When confronting the question whether a debtor can be put into bankruptcy involuntarily, the Bankruptcy Code uses a different measure of financial distress. Creditors can put a debtor in bankruptcy involuntarily only if

---

[6] See In re Johns-Manville, 36 Bankr. 727 (Bankr. S.D.N.Y. 1984).

the debtor is unable to pay debts as they become due. This benchmark is much easier to apply than an insolvency measure, and it overlaps with it substantially. Most loans include terms that accelerate a debtor's obligations under circumstances when it is likely that the debtor's liabilities exceed its assets. When the second condition exists, the first tends to follow. At one time, we distinguished between these two benchmarks of financial distress by calling the first (excess of liabilities over assets) "insolvency in the bankruptcy sense" and the second (inability to pay debts as they become due) "insolvency in the equity sense."

None of this, however, should suggest that those in good financial health make use of bankruptcy law. Bankruptcy law tracks nonbankruptcy law, and a solvent debtor must pay all its creditors 100 cents on the dollar. When an opportunity for abuse exists (when, for example, bankruptcy's procedures offer a way to force a favorable settlement of an irritating antitrust suit or allow a solvent debtor to cap liabilities to its landlord), courts are likely to dismiss the case on the ground that it was filed in bad faith.[7] The *Butner* principle—the idea that bankruptcy law should respective nonbankruptcy entitlements unless a particular bankruptcy policy is being vindicated—limits the number of such cases.

Chapter 3 of the Bankruptcy Code deals with case administration. Sections 301 through 307 tell us how a bankruptcy case begins. Sections 321 through 331 set out the rules governing those who administer the bankruptcy estate. The court must issue an order before the debtor can hire lawyers or other professionals. Under §329 attorneys must file a statement with the court showing how much they will be compensated and the source of the compensation, even if they do not ask the debtor for payment. In addition, Rule 2014 requires that lawyers disclose all their connections with the debtor, creditors, any other

---

[7] See In re Integrated Telecom Express, Inc., 384 F.3d 108 (3d Cir. 2004); In re SGL Carbon Corp., 200 F.3d 154 (3d Cir. 1999).

parties in interest, and their accountants. Such disclosure is needed to satisfy §327(a), which requires that the debtor's attorneys be disinterested.

The disinterestedness requirement complicates the job of any lawyer who wants to continue representing a corporate client after it files a bankruptcy petition. If a business owes its lawyer anything for services provided before the petition, the lawyer may not be able to represent the business in the bankruptcy proceeding. By virtue of being owed money, the lawyer is a creditor within the meaning of §101, and hence may no longer be disinterested. Similarly, a lawyer who is paid for services already rendered outside the ordinary course of business within ninety days before the filing of the petition may be subject to a voidable preference attack, and this may also keep the lawyer from being disinterested. A lawyer who represents any of the corporation's directors or shareholders personally may not be able to represent the corporation in bankruptcy. A lawyer who sits on the corporation's board, or who has partners who sit on the board, may also fail to meet this requirement.

Even if a lawyer herself has had no previous relationship with the debtor or creditors, she must ensure that none of her associates or partners has worked for them, either. Although a lawyer is not disqualified solely because of past representation of a creditor, see §327(c), determining when a lawyer is disqualified is not always easy. Here, as elsewhere in bankruptcy, it is often useful to begin with the nonbankruptcy baseline. In this instance, however, even identifying that baseline is difficult. Nonbankruptcy conflicts rules turn on whether one is representing a client in a transaction or in ongoing litigation. In bankruptcy, much of what goes on is negotiation, but litigation with almost any party is possible.

In all events, disclosure must be full. When a court finds that a lawyer is not disinterested or has failed to make proper disclosure, it can disqualify the lawyer, disallow fees, and force the lawyer to bear the expenses of any investigation triggered by the failure to disclose. One court imposed a $1 million sanction for nondisclosure notwithstanding a finding that the firm had done its work well. Indeed, in the same opinion the court found the firm's work so crucial to the reorganization that it wanted the firm to continue working on the case.[8] Nondisclosure can, in the extreme case, trigger the criminal sanctions imposed by 18 U.S.C. §152(3) for knowingly and fraudulently making a false declaration in a bankruptcy case.[9]

The duty to disclose is an ongoing one. Suppose you discover while representing a debtor that some of its directors have perpetrated a fraud, and you now must investigate all the directors, including the ones that are independent. At this point, you have to find out whether any of your partners or associates has done work for the principal employers of these directors. You have a potential conflict if you must lead an investigation of someone who is a senior officer of a major client. Sensitivity to such issues varies across different judicial districts and even among judges within the same district. This is an area in which all lawyers, but particularly young lawyers, need to be especially vigilant.

In a Chapter 7 case, the provisions of §§321 through 331 must be read in conjunction with §§701 through 705. The principal officer in a Chapter 7 case is the bankruptcy trustee. The trustee acts as the representative of the bankruptcy estate and is charged with managing the assets of the debtor and protecting the rights of creditors and others. The trustee, for example, has the power to bring actions the debtor could have brought outside of bankruptcy. Similarly, in a Chapter 11 case, the provisions of §§321 through 331 must be read in conjunction with §§1101 through 1109. For example, in Chapter 11 cases there is

[8] See In re Leslie Fay Companies, 175 Bankr. 525 (Bankr. S.D.N.Y. 1994). For a general discussion of the law, see Bank Brussels Lambert v. Coan, 176 F.3d 610 (2d Cir. 1999).

[9] United States v. Gellene, 182 F.3d 578 (7th Cir. 1999) (lawyer at prominent New York firm sentenced to fifteen months in prison for failing to disclose his firm's representation of a major secured creditor in another matter).

usually no trustee; instead, under §1107 the debtor in possession takes on the duties and responsibilities of the trustee. Bankruptcy Code provisions authorizing the trustee to take certain actions apply with equal force to the debtor in possession. In the case of a corporation, the old managers of the debtor corporation act as debtor in possession. Thus, when §363 authorizes the trustee to use, lease, or sell assets of the estate in the ordinary course of business without first obtaining court approval, it is also authorizing the debtor in possession to do the same. Sometimes the creditors committee or other party asks to take actions nominally reserved to the trustee when no trustee in appointed. The debtor in possession may lack the incentive to pursue such actions, especially if they are against an insider. The Bankruptcy Code does not address this question explicitly, but most courts have concluded that the bankruptcy court has the power to authorize such actions in appropriate cases.[10]

Sections 341 through 350 set out a number of basic procedures. One of the crucial moments in the life of a bankruptcy case is the initial meeting of creditors that §341 requires. In a Chapter 7 case, for example, the creditors elect a trustee during the §341 meeting. They also decide, under §705(a), whether to form a creditors committee to monitor the course of the case. The bankruptcy judge is forbidden from attending the §341 meeting. Under the 1898 Bankruptcy Act, bankruptcy judges became closely involved in the administration of the bankruptcy case. Many thought that this involvement prevented them from having the degree of detachment needed to decide disputes between the parties. Since 1978, however, increasing concerns about the length of many bankruptcy cases have led to a number of changes, principally in §105, to expedite cases. Bankruptcy judges must, for example, hold such status conferences as are necessary to further the expeditious and economi-

---

[10] See, e.g., In re Cybergenics, 330 F.3d 548 (3d Cir. 2003) (en banc). But see In re Fox, 305 Bankr. 912 (Bankr. App. 10th Cir. 2004).

cal resolution of the case. Bankruptcy judges, however, are not reverting to their earlier roles as much as they are adopting the case management practices that have become commonplace in federal district courts.

Because even the simplest bankruptcy cases take time, rules are necessary to allow the trustee (and the debtor in possession) to act and to keep the creditors from taking matters into their own hands. These rules are largely the province of §§361 through 366. By far the most important of these sections is §362, which imposes an automatic stay on all creditors. It requires creditors to cease all debt collection efforts the moment a petition is filed. The automatic stay looms so large that it is easy to forget that the stay is simply a presumption. The court can lift the stay whenever a creditor shows that there is cause or that its interest is inadequately protected. Moreover, a court has the power under §105 to stay actions that do not come within the scope of §362 so long as a policy embraced in some other part of the Bankruptcy Code justifies it. Sections 363 and 364 authorize the trustee (and hence the debtor in possession in Chapter 11 cases) to sell, use, and lease property and to borrow money. When these transactions fall outside the ordinary course of business, however, the Bankruptcy Code requires notice and a hearing and may impose other requirements as well.

A crucial step in any bankruptcy case is to identify the claims against the debtor and the assets owned by the debtor. Chapter 5 of the Bankruptcy Code tells us how to go about doing this. Sections 501 through 510 focus on claims against the estate. Among other things, this part of the Bankruptcy Code embraces the idea that the general creditors must bear the costs the debtor incurs during the course of the bankruptcy case. Under §507(a)(1) these costs are paid off first, and the remainder is divided among the general creditors. These costs, called *administrative expense claims,* include the expenses of the bankruptcy proceeding proper and those of running the business in the meantime.

Section 506 addresses the rights of a creditor who has properly perfected a security interest in collateral. (*Perfection* has a singular meaning in bankruptcy. To have a perfected interest a creditor must ordinarily give the world notice of the property claim. A mortgagee must typically record its interest in the local real estate records. A creditor with a security interest in personal property must typically file a financing statement in the secretary of state's office.) Outside of bankruptcy, a creditor with a properly perfected security interest in collateral is entitled to be paid to the extent of the value of the collateral before other creditors. As a general matter, properly perfected secured creditors beat (or, to use the words lawyers commonly employ, *prime* or *trump*) the rights of general creditors in bankruptcy as well. The secured creditor, however, has a right to priority only to the extent of the *value* of its collateral. It may not be able to take possession of the collateral itself. If the collateral is worth more than the amount of the debt (that is, if the creditor is oversecured), the creditor has a secured claim equal to the amount of the debt. In addition, §506(b) allows the creditor to enjoy interest on its claim during bankruptcy and also to be paid any reasonable expenses it incurs. The oversecured creditor, however, must have obliged the debtor to pay for the expenses in the security agreement.[11]

If the collateral is worth less than the amount of the debt (that is, if the claim is undersecured), the claim is bifurcated under §506(a). The creditor has a secured claim equal to the value of the collateral and an unsecured claim for the difference. It also has rights against particular assets by virtue of its security interest in those assets. In a simple Chapter 7 liquidation, the security interest—the lien—may simply pass through bankruptcy.

Suppose a bank lends a debtor $100 and takes a security interest in a piece of real property that the debtor owns. A subsequent recession causes the property value to drop to $25, and the debtor files a Chapter 7 petition. Because the debt exceeds the value of the land, the trustee cannot possibly benefit the

---

[11] See United States v. Ron Pair Enterprises, 489 U.S. 235 (1989).

general creditors by keeping the property. The trustee may therefore give the property back (or *abandon* it, to use the language of §554) to the debtor. The Bankruptcy Code provides that the debtor's personal liability to the bank and all other creditors is discharged. The bank, however, remains free to foreclose on the land once it is in the debtor's hands because the lien survives (or passes through) bankruptcy. The doctrine of lien pass-through was first set out in *Long v. Bullard*.[12] The scope of this principle of lien pass-through, however, is more limited than it might appear because of special treatment provided for liens in Chapters 11 and 13.

Sections 541 through 560 establish what assets the estate has. These provisions are built on the central idea that one must begin with the set of rights and obligations that exist outside of bankruptcy and then identify specific bankruptcy policies that require departing from the nonbankruptcy baseline. Section 541 defines the central concept of the *property of the estate*. The trustee (or the debtor in possession) is charged with assembling the assets that are available to meet the creditors' claims and then distributing them. These assets, called the property of the estate, form the bankruptcy estate. Section 541 draws a sharp distinction between individuals and corporations. The future income of individuals does not become property of the estate, while the future income of a corporation does. Drawing this distinction is a crucial feature of bankruptcy's fresh start for individual debtors and it is the focus of the next chapter of this book.

In many cases, property to which the creditors of a debtor are entitled is property to which a third party lays claim. In these cases, the trustee may have to bring an action to vindicate the creditors' right to the property. If the debtor itself could have brought the cause of action, the property is deemed property of the estate under §541. In other cases, the trustee must exercise one of the so-called avoiding powers. Section 544(a) is

---

[12]117 U.S. 617 (1886).

the "strong arm" power of the trustee. Using it the trustee may, for example, set aside unperfected security interests. A creditor who takes collateral may not be able to take the collateral in bankruptcy if it has failed to record its interest through a public filing.

The avoiding powers also allow the trustee to set aside fraudulent conveyances, a power creditors generally enjoy outside of bankruptcy. These include transfers made and obligations incurred for less than reasonably equivalent value while the debtor was insolvent or those done with the intent to hinder, delay, or defraud creditors. §548. Such transactions include not only instances of outright fraud but also those that bear "badges of fraud," indicia suggesting that the transactions had no legitimate business purpose and were aimed instead at thwarting the creditors' ability to be repaid. Another provision allows the trustee to set aside transfers that were made to a creditor on the eve of bankruptcy. §547.

The general provisions of the Bankruptcy Code in Chapters 1, 3, and 5 are not perfectly organized. A number of provisions could well have been placed elsewhere. Section 108, for example, gives the trustee a grace period for taking certain actions. Because the consequences of failing to take action often turn on whether the automatic stay is implicated, this provision is best read in conjunction with §362. Section 365, which deals with executory contracts, is perhaps the provision most conspicuously out of place. Executory contracts inherently involve mutual rights and obligations between a debtor and a third party. They are best seen as combinations of claims and assets. Executory contracts are claims against the estate because they give a third party rights against the debtor. They are simultaneously assets of the estate because they give the debtor rights against a third party. Because both claims and assets fall within the ambit of Chapter 5 of the Bankruptcy Code, the section on executory contracts belongs there. The failure to put §365 in the correct place should not, in principle, affect how it is interpreted, but its faulty positioning may have compounded the difficulties lawyers and judges have faced in applying it consistently.

The remaining chapters in Title 11 set out the different kinds of bankruptcy cases. Chapter 9 is reserved for municipalities. Under §101, *municipality* means any political subdivision or public agency or instrumentality of a state. In addition to cities and towns, debtors in Chapter 9 may include water and power districts. Chapter 9 has not been widely used since the Great Depression, but cases involving it still do arise: one of the important bankruptcies of the 1990s was the case of Orange County in the wake of its speculative investments in derivatives and other exotic securities. The provisions of Chapter 9 are neither long nor complicated. Section 901 identifies the general provisions of the Bankruptcy Code that apply. For example, §1113 does not apply in Chapter 9 cases. Hence, a municipality in Chapter 9 has correspondingly more freedom to reject collective bargaining agreements than a corporation in Chapter 11.

Individuals and corporations can usually choose to file under one of several different chapters. An individual debtor will most often choose Chapter 7 or Chapter 13. An ordinary corporation can file either a Chapter 7 petition or a Chapter 11 petition. The kind of bankruptcy petition that is brought depends on the goals of the person filing the petition. The court, however, enjoys a broad power to convert a case brought under one chapter into a case brought under another. Moreover, under §706(a) the debtor can convert a case that creditors file under Chapter 7 to one under Chapter 11.

As we will discover below in chapter 2, Chapter 7 tries to distinguish the honest but unfortunate flesh-and-blood debtors who need a fresh start from those who can repay their debts or whose use of Chapter 7 would be abusive. An individual who is hopelessly in debt should be able to file a Chapter 7 bankruptcy petition, give up all nonexempt assets, and walk away from nearly all prebankruptcy obligations. Someone who makes enough to repay creditors a substantial sum should not. Section 707(b) implements a "means test" that attempts to distinguish the two. Section 727 gives the honest but unfortunate debtor a *discharge*. Because future income of an individual does not become property of the estate under §541, the effect of §727 is to give the individual debtor the right to enjoy future income free of creditors' claims. Section 726 sets out how the debtor's property is divided among the creditors, but this section and others dealing with the administration of the estate in Chapter 7 often have little relevance in the case of the individual debtor. Many individuals filing Chapter 7 have no assets. The issue to litigate in these cases is the scope of bankruptcy's fresh-start policy, not the division of the spoils among the creditors. Chapter 13 also provides individuals with a substantive fresh start, but it takes a different shape. Chapter 13 allows an individual to keep all assets, but in return the debtor must create a plan under which creditors receive as much out of the debtor's future income as they would have received had the debtor filed under Chapter 7.

Like individuals, corporations may file under Chapter 7. In many cases, a corporation finds itself in Chapter 7 only after first having tried unsuccessfully to reorganize under Chapter 11. See §1112(b). These cases have nothing to do with giving an individual a fresh start. Chapter 7 offers no discharge to a corporation. In a typical corporate Chapter 7 case, the business has ceased its operations or will cease them in short order. Any assets remaining after the secured creditors have taken what they can will usually go to the tax collector, who enjoys a special priority under §507(a)(8). The purpose of allowing corporations to file Chapter 7 petitions is not to give creditors assets but to assure creditors that the corporation has no assets. A Chapter 7 petition is the easiest way for corporate managers who are being constantly harassed to convince a corporation's creditors that the corporation has no assets and lawsuits are pointless. The bankruptcy process can offer scrutiny of the debtor's overall health not otherwise available to individual creditors.

The Bankruptcy Code does not require that a corporation in Chapter 7 be liquidated in the sense that all assets are broken up and sold piecemeal. To the contrary, the trustee is obliged to sell the assets for as much as possible, and sometimes this means selling the assets together as a going concern. In practice, however, operating businesses rarely file Chapter 7 petitions. Those in control of the corporation outside of bankruptcy usually want to retain that control in bankruptcy. Chapter 11 allows the retention of control, while Chapter 7 requires the appointment of a trustee to manage the affairs of the business. It is worth noting that the creditors of large corporations exercise considerable control outside of bankruptcy when the business becomes financially distressed, and they retain much of this control inside of bankruptcy. Indeed, the existing managers are often sufficiently beholden to them that major creditors typically do not demand the appointment of a trustee in Chapter 11 even when the presence of fraud, such as we saw in Enron or Worldcom, gives them an unequivocal right to do so.

Chapter 11 is the vehicle designed to straighten out the affairs of corporations in financial distress. When the corporation cannot continue as a going concern, Chapter 11 provides a mechanism for shutting it down and sorting out its financial affairs in a coherent way. Chapter 11 is better suited than Chapter 7 for corporations that are dissolving when there are problems beyond the simple sale of assets. Consider the following case. Apart from a secured creditor that has repossessed its collateral, the only other creditor is the Internal Revenue Service, which is owed Federal Insurance Contributions Act (FICA) and withholding taxes. The owner-managers of the business are personally (and potentially criminally) liable for these taxes, and they have filed Chapter 11 petitions as well. (Individuals are eligible for Chapter 11 relief, but apart from cases in which the debtor's affairs are tied up with those of a business, Chapter 13 or Chapter 7 is a more attractive place to resolve their financial problems.) We need to sort out who is going to pay what and on what schedule. In such situations, Chapter 11 is often the forum of choice for both the debtors and the IRS. If no one asks for the case to be dismissed or converted, the court is unlikely to do so.

In other cases, the business as a whole may have no future, but discrete divisions may be salable. Chapter 11 is a mechanism that allows for such sales and gives buyers confidence that they will acquire clean title. Finally, Chapter 11 provides a forum for a business that will be kept in intact but needs a new capital structure. Past misfortunes may have left it unable to meet its obligations, but its assets are being put to their best use. By scaling back the business's fixed obligations the creditors as a group are left better off.

Chapter 11 replaced Chapters X, XI, and XII of the old Bankruptcy Act. (The convention is to use Roman numerals for chapters of the 1898 Act and Arabic numerals for those of the 1978 Code.) In Chapter 11, the debtor in possession rather than the trustee ordinarily continues to run the business. In many Chapter 11 cases, the assets are subject to the security interest of one large creditor. In such situations the general creditors are likely to play only a small role, if any. When the debtor is a substantial operating company with a decent chance of survival as a going concern, enough may be at stake so that the general creditors will play an active role.

In theory, the United States Trustee chooses a committee of creditors at the start of every Chapter 11 case, but the committee is active only in cases in which enough is at stake. Section 1102(b) suggests that the creditors committee consist of creditors who hold the seven largest claims and are willing to serve. In practice, however, the United States Trustee often attempts to find a "representative" creditors committee, and §1102(a)(4) allows a small business to insist on becoming a member if its claim against the debtor is large enough to put its own survival at risk. The creditors committee in Chapter 11 may also consist of the members of a committee organized by creditors before the case begins, if that committee is fairly chosen and represents the different kinds of claims that exist. The United States Trustee thus often looks well beyond the seven largest creditors because they may look more like each other than the class of general creditors as a whole. In the largest cases, there may be multiple committees of creditors as well as a committee of the equityholders.

Serving on a creditors committee can be a mixed blessing. Doing so ensures that one is close to the action and knows what is going on. But one may receive information that the debtor considers confidential, and this may interfere with a creditor's ability to act (such as its ability to sell its claim). Moreover, service on the committee is time consuming. Creditors committees in Chapter 11 cases (unlike committees in Chapter 7) can retain professionals such as lawyers and accountants, and the cost of hiring them is an administrative expense entitled to priority under §507. The creditors themselves, however, are not compensated for their efforts. Moreover, as a member of the committee, a creditor is charged with looking out not only for its own interests but also for those of the other general creditors.

Section 1104 allows the court to appoint an examiner, who may be given the powers of the trustee; the United States Trustee chooses the examiner, subject to court approval. An examiner may be retained simply to mediate between the various factions. Examiners are sometimes appointed to investigate whether the debtor should bring a cause of action (such as a fraudulent conveyance action against shareholders) that the debtor in possession might not pursue as vigorously because of its conflict of interest. Such investigations can be enormously expensive and risk duplicating work already done or that will be done subsequently when the action is brought. But they can also lead to substantial recoveries for creditors. In the bankruptcy of Enron, for example, the examiner's investigation cost nearly $100 million and occupied dozens of lawyers and professionals for nearly two years, but the ensuing settlements exceeded $1 billion.

One of the debtor's most important rights in Chapter 11 is its exclusive right to propose a plan of reorganization for the first 120 days after the filing of the petition. The court may extend this period for up to eighteen months. If the debtor does propose a plan, it has another sixty days to secure its acceptance under §1121(c)(3). When exclusivity expires, any party in interest can file a plan. If more than one plan meets all the rules of Chapter 11, then §1129(c) directs the bankruptcy judge to consider the "preferences of creditors and equity security holders in determining which plan to confirm." Terminating the exclusivity period can lead to the proposal and eventual confirmation of a liquidating plan of reorganization. From the perspective of a secured creditor, terminating exclusivity in such a case has the same effect as lifting the automatic stay.

Recognizing that they lack the ability to gather detailed information about a business's operations, bankruptcy judges try to ensure that sensible decisions are made about the debtor's assets by establishing clear benchmarks and taking decisive action when the debtor fails to meet them. At the start of the case, the principal lender may ask that the stay be lifted so it can foreclose on the collateral. The debtor's managers might argue that the stay should continue because the business can be sold as a going concern to another company. The bankruptcy judge might turn down the secured creditor's lift-stay motion but rule that the motion will be granted six weeks hence if no buyer appears in the interim.

The Chapter 11 debtor spends much of its time negotiating with its postbankruptcy suppliers of goods, services, and capital equipment. Chapter 11 provides a forum for the renegotiation of leases, contracts, and labor agreements. Sometimes, the negotiations are indistinguishable from those that take place outside of bankruptcy. Rules ensure that the third party possesses rights that correspond as closely as possible to the rights it would have enjoyed outside of bankruptcy. The rules in §1110 governing aircraft leases are a good example. In other situations, Chapter 11 provides rules that enhance the debtor's bargaining position dramatically relative to the nonbankruptcy baseline. Under such rules, creditors benefit at the expense of third parties relative to the nonbankruptcy baseline. The treatment of collective bargaining agreements under §1113 is a telling example. Negotiations in bankruptcy, however, all tend to have the same effect on the operations of the business going forward. The business that reorganizes in Chapter 11 successfully leaves with a new set of contracts under which it is paying something like the market price for its labor, capital and material. If a business cannot compete effectively under these circumstances, it is unlikely to survive in a market economy.

Sections 1122 through 1129 establish the structure for negotiations among creditors. These sections set out the procedural rights of all the players and their substantive rights in the event they fail to reach agreement. These various rights, the most important of which are in §1129, embody a general principle known as the *absolute priority rule*. This rule tries to ensure that creditors in bankruptcy are paid according to their nonbankruptcy priorities. The debtor's ability to impose a plan over the creditors' objection by satisfying the absolute priority rule is known aptly as the debtor's *cramdown* power.

Sections 1141 through 1146 govern the discharge of old claims and the implementation of the reorganization plan. Just as the discharge provision of §727 in the case of the individual debtor had to be read in conjunction with the exclusion of individual income from property of the estate under §541, the discharge provision in §1141 must be read in conjunction with the absolute priority rule. Together, the discharge of debt and the absolute priority rule implement the central aim of Chapter 11. They ensure that businesses worth keeping intact remain so, despite the incentives each creditor has to look out for its own interest rather than the collective interest of all the creditors.

The Bankruptcy Forum

The Bankruptcy Code is designed so that the debtor's affairs can be sorted out in a single forum. Unlike a federal court sitting in a diversity case, the bankruptcy court has nationwide jurisdiction. Even a creditor who does not have the minimum contacts with California to make it amenable to suit in state court must still file its claim in the bankruptcy court in California if the debtor has chosen to file its petition there.[13] Proper venue for filing a bankruptcy petition includes state of incorporation,[14] and because many large businesses are incorporated

---

[13] See Harder v. Desert Breezes Master Association, 192 Bankr. 47 (N.D.N.Y. 1996).

[14] See 28 U.S.C. §1408.

under or have an affiliate incorporated under Delaware or New York law, large bankruptcy cases are often filed there.

A number of constraints prevent the goal of a single forum from being fully realized. Article III of the U.S. Constitution limits what bankruptcy judges can do given that they do not have life tenure. The jury trial right in the Seventh Amendment limits the ability to resolve disputes expeditiously. The sovereign immunity a state enjoys under the Eleventh Amendment limits the bankruptcy court's power to resolve disputes even when the state is merely asserting its rights as a creditor. Let's look at each of these constitutional limitations more closely.

In eighteenth-century England, the Chancellor appointed commissioners to do much of the work of gathering and administering a bankruptcy estate. Because they were not judges, what these commissioners did cannot be considered an exercise of the judicial power. Modern bankruptcy judges likewise oversee the administration of the bankruptcy estate. They do not enjoy lifelong appointments and cannot exercise judicial power within the meaning of Article III.[15] Disappointed litigants have a right to de novo review in the district courts for matters that are not central to the administration of the bankruptcy case. But for matters that are central to the case, litigants are entitled only to appellate review. A second rationale for limiting the judges' power rests on an idea imported from administrative law. Because bankruptcy law is created entirely by Congress, a ruling under it (as opposed to a decision on matters involving other legal issues) constitutes an adjudication of public rights that an Article III judge need not decide.[16]

The Seventh Amendment requires that the right to a jury trial be preserved in federal court for suits at common law when the amount in controversy exceeds twenty dollars. Many of the questions in a bankruptcy case, including whether a par-

---

[15] See Northern Pipeline Construction Co. v. Marathon Pipe Line Co., 458 U.S. 50 (1982).

[16] See Crowell v. Benson, 285 U.S. 22 (1932).

ticular person has a claim against the debtor, would be the basis of suits at common law if brought outside of bankruptcy. It does not follow, however, that all such claims give rise to a right to a jury trial. A bankruptcy court is a court of equity, and it has the right to use "chancery methods" to decide matters that are central to the bankruptcy process.[17] Other actions, such as fraudulent conveyance suits against third parties, retain their common law character and must be tried by jury unless both parties consent to have the judge decide the dispute.[18] Under 28 U.S.C. §157(e), if a right to a jury trial exists, the bankruptcy judge may conduct the trial only by special designation of the district judge and only if the parties again give their express consent.

The Constitution affects the forum in which bankruptcy disputes are tried in a third way. A state can also appear as a simple creditor. For example, it may allege that the debtor owes sales taxes. Alternatively, the debtor may argue that a provision of the Bankruptcy Code, such as §1146, entitles it to a refund of taxes it has already paid. Were the state a private party, it would, of course, be subject to the power of the bankruptcy court. A state, however, is immune from suit under the Eleventh Amendment unless it waives its sovereign immunity, and waivers of sovereign immunity are not lightly inferred.[19]

In *Gardner v. New Jersey*, the Supreme Court held that "[w]hen the State becomes the actor and files a claim against the fund, it waives any immunity which it otherwise might have had respecting the adjudication of the claim."[20] Much of what takes place in a bankruptcy case—such as a determination

---

[17] See Barton v. Barbour, 104 U.S. 126, 134 (1881).

[18] Granfinanciera v. Nordberg, 492 U.S. 33 (1989).

[19] See Florida Prepaid Postsecondary Education Expense Board v. College Savings Bank, 527 U.S. 627 (1999); College Savings Bank v. Florida Prepaid Postsecondary Education Expense Board, 527 U.S. 666 (1999).

[20] 329 U.S. 565, 573–74 (1947).

that a debt is dischargeable—is not a "suit" within the meaning of the Eleventh Amendment.[21] To the extent that the bankruptcy court is presiding over an *in rem* proceeding concerned with distributing assets of the estate, the Eleventh Amendment does not apply. Nevertheless, the Supreme Court has held that Congress's power to regulate interstate commerce does not give it the ability to intrude upon a state's sovereignty,[22] and the power to enact bankruptcy laws may be similarly limited. Section 106(b) of the Bankruptcy Code purports to give the trustee the power to bring a preference action against a state even when the state does not itself appear in the case, but whether such a grant is consistent with the Eleventh Amendment remains unclear.[23]

For all these reasons, the debtor's affairs may not all be resolved in a single forum. Nevertheless, most of what we shall study plays out in the bankruptcy court and is subject only to appellate review. It is useful to spend some time to see how the rules of procedure bring this about, despite the limitations outlined above.

Federal district courts have original and exclusive jurisdiction over all "cases" under Title 11.[24] The entire process the bankruptcy petition triggers is considered a "case" and thus may be filed only in a federal district court (as opposed to, say, a state court). Section 1334 also gives the district courts original (but not exclusive) jurisdiction over all "civil proceedings" arising under Title 11 or arising in or related to cases under Title 11. A controversy such as a fraudulent conveyance action that

---

[21] See Tennessee Student Assistance Corp. v. Hood, 541 U.S. 440 (2004).

[22] See Seminole Tribe v. Florida, 517 U.S. 44 (1996).

[23] For a case in which the court finds such a power is consistent with the Eleventh Amendment, see In re Dehon, Inc., 327 Bankr. 38 (Bankr. D. Mass. 2005).

[24] 28 U.S.C. §1334.

takes place in the course of settling a debtor's affairs is considered a "proceeding."

Bankruptcy jurisdiction can extend to parties who are neither creditors nor debtors when the dispute is related to a case under Title 11. The reach of related jurisdiction has been broadly defined. Courts sometimes ask simply "whether the outcome of the proceeding could conceivably have any effect upon the estate being administered in bankruptcy."[25] Courts, however, will typically find that the power does not extend to matters that might lead the losing party to seek indemnification from the debtor.[26] A claim that a creditor has against a guarantor of the debtor that would have no impact on the estate is an example of an action that falls outside the jurisdictional reach of §1334.

Bankruptcy courts are adjuncts of the district courts, and §1334 must be read in conjunction with §157(a) of Title 28. Section 157 allows the district court to "refer" any or all bankruptcy cases to bankruptcy judges. It also provides that the district court may refer any or all proceedings arising under the Bankruptcy Code, or arising in or related to a bankruptcy case, to bankruptcy judges. In all district courts this practice is firmly institutionalized. Bankruptcy petitions are, as a practical matter, filed in the bankruptcy courts. The purpose of this circumlocution is to ensure that the dictates of Article III are satisfied. The bankruptcy judge is not acting autonomously and is not exercising judicial power because the bankruptcy judge is merely an adjunct to the district court. Just as a court of equity can appoint a special master, the reasoning goes, the district court can choose to delegate bankruptcy cases to bankruptcy judges.

[25] Kelley v. Nodine, 783 F.2d 626, 634 (6th Cir. 1986). See Lindsey v. O'Brien (In re Dow Corning Corp.), 86 F.3d 482 (6th Cir. 1996).

[26] See In re Federal-Mogul Global, Inc., 282 Bankr. 301 (Bank. D. Del. 2002).

The idea that the district courts have jurisdiction over bankruptcy cases and proceedings is not entirely a formal fiction. Although everything is routinely referred to the bankruptcy courts, §157(d) gives the district judge the power to withdraw the reference in any particular case or proceeding, in whole or in part, for cause. The district court can act either on its own motion or on a timely motion of any party. Although district courts rarely want to hear bankruptcy disputes, they have withdrawn the reference in some important cases.

Withdrawal of the reference is mandatory after a timely motion when "resolution of the proceeding requires consideration of both Title 11 and other laws of the United States regulating organizations or activities affecting interstate commerce." This provision has been read narrowly, as it must be, given that so many disputes in a bankruptcy case involve consideration of federal laws that affect interstate commerce. Courts frequently use a substantial-and-material test: withdrawal is mandatory only when the issues presented require a significant interpretation of federal laws, not when what is presented is the straightforward application of federal law to a particular set of facts. A difficult controversy involving the reach of CERCLA or some other equally complex statute is potentially a subject of mandatory withdrawal, but even then the district court may remand to the bankruptcy court for submission of proposed findings of fact and conclusions of law under §157(c)(1).

Once a case is referred to a bankruptcy judge, many decisions are subject only to appellate review by the district court. Section 157 tells us that bankruptcy judges "may hear and determine all cases under the Bankruptcy Code" referred to them, subject to appellate review under 28 U.S.C. §158. *Case* is used in the technical sense here and refers only to the process that begins with the bankruptcy petition. Individual disputes arise during the debtor's course through bankruptcy are *proceedings*. When these proceedings are central to the administration of the case (or, to use the term in Title 28, when they are *core*), the bankruptcy judge is again subject only to appellate review. Core proceedings include confirmation of plans, matters concerning the administration of the estate, and the allowance or disallowance of claims against the estate. Section 157(b)(2) contains a list of core proceedings, but this list is not by its terms exhaustive.

What remains are noncore proceedings. A typical example is a lawsuit that the debtor has filed against some third party. For these, the bankruptcy judge is subject to de novo review. The bankruptcy judge must submit proposed findings of fact and conclusions of law to the district court. The district court can make a final order only after reviewing de novo those matters to which a party has objected.

Under 28 U.S.C. §158(a), the district courts have appellate review of final judgments, orders, and decrees from the bankruptcy court. The district courts also have jurisdiction to hear appeals from interlocutory orders and decrees, but in these cases leave of the court is required.

The courts of appeals have jurisdiction to hear appeals from final decisions, judgments, orders, and decrees under 28 U.S.C. §158(d). Determining a final judgment for purposes of 28 U.S.C. §158(d) has proven difficult. Suppose there is a final judgment in the bankruptcy court, and the district court hears the appeal and remands to the bankruptcy court. Courts are divided on whether an appeal can be taken to the court of appeals. Section 158(d) does not tell us explicitly whether it is sufficient that the bankruptcy judge's decision be final or whether the district court's decision must be final as well. Most courts recognize that a district court's order generally is not final if it remands the dispute to the bankruptcy court, especially if the remand requires the bankruptcy court to make factual findings or exercise its discretion.[27] Some courts, however, have found that bankruptcy requires a more relaxed standard of finality than ordinary federal civil litigation.[28]

[27] See In re Lopez, 116 F.3d 1191 (7th Cir. 1997).

[28] See Buncher Co. v. Official Committee of Unsecured Creditors, 229 F.3d 245, 250 (3d Cir. 2000).

The uncertainty in the meaning of finality in §158(d) can put lawyers in the awkward position of having to choose between appealing a decision that may prove to be interlocutory or waiving the right altogether if it later proves to have been a final order. Section 158(d), however, does not displace the ordinary rules governing appeals from the district court, and §1292(b) mitigates this problem to some extent. This section allows a court of appeals, in its discretion, to review an interlocutory order, provided the district judge finds that at issue is a controlling question of law as to which there is substantial ground for difference of opinion and that an immediate appeal may materially advance the ultimate termination of the litigation.[29]

This review of appellate review of bankruptcy court decisions, however, is somewhat misleading. Appellate review takes time, and most of the important decisions in a bankruptcy case—whether the business should be shut down or whether the managers should be given another month to turn the operation around—are time sensitive and thus essentially unreviewable. How long to wait before taking action becomes a moot point well before the appellate court can hear the case. When a bankruptcy court approves an asset sale or lease transfer, those who object have no chance of having the decision overturned unless the sale itself is stayed pending the appeal. Even if the case is not formally moot (and it often will be),[30] the reversal of the decision does not itself affect the validity of the sale. See §363(m). Similarly, reversal on appeal of an order approving debtor-in-possession financing does not affect the rights of the postpetition extender of credit who acts in good faith, and appeals of such orders are often moot because a court can fashion

---

[29] Connecticut National Bank v. Germain, 503 U.S. 249 (1992).

[30] See L.R.S.C. Co. v. Rickel Home Centers, 209 F.3d 291 (3d Cir. 2000).

no meaningful relief.[31] Such provisions are necessary to enable debtors to sell assets or borrow while the case is pending. No one will do business with a debtor in bankruptcy if deals can be undone after the fact.

The practical effect of all this is to grant the bankruptcy judge enormous power. From the perspective of financial institutions that have done business with the debtor in the past and expect to continue to do business with it, Chapter 11 is an attractive venue only if the decisions of the bankruptcy judge are predictable. For this reason among others, Delaware and the Southern District of New York have become the venue of choice for many large corporations in bankruptcy.

The Bankruptcy Rules establish the procedures used in the bankruptcy courts. They do not change the substantive rules of the Bankruptcy Code, but they do affect how the issues are shaped. For example, they distinguish the types of hearings that take place before the bankruptcy judge. One type of hearing, called an *adversary proceeding*, is conducted under much the same rules as any other civil dispute. Many sections of the Federal Rules of Civil Procedure that govern pleading, joinder, depositions, interrogatories, and summary judgment have been incorporated into the bankruptcy rules governing adversary proceedings. In Chapter 11 cases, the typical adversary proceeding is a preference or fraudulent conveyance action. For individuals in Chapter 7, an adversary proceeding usually concerns the dischargeability of a particular debt.

Whenever an actual dispute before the bankruptcy court is not an adversary proceeding, it is a *contested matter*. Among the most common is a motion to lift the automatic stay. The procedures for contested matters are more streamlined and are set out in Bankruptcy Rule 9014. For example, no response is required in a contested matter unless the court orders an answer to a motion. The court, however, has the power to invoke the

---

[31] Boullioun Aircraft Holding Co. v. Smith Management, 181 F.3d 1191 (10th Cir. 1999).

more elaborate rules for adversary proceedings in contested matters when appropriate.

Bankruptcy courts also have the inherent power under §105 to impose sanctions in order to maintain control of their courtrooms and of their dockets.[32] Moreover, Rule 11 or its counterpart under the Bankruptcy Rules, Rule 9011, is available at every stage of bankruptcy litigation. In addition, §362(k) of the Bankruptcy Code explicitly grants the bankruptcy court the power to award actual and punitive damages to an individual injured by any violation of the automatic stay.[33]

In the next two chapters, we switch our focus to the two major principles that animate bankruptcy law—the fresh start policy for individual debtors and the absolute priority rule for corporate debtors. We then return to look at various provisions of the Bankruptcy Code in more detail.

[32] See United States v. Mourad, 289 F.3d 174 (1st Cir. 2002); In re Volpert, 110 F.3d 494 (7th Cir. 1997).

[33] Courts, however, are divided on whether "individual" in this context means only human beings. See In re APF Co., 264 Bankr. 344 (Bankr. D. Del. 2001).

Chapter Two

The Individual Debtor and the Fresh Start

Creditor Remedies and Debtor Rights

In our society, extensions of credit are woven into the fabric of everyday life. The telephone company becomes our creditor every time we make a call; we become indebted to the electric company every time we turn on a light switch. Few of us could pay for our education or buy a house if credit were not readily available. But borrowing carries with it the risk that we shall not be able to repay what we owe. A person might be stricken with a catastrophic illness or lose a well-paying job and be unable to cut back on expenses before being overwhelmed by debt. Families with incomes of $30,000 a year, no matter how well intentioned, are not going to be able to pay off $100,000 in debt. They have no assets beyond clothes, a wedding ring, and some household furniture. There are many honest, decent individuals who through improvidence or bad luck end up owing their creditors more than they can ever repay.

For more than a century, our laws have granted such individuals a fresh start. They can file a bankruptcy petition, discharge their debts, and start over again. More than a million individuals file bankruptcy petitions each year. The overwhelming majority of these cases are short, uncomplicated affairs. The debtors never appear in court, no creditor objects, and the court clerk is the only one who ever sees the file. The system provides enormous benefits to the "honest but unfortunate debtor"[1] while imposing only a small cost on creditors.

---

[1] See Local Loan Co. v. Hunt, 292 U.S. 234, 244 (1934).

Having a debt you are owed discharged matters relatively little if there is almost no chance you are going to be repaid anyway. You are better off having the debtor's affairs subjected to scrutiny by a trustee and walking away.

The law that governs the bankruptcy of individuals is complicated not because of the typical case, which again is quite simple and consumes no judicial time, but rather because one must have some way of distinguishing honest but unlucky debtors from those who would abuse the system. When bad behavior is brought to their attention, bankruptcy judges take action. Section 707(b) of the Bankruptcy Code allows the bankruptcy judge to deny debtors a fresh start if the fresh start would work an abuse of the bankruptcy process. To ensure that unscrupulous individuals do not hide assets, we require those who seek the protection of bankruptcy law to disclose the whereabouts of all assets and submit to questioning from creditors. Debtors who are not forthcoming lose, among other things, their right to a fresh start. See §727. Many creditors will stop pursuing the debtor once they are satisfied that the debtor cannot repay them, independent of whether bankruptcy formally discharged the debt. The procedures that bankruptcy law puts in place reassures creditors that the debtor does not have other assets and that nothing is being hidden from them.

For a long time, we believed that Chapter 7 imposed costs on those who used it in such a way that only those for whom the fresh start was intended would use it. To obtain a fresh start, individuals must turn over to creditors all assets other than clothing, wedding rings, and similar types of property that creditors would be unable to reach outside of bankruptcy. For those for whom individual bankruptcy law is primarily designed—lower-middle-class working persons who are hopelessly in debt—the obligation to turn over nonexempt assets imposes comparatively fewer burdens. They do not have much in the way of assets beyond the clothes on the backs and household furniture. In contrast, the same obligation weighs more heavily on those with substantial income who have assembled assets of significant value. For them, the price of bankruptcy is too high if they can pay off existing debt out of future income.

Yet in recent years, doubts began to arise about whether this self-sorting mechanism was working. In a world in which the most important asset any of us owns is human capital, what we own at any one point in time tells us increasingly less about our ability to pay creditors. A recent law school graduate may have far fewer assets than a line cook with a family yet make three times as much. For the former, a debt of $100,000 is neither unusual nor overly burdensome, while for the latter it is crushing.

A number of people argued that bankruptcy law should have an explicit mechanism that gauges whether someone is the honest but unfortunate debtor for whom the law was intended. The law should look explicitly at their income and their ability to repay what they owe. Congress adopted such a mechanism after much debate in 2005. This new test, however, affects only a small portion of those who use Chapter 7.

The strongest objection to the introduction of means testing is not that a discharge should be available to high-income debtors who could pay much of what they owed. Indeed, most courts had already found that the filing of a bankruptcy petition by someone who had the ability to repay debt was itself grounds for dismissing the case.[2] Rather, the problem associated with means testing was one associated with many reform efforts. The game may not be worth the candle. Any mechanism sufficiently fine-tuned to catch bad actors without foreclosing access to the fresh start to people who in fact deserved it is too complicated and imposes too many costs, particularly on those whose right to a fresh start is not in doubt.

The Means Test

Section 707(b)(2) blocks access to the fresh start for consumers who make more than most and who have enough dispos-

---

[2] See, e.g., Zolg v. Kelly (In re Kelly), 841 F.2d 908, 914–15 (9th Cir. 1988).

able income to make substantial repayments to their creditors.[3] It provides a hard-and-fast rule that supplements the discretion that the bankruptcy judge enjoys to dismiss abusive filings by those struggling primarily with consumer debt. The judge determines whether one makes enough to be subject to means testing by taking the debtor's "current monthly income," multiplying it by twelve, and comparing it against the "median family income" of others in the same state. Both terms are defined in §101. The "current monthly income" calculation begins with the average income over the six months before the filing. The "median family income" benchmark draws on census data for the state in which the debtor resides, indexed for inflation and adjusted for household size. When the debtor lives alone, the courts looks at the median income in the state for households of one. When the household consists of two, three, or four, we use whichever has the highest median income. When the household consists of five or more, we again take the highest median of two-, three-, or four-person households and then adjust it upward by a fixed dollar amount for each additional household member.

These adjustments represent just one of the many technicalities associated with §707(b)'s means test. But such adjustments (and many others like them) are necessary for the rule to work sensibly. Someone who lives alone has fewer expenses and less income on average than two who live together. Using the median income of a two-person household for a single debtor would make the median income threshold inappropriately easy for that debtor relative to other debtors. By contrast, the median income for households greater than four is, on average, less than those with smaller households. Simply using that median for larger households would mean that, all else equal, a larger family would be more likely subject to means testing. It

---

[3] For an excellent account of how the means test works, see Eugene R. Wedoff, Means Testing in the New §707(b), 79 Am. Bankr. L.J. 231 (2005).

makes no sense to have a rule that imposes a lower earnings threshold on larger families, especially given that larger families have greater expenses.

Once a debtor is found to make more than most, we still must establish that the debtor earns enough to be able to pay something back to creditors. The benchmark used here is based on the tables the Internal Revenue Service uses to decide how much delinquent taxpayers are able to pay them for back taxes. In calculating allowable living expenses, for example, the IRS allows one person living alone who makes $60,000 to spend $369 on food each month. The amount allocated for housing depends on where the taxpayer lives. In New York City, the amount for a household of two or fewer can be as much as $3,547; in Philadelphia the ceiling is $851.

After this benchmark is determined, the bankruptcy judge makes a number of adjustments. Some judges allow for additional expenses not reflected in the IRS tables, such as expenses for the care and support of elderly, chronically ill, or disabled household members who cannot provide for themselves. Also added are payments to secured creditors to maintain possession of the debtor's primary residence and motor vehicle. Grafting adjustments on top of the benchmarks, however, can create distortions. The IRS tables already include a housing and transportation allowance. Adding payments to secured creditors may result in double counting.

Once we determine the debtor's reasonable monthly expenses according to this formula, we subtract the amount from the debtor's current monthly income, as defined in §101, and see whether what remains is sufficient to make substantial payments to creditors. If there is less than $100 available each month (less than $6,000 aggregated over a five-year Chapter 13 plan), then the debtor remains eligible for a discharge and a fresh start under Chapter 7. If there is more than $167 available each month (or more than $10,000 over the course of a five-year plan), then the debtor whose current monthly income exceeds the median is presumed ineligible for a fresh start. If the income falls somewhere between, we check to see if the amount is sufficient to pay ordinary general creditors 25 cents on the dollar. If the debtor can pay that much back according to this metric, then the debtor again is presumptively ineligible. To rebut the presumption, the debtor must establish special circumstances, such as a serious medical condition, that affect the debtor's expected income or expenses and make the debtor unable to repay creditors.

The means test is embedded in a section devoted to bankruptcy abuse, but this is misleading. The means test is focused exclusively on the ability to repay debt. If two debtors' incomes, expenses, and household size are the same, the circumstances that brought about the financial distress are irrelevant. The person who incurred sudden medical expenses or lost a job is treated the same as the spendthrift who ran up credit card debt by taking too many vacations. Ability to repay, as measured by this formula, is all that matters.

But this is not to say that the spendthrifts who escape the means test are off the hook. Debtors who make more than the median are at greater risk of losing their right to a discharge than debtors who make less than the median. The creditors of the former are permitted to ask the judge to find that the debtor's use of Chapter 7 is abusive for some other reason—say, as a means of escaping a covenant not to compete. Debtors who make less than the median are still subject to the risk that the judge will find their use of bankruptcy abusive, but in these cases, either the United States Trustee or the judge must initiate the inquiry; a disgruntled creditor cannot. The ability to put the issue on the judge's radar screen will likely make a difference. Such disputes, however, seem most likely to arise in the business context, and §707(b) is not likely to apply in such situations, as the power to dismiss for abuse is limited to those whose debts are primarily consumer debts.

Whether this rule-based approach to measuring bankruptcy abuse will work is an open question. Indeed, it will not be easy to measure its costs or its benefits. Such a rule, by its nature, is likely to do much of its work offstage. Someone who would have otherwise used Chapter 7 may now decide not to file at all. To the extent such individuals are not worthy of a fresh start, the benefits will be largely unobserved. The costs may be equally invisible. Even though few of the individuals who filed before means testing went into effect in late 2005 would have fallen within its scope (perhaps only 10 percent), implementing a means test is costly. Debtors have to provide enough information to show whether they are subject to means testing. The burden of turning over income tax returns and pay stubs increases the cost of every Chapter 7 filing. The additional time and lawyers fees might appear small in a single case, but aggregated over a million cases they are substantial.

The Mechanics of the Fresh Start

The Bankruptcy Code advances a number of radically different objectives. It provides corporations with a way to liquidate their assets and dissolve as well as a way to reorganize. It offers individual debtors a fresh start, and it provides creditors with extra tools to ensure that their debtor has not defrauded them. Bankruptcy law also operates interstitially. It respects non-bankruptcy entitlements and in many instances defers to state-law regimes that accomplish similar objectives. For example, state law, not bankruptcy law, governs insolvent insurance corporations. In the case of individuals, states can insist on defining assets that debtors can shield from creditor levy. None of this is, of course, strictly relevant to bankruptcy's fresh start, but it presents a challenge to those who craft the statutory language or attempt to reform it. One must embed the individual's right to a fresh start in a statute that is doing many other things at the same time.

Section 109 sets out eligibility requirements. Because Chapter 7 is also used to liquidate corporations, the eligibility rules for Chapter 7 are quite broad. They need only exclude insurance companies and other entities that are governed by a different insolvency regime and entities, such as railroads, for which there are special rules in the Bankruptcy Code. Hence, Chapter 7 is available to "persons" other than those listed in

§109(b). As we discussed in the first chapter, §101 defines "persons" broadly to include both flesh-and-blood individuals and corporations.

Section 301 states that eligible individuals may commence a case on their own initiative. Section 541 provides that the filing of a petition under §301 transforms assets (including exempt assets) that the debtor owns into property of the estate, but §541(a)(6) creates an exception for the individual debtor's future earnings. The language is deliberately limited to individuals, as the future earnings of a corporation are assets to which creditors are entitled. Section 727 provides a discharge, again only to individuals, not to corporations. Section 522 ensures that individuals keep exempt assets.

Using a single structure to achieve such different objectives creates difficulties as the statute is amended over time. The Bankruptcy Code becomes longer and less accessible, saddled with drafting mistakes and provisions enacted for narrow purposes that are increasingly opaque to nonexperts. Even basic eligibility rules become compromised. The Bankruptcy Abuse Prevention and Consumer Protection Act, for example, requires debtors to take a credit counseling class before filing for bankruptcy. Formally, §109(h) was added as an eligibility requirement. Whatever the merits of credit counseling, making it an *eligibility* requirement is a mistake: eligibility requirements cut broadly and apply to both voluntary and involuntary cases.

While involuntary petitions are uncommon today, they were originally the only type of bankruptcy petition that could be filed, and they still serve a purpose. An involuntary bankruptcy provides creditors with a single forum to assemble the debtor's assets and scrutinize financial and other records. It also allows a creditor to unwind a transfer—such as a large payment to another creditor—that would be permissible under nonbankruptcy law but that violates bankruptcy's norm of pro rata distribution.

If a creditor wants to take advantage of bankruptcy laws, it begins with §303. That provision allows a creditor to bring an involuntary petition against a person who is an eligible debtor within the meaning of §109. Because credit counseling is an eligibility requirement, anyone who has not taken such a course is immune from an involuntary filing. By putting the credit counseling provision in the wrong place, its drafters abolished involuntary bankruptcy petitions. Such mistakes are typically fixed with a technical corrections bill that follows in the wake of major legislation, and we should expect such missteps to be fixed. It might seem that, even if the problem is not fixed, a court will find a way to work around its literal language. A number of justices on the Supreme Court, however, have used bankruptcy litigation as the battlefield of choice when advancing the idea that judges must construe statutes literally.

Once we pass beyond the eligibility requirements, the important provisions can be divided into those designed to prevent abuse and those that ensure the fresh start. A number of other provisions are designed to ensure further that only honest but unfortunate debtors use the bankruptcy law to enjoy the fresh start. Section 727 supplements §707(b) and prevents debtors from receiving a discharge if they have defrauded their creditors or otherwise abused the process. It can come into play when the debtor makes less than the median income and the misbehavior in question does not come to the attention of the bankruptcy judge or the United States Trustee.

Section 727(a)(2) denies a discharge to debtors who transfer property with the intent to hinder, delay, or defraud creditors. Section 727(a)(3) imposes the sanction if the debtor destroys or fails to keep financial records and thereby makes it impossible for creditors to understand the debtor's affairs. Many debtors who end up in financial trouble, however, are honest individuals who are bad record-keepers. Courts typically do not use the financial records exception to deny a fresh start to such debtors.

History shaped many of the exceptions to discharge under §727. The discharge was originally introduced into bankruptcy law to secure the debtor's cooperation; the intent was not to give the debtor a fresh start but to induce the debtor to cooperate with the creditors and help them assemble the debtor's assets.[4] This explains why a debtor who makes a fraudulent conveyance cannot obtain a discharge but a convicted murderer can. (Whether, however, the murderer can obtain a discharge for the civil claim that the victim's heirs might have is a different question that we confront later.) In addition, §727(a)(8) requires a debtor to wait eight years between one fresh start and the next. This limitation on the right to a fresh start prevents the deliberate wrongdoer from abusing the right. It also works in the debtor's interest because it can make it easier to borrow. Creditors who lend to someone who has just emerged from bankruptcy know that the debtor cannot file a bankruptcy petition before they have a chance to be repaid. Section 727 also ensures that individual debtors complete the credit counseling course that §109 requires.

Other provisions ensure that individuals do not use bankruptcy as a delaying tactic. If within forty-five days of filing the petition the debtor fails to supply the information needed to determine whether means testing applies, the case is automatically dismissed. §521(i). The debtor is not allowed to retain possession of property subject to a purchase money security interest unless the debtor reaches a deal with the creditor or redeems the property by paying the creditor the amount of the secured claim in full. That amount is not the amount of the debt, but the amount the debtor would have to pay for the property if purchased at retail. §506(b)(1). For example, if the collateral is a car, the debtor must turn over a cash payment equal to the amount a used car dealer would charge for such a vehicle.

The automatic stay that keeps secured creditors and landlords at bay is sharply curtailed in cases involving individual debtors. It does not apply, for example, to an eviction action

---

[4] The Statute of 4 Anne ch. 17 (1705), which instituted the discharge in bankruptcy, was in fact called "An act to prevent frauds frequently committed by bankrupts."

involving residential property if the landlord obtains a judgment for possession before the filing of the petition. §362(b)(22). A number of provisions are aimed at serial filers, those who file the petition merely to gain the benefits of the automatic stay. If the debtor filed two or more cases in the previous year, the automatic stay does not even go into effect. §362(c)(3).

Balancing the provisions that prevent individuals from abusing the system are those that ensure that eligible debtors in fact receive a fresh start. The principal provisions at work here are two that we have already mentioned—§§541 and 522. We look at each in turn.

Under §541 the debtor may keep assets that do not become property of the estate. Principal among these assets are earnings from future services (§541(a)(6)) and assets held in a trust that the debtor cannot reach under nonbankruptcy law (§541(c)(2)). To understand how difficult it can be to determine future earnings, consider the situation of a debtor who is a partner in a law firm whose practice generates substantial income.[5] A partner's future income from a law practice does not derive exclusively from the partner's own future work. Future earnings from a law practice are generated in part by existing assets, such as employment contracts with the associates in the firm. Earnings also come from the partner's past efforts. There are accounts receivable and a client base that has been built over time. A partner's role at a law firm might consist only of rainmaking; once the client retains the firm, an associate might perform all the subsequent legal work. None of the income derived from prepetition clients would qualify as the partner's future earnings within the meaning of §541(a)(6). The court must distinguish revenues that flow from the business and those that flow from the debtor's postpetition contribution of labor.

Some courts have valued a practice by asking how much would have been realized in the event that the debtor had sold

---

[5] See FitzSimmons v. Walsh, 725 F.2d 1208 (9th Cir. 1984).

the practice.[6] But one must identify the kind of nonbankruptcy sale that provides the relevant benchmark. (An outright sale would obviate the need to make an estimate, but if the individual files in Chapter 11 and plans to continue to run the business, an actual sale is not in the cards.) A lawyer or doctor who sells a practice usually, as part of the sale, agrees to vouch for the buyer, introduce him to clients or patients, and perhaps work with him through a transitional period. In addition, the new buyer will ordinarily insist on a covenant not to compete. Hence, the amount for which a cooperative debtor could sell the practice outside of bankruptcy may not be the relevant benchmark. A better approximation might be the amount the practice would fetch if the debtor ceased all connections with the business but remained free to open a competing practice.[7]

Problems also arise with the effect that the discharge has on liens and other rights that third parties have in the debtor's property. Suppose a bank lends a borrower $100,000 and takes a mortgage on the borrower's $150,000 home. The discharge prevents the bank from pursuing its claim against the borrower, but the discharge does not cut off the bank's lien on the property. After the Chapter 7 proceeding is over, the bank can still foreclose on the property if the borrower is in default. As noted in chapter 1 above, liens pass through bankruptcy.

To ensure that a debtor enjoys a fresh start, however, bankruptcy law has carved out several exceptions to the doctrine of lien pass-through. For example, a right of redemption under §722 allows the debtor to extinguish liens on property intended for personal, family, or household use if those liens secure dischargeable consumer debt. (The debtor, however, must pay the secured creditor an amount equal to the value of the property.) In addition, the debtor is entitled to avoid judicial liens in exempt property and nonpossessory money security interests (other than purchase money interests) in some kinds of exempt

[6] See, e.g., In re Prince, 85 F.3d 314, 323 n.5 (7th Cir. 1996).
[7] See Ackerman v. Schultz, 250 Bankr. 22 (Bankr. E.D.N.Y. 2000).

property such as household goods and tools of the trade under §522(f). Finally, and most important, liens on the debtor's future earnings do not survive bankruptcy. The Supreme Court established this principle in *Local Loan Company v. Hunt*, which held that an assignment of wages did not survive discharge.[8]

The bankruptcy of Tia Carrere raised the same problem as *Local Loan Company* in a different guise.[9] Carrere, an actress, wanted to escape from a long-term contract with ABC requiring her to appear on *General Hospital,* a daytime television soap opera. A clause in that contract prevented her from becoming a regular on *The A-Team,* a prime-time show. The court had to ask if bankruptcy's fresh start freed her from the unfavorable employment contract. If Carrere had foolishly borrowed money from ABC and lost it all, she would have been able to file a bankruptcy petition and keep her earnings from whatever job she happened to take. Similarly, if a creditor of Carrere's had garnished her wages, the garnishment would not survive bankruptcy. Conceptually, Carrere's promise not to appear elsewhere or indeed any covenant not to compete is the same. ABC has what amounts to an ownership interest in Carrere's future income stream. *Local Loan Company* establishes that such interests do not survive bankruptcy. To be sure, if one can discharge a covenant not to compete in bankruptcy, it will be harder for actresses like Carrere to find jobs in the first place. ABC would be less willing to take on new actors if it is not able to keep them. But this does not distinguish *Carrere* from *Local Loan Company.* Any limit on the doctrine of lien pass-through reduces debtors' ability to commit themselves and hence makes it less attractive for others to enter into agreements with them.

In this case and in others like it, the structure of the Bankruptcy Code makes it hard to confront such questions head on. The agreement with ABC falls within the definition of an

---

[8] 292 U.S. 234 (1934).

[9] In re Carrere, 64 Bankr. 156 (Bankr. C.D. Cal. 1986). Carrere ultimately lost.

executory contract under §365, but the Code deals with this question imperfectly. To resolve the issue courts often rely on such factors as whether the debtor's filing was in good faith. Such an approach makes it difficult to craft coherent principles and apply them consistently.[10] We return to this question when we discuss executory contracts in chapter 6 below.

Section 541(c)(2) looks not at future earnings but at a kind of property held in trust that is beyond the reach of both the debtor and the creditors at the time the petition is filed. The paradigm is the spendthrift trust. A parent might establish a trust for a child prone to impulsive spending and provide that the child could not convey future income from the trust in exchange for a fixed sum today. Nonbankruptcy law respects such provisions. Section 541(c)(2) tells us that bankruptcy law respects them as well. If a restriction on the transfer of a debtor's beneficial interest in a trust is enforceable outside of bankruptcy, it is enforceable inside of bankruptcy. The Bankruptcy Code does not limit the reach of §541(c)(2) to trusts that are denominated spendthrift trusts. It applies equally to any beneficial interest in a trust that has the crucial attribute of being beyond the reach of the debtor or the debtor's creditors.[11] In addition, §541(b)(7) excludes from property of the estate contributions that a debtor has made to various retirement and benefit programs recognized under ERISA and other federal law. Provisions in §522 ensure further that retirement funds kept in tax-exempt accounts are similarly free from creditor levy.

After discharge, the debtor enjoys, free from the claims of the creditors, everything that the debtor would ordinarily enjoy in the absence of bankruptcy other than property of the estate. Future income is the most conspicuous example, but there are

---

[10] One can see this by comparing the opinion (and the result) in *Carrere* with Cloyd v. GRP Records, 238 Bank. 328 (Bankr. E.D. Mich. 1999).

[11] Patterson v. Shumate, 504 U.S. 753 (1992).

others. Consider the right of a spouse to take a statutory share of the decedent's estate rather than what was bequeathed in the will. The spouse has this right under nonbankruptcy law, and this right is not property of the estate, so the spouse retains this right notwithstanding the bankruptcy.[12]

We turn now to §522. In addition to keeping everything that is not property of the estate and nullifying liens on future income under the principle of *Local Loan Company*, the debtor is able to keep exempt assets. The Bankruptcy Code provides a list of exempt property that debtors can keep as part of their fresh start. States, however, can—and most do—decide on their own which of the debtor's assets should be beyond the reach of creditors in bankruptcy and out.[13]

State exemptions vary in detail according to jurisdiction. Some are still firmly rooted in the nineteenth century and include such things as homesteads, church pews, and the family Bible. Most of these statutes have been overhauled in recent years. Modern exemption statutes include pensions and insurance policies. Property that is exempt for purposes of §522(b)(2) may extend beyond what a state explicitly calls "exempt." For example, exempt property may extend to all property that the state has put beyond the reach of a debtor's creditors and that otherwise has the attributes of exempt property, whatever label the state (or substantive federal law) applies.

A state may opt to have nonbankruptcy exemptions (both state and federal) govern exclusively. When it does not, §522(b) allows the debtor to choose whether to take advantage of the nonbankruptcy exemptions or keep the property listed in

---

[12] See In re Brand, 251 Bankr. 912 (Bankr. S.D. Fla. 2000); In re McCourt, 12 Bankr. 587 (Bankr. S.D.N.Y. 1981).

[13] The Constitution gives Congress the power to pass only uniform laws on the subject of bankruptcy. The Supreme Court has held, however, that deferring to state exemption statutes does not prevent a bankruptcy statute from being uniform. See Hanover National Bank v. Moyses, 186 U.S. 181 (1902).

§522(d).[14] The largest exemption in §522(d), apart from the one already noted for tax-exempt retirement accounts, is the federal homestead exemption. It protects about $20,000 of equity that debtors build up in their residences (this amount is adjusted every three years to account for inflation).

Section 522(d)(3) allows a debtor to protect household goods, subject to an overall cap (of about $10,000) and a cap on individual items (of about $500). Again, the exact amount changes over time. Other §522(d) exemptions include the debtor's interest in household goods, health aids, tools of the trade, and a motor vehicle, as well as the debtor's right to receive alimony, support payments, life insurance payments, veteran's benefits, and victim's compensation payments. Some exemptions are limited in scope or amount, while others are not.

Beyond the definition of exempt property, §522 also allows the debtor to "avoid the fixing of" certain liens on such property. This power exists whether the debtor uses the special bankruptcy exemptions or the state and federal nonbankruptcy exemptions. More precisely, §522(f)(1)(a) generally allows the individual debtor to free exempt property from most kinds of judicial liens, including liens created by levy on behalf of a general creditor. Not included are liens that secure an alimony or child-support obligation. Moreover, §522(f)(1)(b) allows the debtor to avoid a nonpossessory, nonpurchase money security interest in specified property.

As noted, most states have their own exemption statutes that work in conjunction with federal exemption statutes (such as the provisions discussed here covering ERISA plans and tax-exempt retirement accounts and social security payments). Some state laws put no dollar cap on the property that can be exempt from creditor levy. In Texas, for example, a debtor's homestead is exempt from creditor levy. Texas limits the size of

---

[14] As we have seen elsewhere (in §109, for example), the dollar amounts are adjusted by regulation every three years.

the homestead (one acre) but not its value.[15] Debtors might use bankruptcy to discharge their debts even though they could pay them in full without great sacrifice, given the equity they have in their homes. One can again argue that a debtor who could pay creditors by selling a large house and moving to a more modest home should not be able to take advantage of Chapter 7. But so long as the debtor lived in the state with the large exemption at the time the loan was taken out, the creditor can take this risk into account. If the debtor moves to a state to take advantage of homestead laws after having incurred the debt, however, then the creditor is at risk. Section 522(p) protects the creditor by capping the amount of exempt property the debtor can keep at $125,000 if the debtor establishes a homestead in the state within 1,215 days of the bankruptcy petition.

Defining Discharge and Nondischargeable Debts

A debtor who files a bankruptcy petition is entitled to a discharge of prepetition claims. The debtor is not free of obligations incurred after the filing of the petition. Moreover, some prepetition burdens remain notwithstanding the discharge because they are not "claims" as defined in the Bankruptcy Code. For example, criminal sanctions such as imprisonment survive bankruptcy. A felon enjoys a discharge, but the discharge does not secure release from prison because the state's right to imprison someone is not a claim. Nor can a debtor use a bankruptcy filing to evade a child-custody order.

It is important to understand exactly what it means to discharge a debt. At a minimum, a discharge gives the debtor an affirmative defense to a suit on a prepetition claim. The effect of a discharge, however, is much broader. Section 524 prevents a creditor from making any efforts to collect payment from the debtor once the petition is filed. How the discharge affects fu-

---

[15] Tex. Stat. Ann. §41.001.

ture interactions between the debtor and the creditor, however, remains unclear.

A debtor may need to deal with the creditor after bankruptcy. For example, a debtor might seek a transcript from a school that had made loans to the debtor that were discharged in bankruptcy. The school and the debtor battle over whether the school has the right to refuse to give the debtor the transcript. The school has no duty to engage in further dealings with the debtor, but it is withholding the transcript solely because the debtor has not paid a debt that has been discharged.[16]

The discharge applies only to the debtor. Section 524(e) provides that the discharge does not relieve any third party from an obligation on the debt. A typical example is a guarantor whom the creditor can sue directly.[17] Complications arise, however, when the debtor has an insurance policy and the victim of an accident needs to sue the debtor to recover under the policy. The question is whether §524 bars an action against the debtor when the victim seeks to recover only from the insurance company. Most courts have held that §524 does not prevent victims from recovering in such cases. These courts reason that because the debtor is not personally liable, such actions against a debtor do not interfere with the fresh start.[18]

Section 525 limits the ability of two parties, the government and the debtor's employer, to discriminate against those who have filed bankruptcy petitions, even though they may never have been creditors of the debtor. A state's discrimination against a debtor may take the following form. Before filing for

---

[16] Some courts in the Third Circuit have held that the withholding of a transcript does not violate the automatic stay. See, e.g., In re Billingsley, 276 Bankr. 48 (Bankr. D.N.J. 2002), but courts elsewhere usually find otherwise. See In re Hernandez, 2005 WL 1000059 (Bankr. S.D. Tex. 2005).

[17] See Terwilliger v. Terwilliger, 206 F.3d 240 (2d Cir. 2000).

[18] See, e.g., Houston v. Edgeworth, 993 F.2d 51 (5th Cir. 1993). These cases arise only when the victim is entitled to the proceeds of the insurance policy (and not the bankruptcy estate).

bankruptcy, a debtor injures someone in a car accident and fails to pay the judgment that resulted from the subsequent tort suit. The state suspends the debtor's driver's license, and the debtor files for bankruptcy. The tort obligation is discharged, but the state refuses to reinstate the debtor's driver's license. In *Perez v. Campbell*, the Supreme Court confronted a case such as this in which, under the relevant statute, the state would not reinstate the debtor's driver's license until the judgment was satisfied, notwithstanding the discharge.[19] The Supreme Court held that a state statute designed to ensure that tort judgments were paid was inconsistent with bankruptcy's fresh start policy.

The principle of *Perez* has been codified in §525, which prohibits "governmental units" from denying licenses or otherwise discriminating against someone solely because that person is in bankruptcy or has not paid a debt discharged in bankruptcy. One should not extend *Perez* too far, however. For example, the doctrine of *Perez* should not apply if, under the relevant statute, the state would not reinstate the driver's license until the debtor offered proof of financial responsibility regardless of whether the debtor had paid the tort obligation.[20] This requirement, unlike the one in *Perez*, does not have the effect of inducing the debtor to pay an obligation that has already been discharged.

The reach of *Perez* may be limited for another reason as well. Conditioning a debtor's right to a driver's license on repayment of a debt is ultimately no different from giving a creditor a lien on some other valuable asset of the debtor. We know from the doctrine of *Long v. Bullard* that such liens survive bankruptcy so long as they do not attach to future earnings. In other words, one cannot extend the reach of *Perez* without cutting back on the reach of *Long v. Bullard*.

Although the Bankruptcy Code defines claims broadly and a discharge affects even those who are not creditors, there are

[19] 402 U.S. 637 (1971).
[20] See Duffey v. Dollison, 734 F.2d 265 (6th Cir. 1984).

limits on the scope of the discharge. A debtor may be eligible for a discharge under §727 but still have some debts that are not dischargeable. Section 523(a) contains a list of nondischargeable debts. We have already noted one of these. Debtors who need to borrow to finance their educations often have no other assets. The only asset they can give to lenders is an interest in their future earnings. They can do this, however, only if such debts are not dischargeable. Section 523(a)(8) provides for this result. Such provisions, of course, do much to explain why means testing is likely to affect only a small number of debtors. Many other rules operate to make bankruptcy unattractive to those who are in fact able to repay their creditors.

To ensure that creditors have a chance to participate in the bankruptcy proceeding, a debtor does not receive a discharge of an ordinary claim unless the debtor includes the debt on the schedules it must file with the court and otherwise complies with procedures that ensure that each creditor is notified of the bankruptcy and has the chance to make a timely filing of a proof of claim. §523(a)(3). If a creditor does not know about the bankruptcy and has no chance to share in the assets, it is able to pursue the debtor after bankruptcy. In many cases, however, the debtor has no nonexempt assets; filing a claim is a pointless exercise, and the trustee advises the creditors not to bother, telling them that they will be notified if assets are later found. In such cases, an omitted creditor has not lost any right. As no other creditor was ever given a deadline, there was never a point at which any filing it might have made would have been untimely. Hence, one can argue that such a debt is discharged along with the others.[21]

The other nondischargeable debts in §523 fall into one of two categories (or sometimes a mixture of both). Either the debt arose out of bad conduct, such as a deliberate tort, or the debt

---

[21] This reasoning is set out in In re Mendiola, 99 Bankr. 864 (Bankr. N.D. Ill. 1989), and has become widely adopted. See, e.g., Judd v. Wolfe, 78 F.3d 110 (3d Cir. 1996).

in question is thought to be particularly important. Debts of the latter kind include child support, alimony, and many tax obligations. The dischargeability of tax obligations arises frequently in the case of an unsuccessful businessperson. Too often individuals fail to pay withholding taxes in the waning days of the business. Their money is used to pay suppliers and workers enough to keep the operation open a few weeks longer. The responsible manager of the business is personally obliged to pay these taxes, regardless of whether the business is a sole proprietorship or a corporation. These tax obligations (depending on when the tax is assessed) are typically not dischargeable. For this reason, as well as many others, taking stock of the debtor's tax position and issuing the appropriate warnings are an essential part of advising a debtor who is in financial trouble.

Section 523(a)'s "bad act" exceptions are aimed in part at curtailing abuse of the bankruptcy system. Section 523(a)(2) states that debts incurred through false pretenses or false financial statements are not dischargeable; §523(a)(2)(c) accordingly limits a debtor's ability to borrow and spend when bankruptcy is imminent and the debtor's good faith is therefore suspect. The *fresh cash doctrine* has been a recurring issue in litigation under §523(a)(2). Suppose a debtor has a loan from a bank. The debtor encounters financial difficulties and returns to the bank for an additional loan, which the debtor obtains through false statements. The bank will argue that if the second loan is consolidated with the first, there is only a single debt and that §523(a)(2) makes the entire loan nondischargeable. Courts are divided on whether the whole loan is nondischargeable or only the fresh cash portion, the part that was obtained with the false statement. Section 523(a)(4) deprives the debtor of the fruits of wrongdoing committed while acting in a fiduciary capacity. The difficulty here is deciding what is and is not done in a fiduciary capacity. One unsettled issue is whether selling collateral and spending the proceeds should trigger this section when state law requires that the debtor hold the proceeds in trust for the creditor. Here, as elsewhere, the deciding factor should not be what state law calls a fiduciary duty but rather what bears the attributes of a fiduciary duty, such as the obligation to maintain separate accounts. Other "bad act" exceptions focus on debts that show particularly reprehensible conduct. Debtors who commit willful and malicious torts, including willful conversions of property, cannot discharge them in Chapter 7, nor can debtors discharge obligations that arise from drunken driving.

The list of nondischargeable debts appears to be growing over time. When Congress is presented with the narrow question whether a particular kind of obligation should be nondischargeable, it may seem that it should be. But it is unwise to focus on one type of obligation in isolation. For example, obligations arising from drunken driving are excepted from discharge while those arising from many other tortious acts are not. Chapter 13, as originally acted, provided a superdischarge that made only a few debts nondischargeable. The same dynamic, however, has played out there, and the two lists now increasingly resemble each other.

A debtor may find that the discharge of a particular debt is not desirable. For example, if a debt is discharged, the creditor may try to collect the debt from a friend or a relative who acted as a guarantor of the initial obligation. Alternatively, the debtor may want to keep a car in which an automobile dealer has a security interest. The discharge will free the debtor from the obligation to pay the dealer, but, under *Long v. Bullard*, the discharge will not affect the dealer's right to repossess the car after the debtor's default as soon as the bankruptcy is over. The creditor may be willing to forgo calling the guarantee or to let the debtor keep the car only if the debtor *reaffirms* the debt. A debtor is always free to repay a debt that has been discharged in bankruptcy. The question of reaffirmation concerns whether debtors can legally bind themselves to repay a debt once it has been discharged.

The rules governing reaffirmations, codified in §524(c), (d), and (k), set forth a two-step inquiry. First, the reaffirmation must be effective under nonbankruptcy law. Second, even if it is, the reaffirmation must meet certain requirements. A reaffirmation, to be effective, must be made before the debtor has formally been granted a discharge. In addition, the reaffirmation must come, in the case of an individual, after the debtor has appeared before the bankruptcy court for a discharge hearing. At this time, the debtor will be told that no discharged debt need be reaffirmed. In addition, the consequences of reaffirmation will be set out. This procedure is the bankruptcy equivalent of a *Miranda* warning.

If the debtor is represented by an attorney, the attorney must file an affidavit stating that the reaffirmation agreement is voluntary and does not impose undue hardship on the debtor. In the absence of an attorney, the court must conclude that the agreement will not impose undue hardship on the debtor and is in the debtor's best interest. Courts are generally reluctant to find reaffirmation in the debtor's best interest when the debtor wants to reaffirm in order to keep driving a luxury car. They are similarly reluctant when a debtor wishes to reaffirm in order to keep a creditor from calling on a guarantee that a relative or friend executed in the debtor's favor. Even if all these requirements have been satisfied, the debtor still gets a sixty-day cooling-off period, during which the debtor is free to rescind the reaffirmation.

Wage-Earner Plans Under Chapter 13

Chapter 7 forces individuals to give up existing assets but allows them to keep future earnings. Chapter 13 reverses things. In a Chapter 13 case, the debtor keeps all assets except a portion of future wages. The portion of the wages that the debtor does not keep is turned over to the trustee for distribution to the prepetition creditors. A debtor who completes performance under the plan is then granted a discharge from all debts provided for by the plan under §1328.

Fewer debts are nondischargeable in Chapter 13 than in Chapter 7, but, as mentioned earlier, the number has been increasing over time. In recent years, Congress has excepted drunken driving debts, educational loans, and criminal restitution obligations from discharge in Chapter 13. After a Chapter 13 discharge, one can use Chapter 7 or Chapter 11 within six years if the Chapter 13 discharge was granted on at least a 70 percent payout plan. §727(a)(9). Thus, the main advantages of Chapter 13 are that one can keep existing assets and that one may be able to discharge a greater number of debts.

Over the past decade, Chapter 13 has proved increasingly important for individual debtors in financial trouble. Each year, hundreds of thousands of Chapter 13 petitions are filed and billions of dollars are paid out under Chapter 13 plans. Debtors who file Chapter 13 petitions often face problems quite different from those who file under Chapter 7. Debtors who file under Chapter 13 sometimes do so not only because they need to sort out their obligations to general creditors but also because they have fallen behind in payments to the bank that holds a mortgage on their home. Chapter 13 allows debtors to take advantage of the automatic stay without at the same time giving up nonexempt assets. The decision to use Chapter 13 rather than Chapter 7 also turns on the practices in the different bankruptcy courts. There is enormous variation across districts in how often Chapter 13 is used and how it is implemented.

In contrast to Chapter 7, not every individual debtor is eligible for Chapter 13. Under §109, those whose debts exceed set amounts—a little more than $300,000 and three times that amount for unsecured and secured debt, respectively—may not file for Chapter 13 relief. Chapter 13 is designed for working individual debtors or couples with limited financial affairs, typically consumers or proprietors of small businesses. Individuals with more at stake cannot use it.

As in Chapter 7, a trustee is appointed in every Chapter 13 case. See §1302. The debtor herself, however, is charged with moving the process forward. Under §1321 she must file a plan with the court that sets out the way in which her future income will be used to pay creditors. The plan, which may modify or reduce the debtor's obligations, see §1322(b), must oblige the debtor to pay her creditors from some or all of her future income. Under §1322(a)(1) and (d), plan payments are limited to five years. Payments are generally limited to three years for those who make less than the median income (measured in the same way as in means testing), but this period may be extended to five years on a showing of cause.

The plan must also satisfy a series of important payment conditions. First, the plan must provide for the full satisfaction, in deferred cash payments, of all allowed claims (and administrative expenses) entitled to priority under §507 unless the holder of such a priority claim (or expense) agrees to some other treatment. See §1322. Second, the plan must either consume all of a debtor's disposable income for five years or provide for the satisfaction of all allowed unsecured claims with property (including promises) of a value, as of the effective date of the plan, at least equal to the amount that the creditors would receive from a Chapter 7 liquidation on that date. See §1325(a)(4). In theory, these provisions together ensure that creditors are no worse off than they would be if the debtor filed under Chapter 7, while priority claims may receive even more.

The requirements imposed on Chapter 13 plans protect unsecured creditors in one more way. Under §1325(b)(1) the trustee (or a creditor who is not being paid in full) may insist that the plan require the debtor to pay out all projected disposable income for three years in the case of debtors who make less than the median and five years for those who make more. "Disposable income" is measured differently depending on whether the debtor made more or less than the median income in the period before bankruptcy.

If the debtor made less than the median, disposable income is defined as income "not reasonably necessary to be expended for the maintenance or support of the debtor or a dependent of the debtor." Creditors will not necessarily find it in their interest to insist on such plans. Under §1307 the debtor may convert the case to Chapter 7 or dismiss the case altogether at any time. This power prevents creditors from demanding the dedication of all disposable income when the debtor makes less than the median. Exceptions can arise, however. The debtor may have a debt that is dischargeable in Chapter 13 but not in Chapter 7. Alternatively, a debtor may have already tried to use Chapter 7 but had his case dismissed under §707(b). The "reasonably necessary" standard of §1325(b)(2) is used to determine whether a plan devotes the debtor's entire disposable income to the plan. Like any standard, it lacks clear contours. There is extensive case law, but it developed when the test applied to all debtors, not merely those who made less than the applicable median.

For debtors who made more than the median, payment obligations under Chapter 13 are calculated in a way that parallels the means test in §707(b). The means test, however, looks at income over the six months before the filing of the bankruptcy petition to assess eligibility for Chapter 7's discharge. That amount may be more than the money the debtor makes going forward. The language of §1325(b)(1) requiring that the debtor's "projected disposable income" be the benchmark for determining payment obligations under the plan is at odds with a benchmark based on past earnings.

One more important requirement imposed in Chapter 13 plans protects holders of secured claims. Within a month of filing the Chapter 13 petition, unless the court orders otherwise, the debtor must commence payments to personal property lessors and secured creditors. §1326(a). If the plan allows the debtor to retain property securing a claim, the plan must provide for full payment of the secured claim unless the creditor consents to less. Recall, however, that under §506(a) claims are bifurcated. A creditor's *secured* claim is limited to the value of the collateral. The balance is the creditor's unsecured claim. Payment on the secured claim may occur over time, if paid with interest. The debtor's obligation under the plan must be secured by a lien on the original collateral. Moreover, the debtor must make equal monthly payments under the plan sufficient to provide adequate protection to the secured creditor. §1325(a)(5).

If a plan meets these requirements and otherwise complies with the provisions of Chapter 13—such as the requirements of a plan's good faith, see §1325(a)(3), and feasibility, see

§1325(a)(6)—the court must confirm the plan. Keep in mind, however, that even after confirmation, the bankruptcy case still remains open. The debtor's creditors remain stayed from collection by §362 (and an individual co-liable with the debtor generally is protected by §1301). The debtor's postpetition acquisitions and earnings become property of the estate under §1306.

Debtors who successfully complete performance under a Chapter 13 plan hold their property "free and clear of any claim or interest of any creditor provided for under the plan." §1327(c). Such debtors also earn a discharge under §1328(a). Moreover, a discharge granted under §1328(a) is not subject to all the exceptions to discharge that are in Chapter 7. (These are set out in §523.) For example, debts arising from willful and malicious injury are dischargeable in Chapter 13, while those arising from drunken driving are not. As Congress continues to expand the number of nondischargeable debts in Chapter 13, however, this difference between the two chapters is becoming less important over time.

Debtors who cannot meet payments under the plan may seek to modify the plan under §1329 or request a discharge if creditors have already received as much as they would have received under Chapter 7. The court might grant such a discharge under §1328(b) only if the plan cannot be modified practically and if the debtors failed for reasons beyond their control. Even in such a case, the discharge extends only to debts that could have been discharged in Chapter 7. That is, debtors cannot discharge any debt listed in §523(a). See §1328(c).

Most debtors choose between using Chapter 7 and Chapter 13, but some debtors try to use the two in sequence. This may happen when a debtor owns commercial real estate that has fallen in value since the debtor subjected the property to a mortgage. By filing in Chapter 7, the debtor discharges his personal obligations, including the obligation to the real estate lender for the difference between the amount of the loan and the value of the collateral. After the Chapter 7 discharge, the debtor still faces a lender with a lien on the real property for the entire amount of the debt. The lender can foreclose unless the debtor pays the entire amount owed on the mortgage loan. The discharge of the lender's unsecured claim prevents the creditor only from seeking a deficiency judgment from the debtor on what it is still owed. The debtor, however, can prevent foreclosure if it now files under Chapter 13 and proposes a plan that provides the lender with a payment stream equal to the present value of its secured claim, a claim worth considerably less than the outstanding amount of the mortgage loan. A debtor who has invested in commercial real estate may initially owe more than the Chapter 13 limit for debt obligations, but Chapter 7 discharges those debts and hence puts the debtor under the limit. These "Chapter 20" cases take advantage of the ability both to insulate future income from creditors under Chapter 7 and to strip down liens in Chapter 13. There is no per se barrier to using them in sequence.[22] A court, however, might refuse to confirm the Chapter 13 plan in a Chapter 20 case on the ground that the plan was filed in bad faith.

A Chapter 13 plan may propose the debtor's retention of collateral for a secured claim and generally "may modify the rights of holders of secured claims." §1322(b). But Chapter 13 protects holders of secured claims from modifications that leave them worse off. The most basic protection is found in §1325(a)(5), which provides that the plan must distribute to the holder of the secured claim property that has a value, as of the effective date of the plan, at least equal to the amount of the claim. Moreover, under the same provision, if the debtor is to retain the collateral, the plan must grant the holder of the secured claim a continuing lien on the collateral until the new obligation is fully paid. Put plainly, a debtor cannot retain collateral unless the plan proposes to pay an amount equal to the value of the collateral, though not necessarily at once. The requirement of a continuing lien supports this full-payment obli-

---

[22] See Johnson v. Home State Bank, 501 U.S. 78 (1991).

gation in the event the debtor fails to complete payments under the plan.

Home mortgages often figure centrally in Chapter 13 cases. A debtor who has fallen behind on his mortgage payments is one of those most likely to file under Chapter 13. When a debtor encounters hard times, it may be that outside of bankruptcy he can prevent foreclosure and loss of his home only by paying off a bank's entire loan in full or by reaching a negotiated settlement with the bank. Particularly when the home has fallen in value, the debtor may find the bank uncooperative. The debtor might file for bankruptcy under Chapter 7, but he will find little relief there, as liquidation of the estate will throw the house back to the bank and state law. Chapter 13 offers the debtor breathing room and a last chance to sort things out.

Filing a Chapter 13 petition merely to take advantage of the automatic stay, however, can be found abusive if it is done without any attempt to put in place a plan to restructure debts.[23] One of the most common abuses of Chapter 13 is the serial filing, in which debtors repeatedly file just on the eve of foreclosure, and courts have had to devise a number of tools to deter the most flagrant forms of misbehavior.[24]

In addition, Chapter 13 contains a number of special provisions that extend more protection to home mortgage lenders than to other secured creditors. The primary limitation on a debtor's right to affect a home mortgage is the general prohibition on modification of the mortgage. See §1322(b)(2). For other kinds of mortgages, a plan will bifurcate an ordinary undersecured claim under §506(a) into a secured and unsecured claim, then treat each part separately. The plan will provide the holder with two new loan obligations, one on account of the secured claim and one on account of the deficiency. As an unsecured claim, the deficiency may well be paid only a few cents

---

[23] See In re Felberman, 196 Bankr. 678, 681 (Bankr. S.D.N.Y. 1995).

[24] See Casse v. Key Bank National Association, 198 F.3d 327 (2d Cir. 1999).

on the dollar. The terms of these loans can differ from each other and from those of the original loan. These new obligations replace the old claim, which may be discharged even if the terms of the original loan are never fully satisfied. Under §1322(b)(2), however, the debtor's ability to modify the rights of holders of secured claims does not extend to rights associated with "a claim secured only by a security interest in real property that is the debtor's principal residence." Section 1322(b)(2) prevents a plan from altering *any* of the terms of the original loan, even if they are not strictly speaking part of the secured claim. An example of such a term would be one that gives the creditor an action against the debtor for the difference between the value of the collateral and the amount of the debt.[25]

Chapter 13 does, however, provide some relief to debtors for their home mortgages. Under §1322(b)(5), a Chapter 13 debtor may cure some defaults on a long-term home mortgage. The cure must occur within a reasonable time and must reinstate the mortgage on its original terms. The exception does not apply if the last mortgage payment becomes due before the final payment under the Chapter 13 plan. In short, Chapter 13 gives debtors a way to keep their homes after a default, even a default that would give the lender a right to foreclose under state law. But during the Chapter 13 plan period and afterward, debtors must continue to pay off the mortgage in full, even if the value of the home has fallen far below the outstanding amount of the debt. The ability to cure only returns debtors to the situation they were in before they defaulted. Unless there has been a change in their circumstances, debtors can quickly find themselves unable to meet these same obligations once again.

When creditors pursue their nonbankruptcy remedies, sooner or later they must have gone so far in the foreclosure process that a debtor can no longer file for bankruptcy and cure

[25] Nobelman v. American Savings Bank, 508 U.S. 324, 329 (1993).

outstanding defaults. Section 1322(c)(1) provides that a debtor loses the right to cure defaults once the residence is sold at a foreclosure sale that is conducted in accordance with applicable nonbankruptcy law. Home mortgages can run for twenty years or longer. In most cases, the term of the mortgage is longer than the term of the plan and the rule of modification or cure just described will apply. For the case in which the remaining term of the home mortgage is less than the length of the Chapter 13 plan, "the plan may provide for the payment of the claim as modified pursuant to §1325(a)(5)," notwithstanding the §1322(b)(2) antimodification clause. §1322(c)(2). Chapter 13 thus gives the debtor some maneuvering room with home mortgages that are near the end of their term.

The complexity of Chapter 13 should not obscure two striking features of the way it works in fact. First, there are widespread differences in Chapter 13 practice. From one circuit to the next, from one state to the next, the role Chapter 13 plays varies dramatically. Fewer than one bankruptcy case in six is a Chapter 13 in the Eastern District of Kentucky, while two out of every three is a Chapter 13 in the Western District of Tennessee. Second, Chapter 13 often falls far short of its ambitions. By some accounts, only one plan in three succeeds.

In addition to Chapter 13, a special chapter of the Bankruptcy Code protects small farmers and fishermen. Chapter 12 balances two competing concerns. First, it tries to give family farmers the ability to keep their farms and fishermen their boats even when they owe a secured creditor more than their assets are worth. Second, it tries to ensure that the property interests of the secured creditors are respected and that these creditors receive the value of their secured claim. These two goals might seem incompatible. If a farm is worth less than what the secured creditor is owed, then giving the secured creditor less than the entire farm seems undercompensatory. The residual interest that the farmer holds has *some* value. To the extent that the interest the farmer keeps has value, the secured creditor would seem to receive less than the full amount of its secured claim. Chapter 12, however, is premised on the notion that a reorganization plan that leaves a farm 100 percent leveraged is permissible.

Farmers have enjoyed special bankruptcy protection for many years. The politics of the 1841 bankruptcy statute were tied to the farm crisis that existed at the time. Similarly, the Frazier–Lemke Act protected farmers in the 1930s. A characteristic of much farm relief legislation has been that it remains in effect for only a finite number of years and then must be reenacted. For many years, Chapter 12 had only limited life, but Congress regularly renewed it. In 2005, it was made a permanent part of the Bankruptcy Code. At the same time its protections were extended to fishermen.

Chapter Three

Corporate Reorganizations
and the Absolute Priority Rule

Introduction

We saw in chapter 2 that the animating principle of bank-ruptcy law for individual debtors is the fresh start, the right to discharge past debts and free future income and other exempt property from the claims of creditors. In this chapter we see that a different principle—the absolute priority rule—animates the law of corporate reorganizations. The absolute priority rule is so central to Chapter 11 and the negotiations surrounding it that we shall spend the bulk of this chapter trying to under-stand its origins as well as its shape today.

A corporation in Chapter 11, like an individual in Chapter 7, receives a discharge at the end of the bankruptcy proceeding, but the discharge has radically different consequences in the two cases. In the case of the individual debtor, the discharge works in conjunction with other parts of the Bankruptcy Code to ensure a fresh start. Discharging old debt does not itself keep creditors from reaching the debtor's future income. What mat-ters in the case of an individual is not simply that debts are dis-charged under §727, but also that future earnings do not be-come property of the estate under §541. In contrast, a corpora-tion's future earnings *do* become property of the estate. For this reason, the discharge itself does not put future income beyond the reach of those who held rights against it before the petition was filed. The discharge of corporate debt provided for in §1141 must serve a purpose altogether different from the dis-charge of individual debt in §727.

A limited liability corporation is not a flesh-and-blood individual, but rather a juridical being that owns assets against which many individuals have rights. We must focus on shareholders and creditors and others and ask what happens to their rights in the wake of the discharge. In the case of an individual in Chapter 7, we have to look at the exclusion of an individual debtor's future income provided by §541 to understand the effect of §727's discharge. Similarly, in the case of a corporation in Chapter 11, we have to look to the other parts of the Code that allocate rights to the corporation's future earnings to understand the effect of §1141's discharge. Section 1141 does not tell us how the earnings of the reorganized business are split among the old creditors and shareholders. Instead, it is the absolute priority rule, as codified in §1129 and other parts of Chapter 11, that determines how those who held rights against the old corporation will enjoy rights in the reorganized corporation.

Before we look at the absolute priority rule, it is important to understand the purpose of Chapter 11 for corporate debtors. In the case of the individual debtor, Chapter 7 is meant to provide a substantive right: it allows an individual to enjoy a new life free of the burdens of unmanageable debt. A corporation is different. We may care about the workers or the shareholders or the creditors, but the corporation itself is merely a legal fiction. It is not a sentient being, and there is no virtue in preserving a corporate charter for its own sake.

Moreover, Chapter 11 cannot remedy the problems of an unsound business venture. Suppose an entrepreneur decides to open a new restaurant in a strip mall in southern California. The restaurant specializes in Chicago dim sum. Customers eat in sequence small plates of food that provide a sample of every ethnic neighborhood in the city. The typical meal begins with a miniature bratwurst. Next is a small deep-dish pizza, followed by mu shu pork, and then a small portion of barbeque ribs, and then a piece of Baklava from Greektown for dessert. As it happens, aging, calorie-conscious baby-boomers in California have little interest either in going to this strip mall or in sampling this kind of cuisine. Chapter 11 can do nothing to make this restaurant or Chicago dim sum a success. It does not matter whether the restaurant has no creditors or dozens of them. No one wants to dine at this restaurant, and bankruptcy law can do nothing to change this. The assets of the restaurant are best put to another use.

Some businesses that cannot pay their debts may nevertheless be enterprises that are worth keeping intact. The archetypal case is a railroad. (As we shall see shortly, reorganizations of railroads in the late nineteenth century were the progenitors of modern Chapter 11.) The assets of a railroad—rights-of-way over narrow strips of land, hundreds or thousands of miles of iron rails, millions of wooden ties, and assorted bridges across the country—have relatively little scrap value. For this reason, a railroad may be worth keeping intact even if it does not carry enough traffic to pay back its construction costs. Building the railroad may have been a mistake, but, once built, the best use of the assets may still be as a railroad. Unlike a restaurant in a bad location that serves bad food, the railroad's assets may have no better use. Nevertheless, everyone has to confront the fact that the railroad cannot pay off its creditors. There needs to be a forum in which the rights of creditors and shareholders are sorted out.

If creditors of the railroad had the right to invoke the rules of various states governing debt collection, any given creditor would have a chance of being paid in full. It could grab the nearest assets of the railroad and sell them for scrap. But a remedy premised on each creditor's pursuit of its own interests could lead to the dismemberment of the railroad. The creditors are better off if the railroad is kept in one piece. They need to enforce their claims against the railroad in a way that preserves the railroad's value as a going concern. The struggle to sort out competing claims to the assets should not keep the assets from being put to their best use.

Ensuring assets are put to their best use requires recognizing that some parties are not going to be paid in full, and a coherent bankruptcy law has to identify them. The basic distributional rule of Chapter 11—the one as central to it as the fresh start policy is to individuals—is the absolute priority rule. The substantive idea behind the absolute priority rule can be put simply: senior creditors are paid before junior creditors, and creditors are paid before shareholders. The rhetoric of the fresh start often creeps into discussions of Chapter 11, but one should not be misled by the notion of "rehabilitating" a corporate debtor.

Some might wish for a bankruptcy law that brings together all affected by the failure of a business, whether a creditor or not, and ensures fair treatment for everyone. Our bankruptcy law, however, is squarely focused on vindicating legal rights established outside of bankruptcy. The notion that Chapter 11 does otherwise or takes into account interests beyond those of people who hold substantive rights outside of bankruptcy is simply wrong. One should not allow such wishful thinking to obscure its fundamental harshness. Respecting nonbankruptcy entitlements while ensuring that a viable business continues is a tough task, and the procedures needed to bring it about are correspondingly complicated. The easiest way to understand them is to see where they came from. Hence, we look first to history.

Equity Receiverships and the Origins of Chapter 11

We can trace the roots of Chapter 11 back to the problems attending the rise of the great railroads in the late nineteenth century. These were the first giant corporations. They connected all parts of the United States and revolutionized the way people lived. Before the railroads, milk would spoil long before it reached the urban marketplace. Ranchers and farmers had only a small market for their meat and produce. The railroad created a national marketplace. The dinner table of New Yorkers included for the first time meat from cattle raised in Kansas and bread from grain grown in Missouri.

Railroads, however, required capital on an unprecedented scale. Laying a single mile of track cost $20,000 or more—

sometimes much more. Even by 1860, private investment in railroads exceeded $1 billion. Investment bankers such as J. P. Morgan, August Belmont, and Kidder Peabody had to turn to large commercial centers of Europe for the capital to finance the transcontinental railroads that were to be built over the next three decades. These investment bankers sat on the boards of the various railroads and represented the interests of their European investors.[1] Because they counted on repeated dealings with these investors, they had the incentive to represent them well.

The period between 1865 and 1890 was one of enormous growth for railroads. The period also saw the consolidation of different lines in haphazard and unpredictable ways. More than 75,000 miles of track were laid down in the 1880s alone. This was a time of both increasing competition and increasing government regulation. Competition among the different lines intensified; cartels came into existence and then fell apart. At the same time, the early 1890s brought on one of the United States's worst economic downturns. All these factors created an industry that by the mid-1890s was insolvent. Most of the railroads that had been built could not meet their fixed obligations. More than half the railroads in the United States went through reorganization during this period, some more than once.[2]

The typical railroad needing reorganization had few general creditors. There were different classes of bonds, each widely held by diverse investors, many of whom were in Europe. One bond was secured by track between points A and B, another by track between B and C, a third between C and D, and so on. Points B through Y were in the middle of nowhere, and the terminals at points A and Z connected to solvent railroads owned by the shareholders. The collateral of individual creditors

---

[1] See Alfred D. Chandler Jr., The Visible Hand: The Managerial Revolution in American Business 146 (1977).

[2] For a history of railroad reorganizations of the 1890s, see Stuart Daggett, Railroad Reorganization (1908).

added value to the ongoing railroad. This value, however, could not be realized by foreclosing on the collateral; only through the active participation of all parties could the value of the constituent parts be maximized.

Bringing about a successful reorganization was hard. The value of the railroad had to be estimated against a background of rapid technological and regulatory change. The claim of the many different kinds of bondholders turned on how much their collateral contributed to the earnings of the railroad as a whole. Moreover, many of the investors lived abroad and could not actively participate in the reorganization. They had to rely on their investment bankers and their lawyers to represent them. Although Congress had the power to enact federal bankruptcy law, none was in place during this period. Faced with dispersed interests with uncertain value and no statutory guidance, the lawyers used the equity receivership to reorganize the railroads.

Because the railroads were the first experiments in large aggregations of capital from diverse investors, many of the terms of the investment contracts were left blank or imported mechanically from real estate transactions. The law of equity receiverships had to supply the missing terms, and these had to respond to the distinct problems that arose when the railroad needed a new capital structure. What emerged in the end were the basic features of Chapter 11.

Consider a railroad that owes $100 million to several dozen different kinds of bondholders, each of whom has a security interest in different assets of the railroad. In the aggregate, these bonds cover all the hard assets of the railroad. The railroad also owes a diverse group of general creditors $1 million. The railroad cannot meet payments on the $101 million debt. The bondholders realize that the time has come to restructure the railroad. They call on their lawyers and their investment bankers. The lawyers persuade a general creditor to ask a federal court to appoint a receiver for the railroad. The receiver the court appoints is often the group of manager-shareholders that has been running the railroad. In the meantime, lawyers and the investment bankers form committees, each representing the interests of a different group of shareholders or creditors.

Each bondholders committee then tries to persuade those holding its bonds to deposit them with it and give it the power to assert all the rights of the bondholders in the reorganization. Let's assume that in our case, 90 percent of the bondholders give their bonds to their respective committees. Similarly, another committee holds 90 percent of the stock. The various committees then meet and create a new committee, the reorganization committee, on which members of each of the other committees sit and that is empowered to act on behalf of the other committees. The reorganization committee now controls 90 percent of all outstanding securities. It then proceeds to form a plan of reorganization.

Under the plan, each participant in the reorganization who holds a $100 bond in some asset of the railroad will give it up in exchange for a $50 bond secured by all the assets of the railroad. The participating shareholders are given the option to acquire equity of the reorganized railroad in exchange for their shares in the old railroad and $1 million in new cash. Through their representatives on the reorganization committee, all the participating creditors and shareholders consent to this plan.

The reorganization committee then borrows $10 million from a bank on a short-term basis. At this point, the receiver conducts a foreclosure sale in which the assets of the railroad are sold to the highest bidder. At the sale, the reorganization committee is the only bidder. It bids $10 million for the entire railroad and takes over the assets of the railroad after it pays the receiver. The receiver takes the $10 million and distributes it to the bondholders. (Nothing goes to the general creditors, because the sale price is not enough to pay the bondholders in full.) Because the reorganization committee itself owns 90 percent of the bonds, the receiver gives back to the reorganization committee $9 million of the $10 million the committee paid to buy the railroad. The receiver pays the other $1 million to the nonparticipating bondholders who did not give their bonds to their committees.

The old corporation is now a hollow shell and the old shareholders dissolve it under state law. Because the legal entity that was the railroad now no longer exists, all claims against it are worthless. The stockholders who did not turn over their rights to the relevant committee are out of luck, as are the general creditors who did not have any chance to participate at all. At this point, the reorganization committee has the assets of the railroad and the $9 million it received from the receiver. The committee now forms a new corporation and transfers all the assets of the railroad to it. The new corporation creates $45 million in bonds and gives them to the old participating bondholders as promised in the reorganization plan. All the stock in the new railroad is given to the old shareholders when they come up with the $1 million in cash they promised in the reorganization plan. With this $1 million and the $9 million the receiver gave it, the committee repays the $10 million bank loan. The reorganization committee now goes out of existence.

If we focus entirely on legal forms, we see a new corporation with a new set of ownership claims against it. In substance, however, the story is quite different. If one collapses the various steps in this elaborate dance, most of the bondholders and shareholders have simply exchanged their old claims against the railroad for new ones that take better account of the condition in which the railroad finds itself. We have exactly the same railroad with the same managers and the same investors, but the ownership rights of the investors have been adjusted so that they are in line with the revenue that the railroad actually earns.

Under Chapter 11 of the Bankruptcy Code, we would say that the railroad's old obligations to its creditors have been discharged. As we noted at the start of this discussion, however, "discharge" in this context means something quite different from what it does in the case of the individual who is given a fresh start. The discharge is only one part of the mechanism that allows the business to acquire a new capital structure.

The debates over the railroad reorganization therefore revolved not around the meaning of a fresh start for corporations but around other issues. First, there was the question of the rights of those who did not participate in the reorganization. In our example, these included 10 percent of the bondholders and the diverse general creditors. The bondholders who did not participate argued that they were given only ten cents on the dollar, while those who did participate were given fifty cents on the dollar. To the response that they could have participated and enjoyed fifty cents on the dollar if they had wanted, these bondholders would argue that the reorganization forced them to choose between the lesser of two evils. Either their claims would be cashed out at ten cents on the dollar at a fictitious foreclosure sale or they would have to submit to whatever terms the reorganization committee dictated. None of the individual bondholders had enough of an investment in the railroad to go through the effort necessary to keep the reorganization committee from doing whatever it pleased. As a result, insiders remained in control of the process and ended up in control of the railroad.

The equity receivership thus had to navigate between two dangers: that of insiders taking advantage of the scattered bondholders and that of a few dissident bondholders free riding on the efforts of others to recapitalize the railroad. Under the solution that ultimately emerged in the equity receivership, the judge insisted on an *upset price*, a minimum price that the reorganization committee would have to bid at the foreclosure sale to acquire the assets of the railroad. By ensuring that the upset price was sufficiently high, the minority bondholders would be given an amount commensurate with the value of their nonbankruptcy rights.[3] The defect of this approach in practice was that judges tended to keep the upset price low. They feared that a high upset price would undermine the successful reorganization because it would require the reorganization committee to come up with more cash than it could raise.

---

[3] See First National Bank of Cincinnati v. Flershem, 290 U.S. 504 (1934).

The 1978 Bankruptcy Code replaced this way of protecting dissenters in a class of creditors. Congress folded into the corporate reorganization a procedure that had been used in plans under the 1898 Bankruptcy Act. Under the 1898 Act, the debtor would meet with creditors, fill out schedules of assets and liabilities, and subject itself to examination. At this point, the debtor would propose a plan, or *composition*, in which the creditors' claims were scaled back. If the plan was accepted by a majority of the creditors and if the majority held more than half of the outstanding debt, the court would approve it if, among other requirements, the plan was in the best interests of the creditors.[4] Courts interpreted "best interests" to mean that those creditors who did not vote in favor of the plan had to receive as much as they would receive in an orderly liquidation of the business.[5] This method of protecting dissenters in a class of creditors, codified in §1129(a)(7), replaced the use of an upset price in the equity receivership (and its statutory successor in old Chapter X).

More important in the dynamics of modern Chapter 11 are the procedures that emerged in response to the complaints from the general creditors who had no chance to participate in the reorganization at all. It might seem that the general creditors have nothing to complain about. The railroad is worth less than $100 million, the amount the bondholders were owed. Even if the railroad's assets were sold for cash at their fair market value, the general creditors would receive nothing. Given the sorry condition of the business, they are not entitled to anything. This risk is one they should have taken into account when they extended credit to the railroad.

Nevertheless, we must at least have in place procedures that ensure that the railroad is indeed worth less than $100 million. We need to be sure that the senior creditors and the sharehold-

---

[4] Act of July 1, 1898, ch. 541, §12b, 30 Stat. 541, 549.

[5] See Fleischmann & Devine Inc. v. Saul Wolfson Dry Goods Co., 299 F. 15 (5th Cir. 1924).

ers have not restructured the railroad in a way that slighted others' rights. To ensure the protection of such rights, courts fashioned over the course of many decades a set of rules, loosely identified as the *fair and equitable principle*. Section 1129(b) codifies this principle. It requires that a plan be fair and equitable before it can be confirmed over the objection of a class of claims. To understand what "fair and equitable" means, one must know the sequence of cases from which the principle emerged. The most important of these is *Northern Pacific Railway Company v. Boyd*.[6]

In 1886 a man named Spaulding had supplied $25,000 worth of materials and labor to the Coeur D'Alene Railroad for which he was never paid. The assets of the Coeur D'Alene, after several restructurings, ultimately became part of the Northern Pacific Railroad. Spaulding believed he could hold the Northern Pacific Railroad liable for this debt. Before he acquired a judgment against it, however, the Northern Pacific Railroad became insolvent and went through an equity receivership, out of which emerged a new entity called the Northern Pacific Railway.

Spaulding's successor, a man named Boyd, did not participate in the reorganization of the Northern Pacific Railroad and instead sued the new entity. The dispute finally reached the United States Supreme Court in 1913. The Court found first that the old Northern Pacific had indeed been responsible for the obligations of Coeur D'Alene. The Court then had to ask whether the new Northern Pacific was responsible for the debts of the old.

Boyd argued that the court-supervised sale could not extinguish his rights because the old shareholders remained the shareholders of the new entity. He invoked the common law rule, based on fraudulent conveyance doctrine, that a landowner who purchases back his property at a foreclosure sale takes subject to the claims of junior creditors, even though a

---

[6] 228 U.S. 482 (1913).

third party buying at arm's length would not. Boyd had not participated in the reorganization or relinquished his claims. Thus he could hold the Northern Pacific Rail*way* answerable for the obligations of the Northern Pacific Rail*road*.

Lawyers for the Northern Pacific Railway argued that the sale had to be respected. The real estate analogy was inapt, they asserted. The Rail*way* was an entity that was distinct from the Rail*road*. One should respect the formal differences, even though the shareholders of the two were the same. The judicial sale was regular in form and free from fraud. The assets had been sold for a fair price and that price was for less than what the secured creditors were owed. Had Boyd participated in the reorganization, he would have received nothing. Recharacterizing the transaction would only foster strike suits and make reorganizations of insolvent railroads impracticable. The Northern Pacific Railway lost below and appealed to the Supreme Court.

In *Boyd*, a divided Court found that the common law principle limiting the effect of debtor purchases at a foreclosure sale existed in the law of corporate reorganizations as well:

> As against creditors, [the sale] was a mere form. Though the Northern Pacific Railroad was divested of the legal title, the old stockholders were still owners of the same railroad, encumbered by the same debts. The circumlocution did not better their title against Boyd as a nonassenting creditor. They had changed the name but not the relation.[7]

Nor did it matter that the assets were worth less than what creditors senior to Boyd were owed:

> [T]he question must be decided according to a fixed principle, not leaving the rights of the creditors to depend upon the balancing of evidence as to whether, on the day of sale the property was insufficient to pay prior encumbrances.[8]

[7] Id. at 506–07.
[8] Id. at 507–08.

The Court did not go so far as to say that all of real estate foreclosure law should be mechanically transplanted to the law of corporate reorganizations. The Court held only that a complete freezeout of an intervening creditor was not permitted. Indeed, the Court itself was quick to note that its holding was narrow:

> [We do not] require the impossible and make it necessary to pay an unsecured creditor in cash as a condition of stockholders retaining an interest in the reorganized company. His interest can be preserved by the issuance, on equitable terms, of income bonds or preferred stock. If he declines a fair offer he is left to protect himself as any other creditor of a judgment debtor, and, having refused to come into a just reorganization, could not thereafter be heard in a court of equity to attack it.[9]

In contrast to real estate foreclosures, a plan of reorganization could include shareholders if the creditor were given a fair offer in a just reorganization. Exactly what these terms meant, the Court did not explain. Lower courts had to identify on their own the contours of the "fixed principle" that should be at work and out of this emerged a set of ideas of what constituted a fair and equitable plan.

After *Boyd*, a plan could not bypass junior creditors unless such creditors consented or had their day in court. Ex post assertions of fairness by a coalition of senior creditors and shareholders would not suffice. The question remained, however, whether or under what conditions a nonconsensual bypass of junior creditors was permissible *even given* their day in court. The Court ultimately confronted this question in *Case v. Los Angeles Lumber Products.*[12]

In *Case*, the debtor was a holding company whose principal asset was the Los Angeles Shipbuilding & Drydock Corpora-

---

[9] Id. at 508.
[12] 308 U.S. 106 (1939).

tion. This corporation had built ships for the navy during World War I but languished during the 1920s and 1930s. It sought to reorganize itself in 1937. The only creditors were holders of twenty-year bonds due in 1944. Holders of more than 90 percent of the face amount of the bonds voted in favor of the plan. The plan gave 23 percent of the stock in the new corporation to the old shareholders. These shareholders planned to continue to play a managerial role in operating the business, but they were not contributing any new cash.

The district court had held that the plan was fair and equitable. It noted that only two bondholders had objected to the plan, and the court did not want to give a couple of dissenters the ability to hold up a reorganization approved by a substantial majority of the bondholders. The court justified the continued participation of the old equityholders on the grounds that the shareholders were willing to assume managerial responsibilities in the company and that they were "the only persons who [were] familiar with the company's operations and who [had] experience in shipbuilding." In addition, the court noted,

> [m]ost of the present bondholders are widely scattered with small holdings, and their position would be benefited by being associated with old stockholders of financial influence and stability who might be able to assist in proper financing.[13]

The reorganization was brought about, it seems, from the need for additional capital, not by the threat of foreclosure by existing creditors. Because of a previous workout, interest payments were owed only if earned, and the creditors lacked the power to foreclose until 1944.

When *Case* reached the Supreme Court on appeal, the Court had a vehicle to confront the different interpretations of the

---

[13] In re Los Angeles Lumber Products Co., 24 F. Supp. 501, 513 (S.D. Cal. 1938), aff'd, 100 F.2d 963 (9th Cir.), rev'd, 308 U.S. 106 (1939).

[15] 308 U.S. at 122.

"fair and equitable" principle that had been debated in the wake of *Boyd*. Under one view, the approval of the plan by 90 percent of the creditors was enough. Requiring unanimity was unreasonable, and the old shareholders had to be given some of the going-concern value or they would not cooperate in reorganizing the corporation. A court should confirm a plan if a class of diverse investors approved the plan, if each investor received what it would receive in a liquidation, and if the overall process was regular.

The competing view was altogether different. Under this view, allowing the old equity to continue was a source of mischief. Rather than making it possible to obtain their help after the reorganization, it gave old shareholders an opportunity to hold up other investors. In a business such as a shipyard, shareholders do not control the day-to-day operations. Professionals can be brought in to do the job. Only in the narrowest of circumstances should old equity be permitted to continue in the face of any dissent.

Speaking through Justice William O. Douglas, the *Case* Court sided squarely with the second view. The Court first rejected the idea that dissenters are entitled only to their share of a debtor's liquidation value, leaving others to decide how any surplus would be divided. The Court held instead that the fair and equitable standard afforded each creditor its "full right of priority" in the business as a going concern. *Case* thus forged a link between the phrases "fair and equitable" and "absolute priority," a link that lawyers, judges, and Congress have accepted ever since.

Once Justice Douglas established this link, he was led to cut back sharply on the shareholders' ability to participate in the reorganization of an insolvent company over a creditor's objection. The absolute priority rule allowed shareholders to participate in the new venture only if they paid fair value for their continuing interest in a reorganized debtor. Moreover, to ensure that the shareholders paid fair value, the Court required that such payments be easy to value. If a creditor objected to an insolvent debtor's plan of reorganization, the plan could not include a distribution to old equity unless each stockholder's participation was based "on a contribution in money or in money's worth, reasonably equivalent in view of all the circumstances to the participation of the stockholder."[15]

Under pre-Code law, a single dissenting creditor could insist that a plan be fair and equitable. This gave one creditor considerable holdup power. Indeed, in *Case* itself, one of the dissenting creditors had a long history of buying claims at a deep discount and holding up reorganizations until he was paid in full. Under the Bankruptcy Code, the "full right" of absolute priority Justice Douglas identified now comes into play only if a class as a whole opposes the plan.

The "fair and equitable" language in §1129(b) embodies the absolute priority rule. Those with rights against the assets of a corporation under nonbankruptcy law receive interests in the reorganized corporation according to the priority they enjoyed under nonbankruptcy law. A creditor who is entitled to be paid before another creditor outside of bankruptcy (by virtue, say, of a security interest) is entitled to be paid first in bankruptcy as well.

Similarly, general creditors are entitled to be paid before shareholders. The effect of the discharge, in other words, is almost the opposite of what we see in the case of the flesh-and-blood individual debtor. In the case of an individual, the discharge (coupled with the exclusion of future income from property of the estate) allows individuals to preserve their right to future earnings in the face of creditors' claims. In the case of a corporation, discharge (coupled with the absolute priority rule) allows creditors to extinguish the shareholders' right to future earnings when the assets are not worth enough to pay the creditors off in full. We will look more closely at the mechanics of §1129 in the next section.

Chapter 11 and the Absolute Priority Rule

Section 1129(b) comes into operation when a reorganization plan fails to garner the acceptance of all adversely affected (or *impaired*) classes of claims and interests and thus fails to satisfy §1129(a)(8). Section 1129(b) first requires that a plan not "discriminate unfairly." If two classes contain claims or interests of identical priority, absent some special circumstance that would justify subordination of one class, a plan cannot provide less to one class on a pro rata basis unless that class consents. The requirement stops short of mandating identical treatment for classes at the same priority level. A plan does not discriminate unfairly merely because it gives cash to one class of general creditors and long-term notes to another. The plan will pass muster if there is a reason for the different treatment and if the cash payments and the notes give claims in each class the same pro rata share of the debtor's assets. A tort victim who needs surgery, for example, might be paid in cash, while an institutional lender might receive a note, as it has no similar need for payment in cash.

Section 1129(b) then requires that each class that rejects the plan be treated in a way that is "fair and equitable." These words are a term of art and, standing alone, are sufficient to require absolute priority among the different stakeholders. The section goes on to add specific requirements to ensure that absolute priority is respected. Through them, the core ideas of the judicially created fair and equitable doctrine remain fixed even if the edges of the doctrine continue to evolve.

With respect to a class of allowed secured claims, the fair and equitable principle requires, at a minimum, that each holder of a secured claim receive a stream of payments with a discounted present value equal to the value of the collateral. See §1129(b)(2)(a). Moreover, this stream of payments must be secured by a lien on the creditor's collateral. If the collateral is sold, the creditor's lien attaches to the proceeds. Alternatively, the plan could propose a different treatment that provides for the realization of the *indubitable equivalent* of the secured claim. This language is taken from Learned Hand's opinion in *In re*

Murel Holding.[16] The test, however, is sufficiently stringent that it is likely to be of use to the debtor only under narrow circumstances.

A reorganization plan must meet an additional requirement to be confirmed over the objection of a class of secured claims. The plan must also provide a stream of payments equal to the face amount of the secured claim. In most cases, this requirement is redundant. In a world in which discount rates are positive, a stream of payments over time equal in value to a given amount must total more than the face amount owed. Hence, this requirement matters only if the secured claim is for more than the value of the collateral despite the operation of §506(a), which generally equates the two. A mismatch can occur if a secured creditor makes what is called the §1111(b)(2) election. Under this provision, a secured creditor can elect to have its entire claim treated as secured regardless of the collateral's value. As a result, the stream of a plan's payments must not only be equal in value to the collateral, as determined by the judge, but the face amount of the stream of payments in the aggregate must equal the total amount of the claim that the collateral supports. The election is a way in which the secured creditor gives up its deficiency claim and in return limits the extent to which its lien can be stripped down as a result of judicial undervaluation of the collateral.

Section 1129(b)(2)(b) fleshes out the fair and equitable standard for a class of unsecured claims that rejects the plan. If the plan awards any property to old equity (or to a junior class of claims) on account of the old equity interest (or junior claim), the plan must provide each holder of an unsecured claim with property that is at least equal in value to the amount of the claim. In other words, unless the plan proposes to pay unsecured claims in full, those junior to them must be wiped out if the plan is to be crammed down over objection by the holders of unsecured claims. This provision seems straightforward

---

[16] 75 F.2d 941 (2d Cir. 1935).

enough. But complications arise when holders of old equity wish to remain and are contributing new value. They can argue that they receive new equity on account of the new capital, not "on account of" their old interests. Hence, holders of old equity argue, notwithstanding §1129(b), the plan does not have to pay the unsecured claims in full.

If the equityholders enjoy the exclusive right to buy the equity, however, they have an option, which is itself a form of property. In the last chapter of this book we shall return to the question of equity participation when a class of claimholders votes against the plan. For the moment, it is worth noting that in the continuing evolution of the fair and equitable principle, courts have further protected creditors by insisting that market benchmarks be used to ensure that equity is paying top dollar. A judge might, for example, lift exclusivity and entertain other plans as soon as the debtor proposes a plan in which the old equity participates and a class of claimholders objects.[17]

Section §1129(b)(2)(c) applies to a class of preferred stock interests. Under corporate law, preferred stock, though classified as equity and thus as an interest, is a hybrid between debt and equity, inferior to the former but superior to the latter. The "preference" is typically a right to insist that neither dividends nor any other payments go to the corporation's common shares unless and until the corporation pays the preferred shareholders specified amounts analogous to interest and principal on a debt. The fair and equitable standard requires that a reorganization plan honor these preferences—called *liquidation preferences* or sometimes *redemption prices*—with provision of full payment, though not necessarily in cash. If the plan fails to do this, then the holders of more junior interests, those who hold common stock, may not receive any property on account of their old interests.

---

[17] Bank of America v. 203 North LaSalle Street Partnership, 526 U.S. 434 (1999).

For its part, common equity also is protected by the fair and equitable standard of §1129(b)(2)(c), though in a more limited way befitting common equity's status of lowest priority. A plan is not fair and equitable to a class of common equity interests unless the plan provides property with a value at least equal to the value of those interests. This is simply a requirement that creditors not capture the entire value of a solvent debtor. This matters only rarely, as debtors that can pay their creditors usually do not end up in bankruptcy.

As you consider these provisions, keep in mind that the fair and equitable standard is a *class-based* right. The holder of an individual claim or interest can demand at least what it would have received in a Chapter 7 liquidation. If, however, a class votes to make a sacrifice of its priority, a dissenter within the approving class cannot block the plan on the basis of that sacrifice.

The absolute priority rule sets the ground rules for Chapter 11, but it does not identify all the effects of filing a Chapter 11 petition. For example, a secured creditor may worry that if it works too closely with the debtor in crafting a nonbankruptcy workout, it will be charged with being an insider or be subject to labor laws or environmental laws.[18] A nonbankruptcy restructuring of the debt may also bring unfavorable tax consequences for the secured creditor that can be avoided in bankruptcy. If the secured creditor wants to continue to finance a business, it may be better off doing it under the umbrella of Chapter 11 as a debtor-in-possession (commonly abbreviated as a "dip") lender. Then it would be able to retain significant control, its priority would be respected, and payments to junior debtholders would be suspended. Finally, the secured creditor must face the possibility that a nonbankruptcy workout will

---

[18] See United States v. Fleet Factors Corp., 901 F.2d 1550 (11th Cir. 1990). Lawmakers and judges, however, are sensitive to the possibility of demanding too much of creditors here. See, e.g., Monarch Tile, Inc. v. City of Florence, 212 F.3d 1219 (11th Cir. 2000).

only postpone the inevitable. If the secured creditor makes compromises in the workout, it may be worse off in a subsequent Chapter 11 case relative to those who refused to compromise. A long-term secured creditor may be better off in Chapter 11 than it would be if it had to wait and watch while the debtor paid off short-term obligations that were junior to the one owed it.

The ambition of every lawyer whose client files a Chapter 11 petition is to persuade each group of creditors to consent to a plan of reorganization. Whether a group consents depends on its rights under the plan versus the rights it would have if it refused to go along with the plan. The absolute priority rule is central to the law of corporate reorganizations because it is the source of the substantive rights as well as the procedural protections that each participant in a reorganization enjoys. Parties can insist that the priority rights they enjoyed outside of bankruptcy be respected inside. Nevertheless, every junior party, including the shareholders, can invoke elaborate procedures before their rights are compromised. The absolute priority rule allows the senior parties to insist on full payment, but it also grants all junior parties those procedural protections necessary for a "just reorganization." Resolving this tension between substantive and procedural rights that began with *Boyd* remains central to answering the hard questions that arise under Chapter 11.

The law and practice of Chapter 11 establishes a framework for negotiations. The dynamics of any negotiation are defined by what there is to bargain over and the place of each of the parties in the pecking order. Before a plan of reorganization can take place, we must find out what assets the debtor has and we must know the relative positions of each of the parties. In the next few chapters, we step back from the dynamics of reorganization practice per se and explore how we go about establishing the stakes the parties are fighting over and their rights vis-à-vis one another. Once we understand these, we will return to the reorganization process itself and explore it in greater detail.

Chapter Four

Claims Against the Estate

We now turn to the way bankruptcy law establishes the debtor's *liabilities* and *assets*—what the debtor's obligations are and what assets exist to meet them. We must determine who gets what. Figuring out the "who" is the problem of claims, which we examine in this chapter. Figuring out the "what" is the problem of assets, which we focus on in the next chapter. In both cases our starting point is nonbankruptcy law. The *Butner* principle is perhaps most powerful when we look at the subject of claims in bankruptcy. As the Supreme Court notes, "[c]reditors' entitlements in bankruptcy arise in the first instance from the underlying substantive law creating the debtor's obligation."[1] Another Supreme Court case—*Chicago Board of Trade v. Johnson*[2]—tells us to use the nonbankruptcy baseline to identify the debtor's assets.

Establishing a Claim Against the Estate

A creditor often first learns of a bankruptcy filing when it receives notice of it from the bankruptcy clerk. Rule 2002. When a debtor files for bankruptcy, it must fill out schedules that list its liabilities and the names and addresses of its creditors. If you are a creditor and are included on this list, you will be sent notice of the bankruptcy and you will be given a chance to take the appropriate procedural steps to vindicate your rights. Your first step would be to file a form known as a proof of claim. Once that is filed, the claim is "allowed" in the absence of objection. The consequences of failing to file a proof of claim de-

---

[1] Raleigh v. Illinois Department of Revenue, 530 U.S. 15, 20 (2000).
[2] 264 U.S. 1 (1924).

pend on whether your debtor is an individual or a corporation, whether your debtor is in Chapter 7 or Chapter 11, and whether you are listed on the debtor's schedules.

Take first the case of an individual debtor who files a Chapter 7 petition and fails to list your claim. If you do not file a proof of claim, you will not share in the distribution of assets. But if you do not know about the bankruptcy, §523(a)(3) prevents your claim against the debtor from being discharged.[3] You can pursue the debtor after the bankruptcy is over.

Your rights against a corporation in Chapter 7 are different. A corporation has no life after bankruptcy. If a corporation files a Chapter 7 petition, you must file a proof of claim to share in the distribution of the debtor's assets regardless of whether your claim is listed or whether you learn of the bankruptcy. To be sure, no corporate debts are discharged in Chapter 7.[4] The discharge, however, is irrelevant. The corporation distributes all its assets in Chapter 7 and then dissolves. At the end of the Chapter 7 case, all the assets are gone and there is nothing left to satisfy your claim.

There is a procedural difference in Chapter 11. A creditor must file a proof of claim only if its claim is not listed in the schedules or is disputed, contingent, or unliquidated. §1111(a); Rule 3003(c). The substantive outcome, however, is the same for a creditor whose claim is not listed or whose claim is contingent. Even though the corporation has a continuing life after bankruptcy, all the debts of the corporation are discharged in Chapter 11, even if they are not scheduled. A creditor who is not listed on the schedules is obliged to file a proof of claim and is left out of the distribution if it fails to do so.

Ordinarily, the treatment of claims is straightforward. The amount each creditor is owed is listed on the schedules and is not disputed. All one has to do is figure out how to divide

---

[3] As we discussed in chapter 2, an exception may exist in the no-asset case. See p. 53 *supra*.

[4] Under §727, only individuals enjoy a discharge in Chapter 7.

whatever assets there are among the various claimants. Suppose there are 100 creditors, and all are listed and properly notified. The debtor owes them $10,000. The average claim is $100, but some are owed $10 and one is owed more than $1,000. All the debtor's assets are sold for a total of $1,000.[5] Only 10 cents in assets is available for every dollar of liability. How do we divide the pie, as small as it is? Since at least the sixteenth century the rule has been one of pro rata distribution: in this case, then, each creditor receives 10 cents for every dollar it is owed. A creditor that is owed $1,000 gets $100. A creditor that is owed $50 gets $5. Rule 3010 provides that no dividend of less than $5 is paid. It costs that much just to cut the check.

The rule of pro rata distribution provides a way to approximate the rights of each of the general creditors. We should bear in mind, however, that it is only an approximation. We do not know what the nonbankruptcy right would be for each creditor because bankruptcy has put a halt to the race among them. We know that without the automatic stay, some of them would have been paid in full and others would have received nothing, but it is not worth the effort to figure out who would have come first. There are other complications. Smaller creditors might have been more likely to be paid in full because they would not have had to seize much to satisfy their claims. For this reason, some might argue that we should give them more than their pro rata share. Large creditors, however, have more to lose and therefore might spend more time and effort monitoring the debtor. For this reason, one could argue that large creditors should receive more than their pro rata share. In the end, we have the pro rata sharing rule because trying to answer arguments like these is more trouble than it is worth. The kinds of distributions in these cases are in the neighborhood of 10 cents on the dollar for general creditors.

---

[5] Unless specified otherwise, figures exclude the costs of bankruptcy.

Now we will flesh out the story somewhat. Suppose that a fully perfected secured creditor is owed $500. It has a fully and properly perfected security interest on every asset that the debtor has. In this case, the secured creditor gets 100 cents on the dollar, or $500, out of the $1,000 pie. From the remaining $500 we subtract the fees that the trustee gets (and, more important, the fees of the lawyer for the trustee, who is frequently a lawyer at the trustee's firm). Whatever is left is divided among the general creditors pro rata. If the remainder is $150 and the general creditors are still owed $10,000, then the distribution is at the rate of 1.5 cents on the dollar. If you are owed $1,000, you get $15. If you are owed $600, you get $9.

We also need to put a value on disputed claims, such as a lawsuit against the debtor that is in litigation. To see how the Bankruptcy Code handles these claims, it is useful to look at a straightforward example. Assume that a software producer is suing the debtor for unfair competition. If the debtor owes anything, it will owe $12,000. But the debtor argues that all it did was engage in some hardball competition. The liability is an all-or-nothing affair. The software producer's chances of winning in state court are roughly one in three. The trial is still many years away.

Under §101, the software producer is viewed as a creditor who holds a claim against the debtor. The claim, however, is both disputed and unliquidated. After the producer files its proof of claim and the debtor files its objection, the bankruptcy judge may conduct a streamlined trial and decide the merits of the dispute. §502(b). The shortened process makes sense. Even if the producer wins, it is not going to be paid in full. In most Chapter 11 bankruptcies, general creditors are lucky to receive more than 20 cents on the dollar. In deciding the merits of the producer's claim, the bankruptcy judge follows nonbankruptcy substantive rules and bankruptcy's procedural rules. The judge turns to state law to find out what conduct constitutes unfair competition, but the judge may decide factual questions rather than leaving them to a jury. A bankruptcy court is entitled to use chancery methods in putting a value on a claim.

A bankruptcy judge is not, however, required to *fix* a value on the claim. Under §502(c) the judge can estimate the value for the purposes of the bankruptcy proceeding and allow the creditor to reappear if it gets a judgment for a different amount. In the meantime, the creditor participates as if its claim is equal to the estimate. There can even be a distribution according to the estimate, perhaps with some way (such as the issuance of new equity) to increase the distribution after the case is over.

Estimating the producer's claim is not easy. It is a $12,000 lawsuit, but it has only one chance in three of succeeding. Assume that other general creditors are owed $3,000 and that the assets are worth $1,000. If we value the producer's claim at its present probability of success, it would have a claim for $4,000. The producer's claim, even discounted, makes it the largest unsecured creditor. The producer would dominate the bankruptcy proceeding even though in the end its lawsuit would probably not succeed and the debtor would owe it nothing.

Giving the producer a voice according to its present probability of success therefore seems unattractive, but there may be no better alternatives. If the producer prevailed in the end, it would be entitled to 80 percent of the debtor's assets and would virtually be able to dictate the plan of reorganization. Valuing the producer's claim at its present probability of success would be undervaluing it if the producer ultimately wins. By the same measure, we would be overvaluing it if it turns out that the producer loses. Discounting the producer's claim by its present probability of success would give the producer too large a role in some instances and too small a role in others.

It might be useful to view the estimation of claims as a coerced settlement. Outside of bankruptcy, most civil cases are settled. Every settlement reflects an estimate by both parties of their chances of success on the merits. Disregarding concerns about reputation and other complications, the settlement value of the producer's claim against the debtor is about $4,000. It might make sense for a bankruptcy judge to estimate a claim according to its present probability of success. Even though this amount will necessarily be different from the outcome of any litigation, it may match the settlement that we would have seen in the absence of bankruptcy.

There is, however, a good reason to estimate the value of the producer's suit at zero for purposes of determining the kind of role that the producer plays in drawing up the plan of reorganization. The producer should not be allowed to force a settlement on terms more favorable than would be possible outside of bankruptcy. What may be crucial is not that the producer's present probability of success is less than 50 percent, but that it is less than 100 percent. Even though creditors in some sense always deal at arm's length with their debtor, in bankruptcy they are acting as equityholders. They are the residual claimants. Giving the producer a voice in the reorganization is analogous to allowing a shareholder to sue the corporation. Estimating the producer's claim at zero makes the most sense when the producer is allowed to pursue the claim, unaffected by the bankruptcy process. Courts are most likely to take this approach when the claim is large and the probability of success low.[6]

A person with a personal injury or wrongful death claim has a procedural right in bankruptcy that a contract creditor does not. Unlike a contract creditor, a tort victim has the same right to a jury trial in bankruptcy as would exist under nonbankruptcy law. 28 U.S.C. §1411. As elsewhere in bankruptcy, this additional procedural right may generate substantive consequences. In mass tort cases involving A.H. Robins and Manville, however, the courts limited the scope of the trial right. The courts used §502(c) to estimate the total liability to tort victims. These courts then allowed a fund of this amount to be established that would serve as the victims' sole source of compensation. They confined the scope of the jury trial right to the adjudication of individual claims against the fund.

Apart from these differences, a tort creditor occupies the same position as a contract creditor. Tort victims enjoy no spe-

---

[6] See Bittner v. Borne Chemical Co., 691 F.2d 134 (3d Cir. 1982).

cial priority outside of bankruptcy and hence none in. They are simply general creditors with disputed claims. One can argue that as a matter of nonbankruptcy law this is a bad idea. The purpose of tort law is to make businesses internalize the costs of hazardous activities. If creditors through loan covenants or some other kind of monitoring can influence a business's behavior, giving tort victims a priority right may have the effect of reducing the number of torts the business commits. Other creditors might complain that there is nothing they can do to make the business more careful, but the risk of having another creditor take priority over them gives them an incentive to think twice about whether there is in fact anything they can force the business to do. If a victim of an accident involving a truck takes priority over a creditor with a security interest in the truck, that creditor will have an incentive to make sure that the truck is properly maintained, that the driver is well qualified, and that the debtor carries insurance. As Samuel Johnson might note, the prospect of being beaten out by another creditor, like the prospect of being hanged in a fortnight, concentrates the mind wonderfully. But existing law does not work this way. Inside of bankruptcy and out, tort victims are general creditors.

Some debtors may have committed some act before the petition that will injure some as yet unidentified person long after the bankruptcy case is over. The technical question is whether the victim has a claim arising before the filing of the petition for purposes of §101. An aircraft manufacturer has made thousands of planes that are still flying. Some will crash in the future and expose the manufacturer to liability. These as yet unknown victims may not have a prepetition connection with the debtor sufficient to give rise to a claim within the meaning of §101.[7]

---

[7] See Epstein v. Official Committee of Unsecured Creditors, 58 F.3d 1573 (11th Cir. 1995); Hexcel Corp. v. Stepan Co., 239 Bankr. 564 (N.D. Cal. 1999).

The effect of finding that future victims possess claims depends on the kind of case involved. First is the mass tort case in which a corporation is liquidating in Chapter 7. If future victims do not have prepetition claims within the meaning of the Bankruptcy Code, they will receive nothing in Chapter 7 even though they would receive something if the corporation dissolved under nonbankruptcy law. In a nonbankruptcy dissolution of a corporation, a fund usually must be set up to cover any liabilities that appear on the corporation's books. So long as the accountants have recognized the obligation (as they should if matters have deteriorated sufficiently), the tort victim will be able to recover from this fund even though the victim does not know about the injury until after the corporation goes out of existence.

Second is the case in which the business is in Chapter 11 and will have a postbankruptcy life. Here, tort victims may be better off if they do not have a prepetition claim. To be sure, if tort victims lack a prepetition claim, they will be unable to share in the distribution in bankruptcy, but they will be able to pursue the corporation in its postbankruptcy incarnation. Remember that only "claims" are discharged under §1141. Such victims may be able to recover more than they would have received had they participated in the bankruptcy case.

In the wake of the Manville bankruptcy, §524(g) of the Bankruptcy Code was amended to allow the bankruptcy court to enjoin subsequent actions against reorganized corporations and even third parties such as insurers, but this provision by its terms applies only to mass torts involving asbestos. In other cases, the law is less settled.[8] Courts are especially unsympathetic to plans that release nondebtors from liability as part of a

---

[8] Such releases are possible under limited circumstances. See Class Five Nevada Claimants v. Dow Corning Corp., 280 F.3d 648, 658 (6th Cir. 2002).

reorganization.[9] Moreover, even when a debtor attempts to sell assets free and clear of claims against it, the bankruptcy court cannot insulate buyers from potential successor liability under state law.[10]

Several technical complications arise when we try to put a dollar value on each creditor's claim. The best way to understand how the process works is to imagine that the filing of a bankruptcy petition is a presumptive event of default that accelerates all the debtor's obligations.[11] As part of this process, we must decide two basic issues: how interest affects the calculation of claims, and what caps are placed on some types of claims.

Suppose I borrowed $100 from First Bank last year when interest rates were 7 percent. This year I borrowed $100 from Second Bank at 12 percent. Although I am not in default on either loan, I file a bankruptcy petition. My assets are worth $150. Who gets what? Should the two banks receive the same amount? In the absence of a bankruptcy filing, First Bank is in a worse position than Second Bank. Other things being equal, it would rather have my promise to repay $100 at 12 percent than at 7 percent. In Chapter 7 of the Bankruptcy Code, however, we ignore these differences. Section 502(b)(2) does not allow claims for unaccrued interest. Both banks would have claims of $100. Because the assets are worth $150, each bank would get 75 cents on the dollar. Treating the two lenders equally makes sense. If the debtor defaulted outside of bankruptcy, the obligation to pay back the principal of both loans would be accelerated. At this point, both lenders would be in the same position.

---

[9] See, e.g., Gillman v. Continental Airlines, 203 F.3d 203 (3d Cir. 2000).

[10] Western Auto Supply Co. v. Savage Arms, Inc., 43 F.3d 714 (1st Cir. 1994); Zerand-Bernal Group, Inc. v. Cox, 23 F.3d 159 (7th Cir. 1994).

[11] As we shall see in the last chapter of the book, §1124 gives debtors the right to de-accelerate loans in Chapter 11.

Both would have the right to recover $100 immediately. When it ignores differences in the interest rates, all that bankruptcy is doing is treating the filing of a petition as a default. This seems a sensible off-the-rack rule that most lenders would include in their loan agreements.

We can think of a Chapter 7 bankruptcy liquidation as financial death. We call in all the loans, gather the assets, and have a general day of reckoning. Sometimes it will not be easy to distinguish principal from unaccrued interest. The simplest case arises when there is a zero-coupon note. I borrow $900 and I promise to pay you $1,000 in a year's time. On the face of it, the principal amount of the loan is $1,000 and the interest rate is 0 percent. We can be confident, however, that the principal is in fact $900 and the interest rate is 11 percent. In the case of zero-coupon notes, only the principal and interest already owed is accelerated. If I default immediately, you have a claim for $900. If I default in six months, you have a claim for $950. More complicated cases arise when the interest rate is not 0 percent but is still substantially below market, and when the note is issued not for cash but in exchange for other securities.[12] Also less clear are cases in which a consumer buys on the installment plan and the interest-rate component is hard to identify.

The second issue that arises when putting a dollar value on creditors' claims concerns the caps that the Bankruptcy Code places on damages for two classes of creditors. Sections 502(b)(6) and (7) limit what both landlords and employees can recover if the debtor rejects a long-term contract with them in bankruptcy. Suppose you lease land to a debtor for $5 a year for a term of years. A year or so later, the bottom drops out of the real estate market. The land falls in value, and now you could rent it out at only $1 a year. The debtor files a bankruptcy

---

[12] See Thrifty Oil Co. v. Bank of America National Trust & Savings Association, 249 Bankr. 537 (S.D. Cal. 2000); Brown v. Sayyah (In re ICH Corp.), 230 Bankr. 88 (N.D. Tex. 1999).

petition. Your damages by the ordinary contract rule (the contract–market differential) are $4 for each year remaining on the lease. The Bankruptcy Code, however, limits your recovery. The limit depends on how long the lease lasts. Your cap will never be less than one year's rent ($5). If 15 percent of all the payments remaining turn out to be greater than one year's rent, you get 15 percent of all the payments remaining. But in no event can the amount you get exceed three years' rent. When the rental payments under the lease are constant, your damages are the lesser of (1) actual damages according to the contract–market differential or (2) one year's rent if fewer than 6.7 years are left on the lease, 15 percent of the remaining payments if between 6.7 and 20 years are left, and three years' rent if more than 20 years are left.

The usual justification for capping a landlord's damages is that they are hard to measure, but this assertion is not sound. Section 502(b)(6) does not free you from estimating damages. Moreover, it assumes that judges are apt to think damages are too high, but not too low. If there is a ceiling on damages, it would seem that there should also be a floor. There may, however, be a better justification for such limits in the case of employees under §502(b)(7). The employees most likely to be affected by the breach of long-term employment contracts are employees with golden parachutes, and they frequently are insider-shareholders. When these contracts are unusually favorable, there may be a significant chance of self-dealing that violates the rights of creditors as a group. The cap in the case of an employee under a long-term contract may be a means of policing misbehavior that cannot be controlled directly. In considering the merits of capping landlord and employee damage claims, you should bear in mind that this limitation applies only to damages flowing from termination of the agreement. It does not limit the damages landlords or employees might be able to get from other causes, such as the damages that arise if the debtor damaged the premises before filing or terminated an employee without justification.

As mentioned in the beginning of this section, assessing claims against the estate involves asking who is owed what and whether someone has priority. The most common kind of privileged party is a creditor with a perfected security interest. Some priority rights are established in the Bankruptcy Code itself, in §507(a). Workers, for example, enjoy priority with respect to several thousand dollars in back wages and benefits. The tax collector has special priority as well. Special priority rules are hard to defend as a matter of first principle and are often the product of special interest lobbying, but these priorities usually do not play a significant role in large reorganizations. As a practical matter, employees will have to be paid if the business is to remain open, and usually little is owed in the way of back taxes. The typical Chapter 11 case is quite a different matter. Small companies make up the vast majority of the Chapter 11 docket, and the entrepreneurs in charge of them often try to keep the businesses afloat by using money that should have gone to the IRS to pay withholding taxes. The obligations then commonly exceed the value of the estate, leaving general creditors with nothing. For this reason, the rhetoric frequently used to describe Chapter 11—that it protects small general creditors and ensures a fair distribution of assets to them—is misleading, at least in the typical case.

Secured Claims

Secured credit, put simply, is a loan supported by a contingent property interest. Outside of bankruptcy, default on the loan satisfies the contingency and triggers the creditor's right to take the property the debtor has pledged as collateral. The creditor then conducts a foreclosure sale. If the proceeds from the sale are greater than the outstanding loan, the creditor remits the excess. If the proceeds from the sale are less than the outstanding loan, the creditor maintains a claim against the debtor for the deficiency. Section 554 allows the bankruptcy trustee to abandon collateral and permit a secured creditor to take the assets and then foreclose under state law. The secured creditor still participates in the bankruptcy process on account of its deficiency claim. Unless the secured creditor agrees otherwise at the time of the loan, that creditor possesses all the rights of an unsecured creditor. Collateral gives a creditor extra rights. Thus, to the extent its collateral falls short of repaying the loan in full, the secured creditor participates in the bankruptcy process as the holder of an unsecured claim.

A trustee may not wish to abandon collateral, however. She may instead intend the debtor to keep the property as part of a reorganization or adjustment of the debtor's obligations. When the collateral is to remain part of the estate, bankruptcy law provides a procedure that takes the place of a foreclosure sale's valuation of property. Section 506(a) of the Code instructs the bankruptcy court to value a creditor's interest in property of the estate and to designate the creditor's claim a "secured claim to the extent of the value of such creditor's interest." Any remaining claim amount is designated as an unsecured claim. The same process separates into secured and unsecured portions any claim held by someone who enjoys a setoff right. In the most common case, the debtor maintains a deposit account at a bank from which it has borrowed money. The bank has the ability under nonbankruptcy law to "set off" against the loan whatever is in the account. The Bankruptcy Code treats the portion of claim subject to a setoff right as a secured claim and the balance as an unsecured claim. If, for example, the bank had lent the debtor $300 and the debtor has $100 in its account, the Bankruptcy Code gives the bank a secured claim for $100 and an unsecured claim for $200.

In broad strokes, the bifurcation process of §506(a) mimics nonbankruptcy law. The secured creditor receives the full value of her collateral and shares in the debtor's other assets to the extent that the collateral value is less than the creditor's claim. When the collateral is not sold, however, the court must value the collateral, and this is not a simple task. The secured creditor will argue for a high valuation (and thus a larger secured claim), while the debtor's other creditors, represented by the trustee, will argue for a low valuation. The bankruptcy judge begins with an objective benchmark: the replacement value of the asset. Apart from the cases in which the debtor is an individual in Chapter 7 or Chapter 13, see §506(a)(2), this amount must be adjusted downward. The price a third party would charge for the replacement property would include costs associated with an actual sale, and these should not be counted in determining the secured creditor's rights. For example, the price a dealer would charge if the debtor sought to replace the property would include its costs of shipping and storing the property and any costs associated with warranties it provided. The judge must deduct such costs from the replacement value.[13]

It is essential to distinguish between the rights that a secured creditor enjoys against the debtor by virtue of its claim and the rights that such a creditor enjoys against particular assets by virtue of its lien—its property interest—in those assets. In a simple Chapter 7 liquidation, the lien that the creditor enjoys is unaffected: it passes through bankruptcy. The doctrine of lien pass-through was first set out in *Long v. Bullard*.[14] Recall the example in chapter 1 above. A bank lends a debtor $100 and takes a security interest in a piece of real property that the debtor owns. A recession hits and the property drops in value and is now worth only $25. The debtor files a Chapter 7 petition. The trustee abandons the property, giving it back to the debtor. The Bankruptcy Code provides that the debtor's personal liability to the bank and all other creditors is discharged. The bank remains free to foreclose on the land once it is in the debtor's hands because the lien survives, or passes through, bankruptcy.

Although the question whether liens pass through bankruptcy is straightforward, the extent to which they do is controversial. Return to our example. Assume that immediately

[13] See Associates Commercial Corp. v. Rash, 520 U.S. 953, 965 n.6 (1997).

[14] 117 U.S. 617 (1886).

after bankruptcy, the debtor is able to raise $25 from friends to pay off the bank. Can the bank insist that even though its claim has been discharged, the lien survives at its original amount of $100? The debtor will argue that the lien was stripped down as it passed through bankruptcy. On the face of it, the debtor might seem right. Section 506(d) of the Bankruptcy Code permits lien strip-down of a claim bifurcated by §506(a): "To the extent that a lien secures a claim against the debtor that is not an allowed secured claim, such lien is void." This language seems to provide that the bank's lien is void to the extent that it exceeds the amount of its secured claim. The debtor originally owed the bank $100, but the bank's secured claim is for only $25. Hence, the lien is void to the extent it exceeds $25. The debtor could pay the bank $25 and remove the lien on the property.

The bank, however, can argue that §506(d) was not aimed at lien strip-down at all. Rather, the provision was designed to prevent liens from surviving bankruptcy if the underlying claim was disallowed. Consider the following example. A lawyer provides legal services at an exorbitant fee and secures it with a lien on the debtor's property. Another section of the Bankruptcy Code disallows the lawyer's claim, but only §506(d) voids the lawyer's lien. Under this view, the purpose of §506(d) was not to strip down liens but rather to make sure that a creditor's lien fares no better than her claim. Section 506(d) ensures that the lawyer is both denied a pro rata share of the debtor's assets in bankruptcy and prevented from seizing collateral after the bankruptcy is over. The language, aimed at this specific kind of abuse, was never intended to deal with a valid creditor's lien and should not be read to do so.

Stripping down a lien in bankruptcy has the effect after the fact of benefiting debtors at the expense of creditors. If the bankruptcy judge places too high a value on the land, the debtor can surrender the land to the secured creditor. If the bankruptcy judge errs on the low side, the debtor can pay the bank this amount and keep the land. In other words, debtors can systematically take advantage of judicial valuations that are too low but not be stuck with valuations that are too high. Lien stripping runs contrary to established practice in bankruptcy before the 1978 Bankruptcy Act. It also runs contrary to the notion in real estate law that when a debtor defaults, the value of the land is set through a foreclosure sale rather than through a judicial valuation.

The Court accepted the bank's argument against lien strip-down in *Dewsnup v. Timm*.[15] The majority's opinion noted that had it simply looked at §506 "on a clean slate," it would have agreed with the debtor and stripped down the lien to the value of the property. But in light of the historical practice against lien strip-down and a plausible argument that the provision was aimed at an altogether different problem, the majority concluded that strip-down was not allowed.

Because of the special treatment accorded liens in Chapters 11 and 13, *Dewsnup* has limited impact. Nevertheless, it sparked a major debate over statutory interpretation. In a strong dissent, Justice Antonin Scalia rejected the bank's interpretation of §506(d). To have the effect that the bank claimed, Justice Scalia wrote, the provision should have been phrased this way: "To the extent that a lien secures a claim against the debtor that is not an allowed claim, such lien is void." In Justice Scalia's view, we should not treat the allowed *secured* claims of creditors like the bank as if they were the same as "allowed claims." The result here may be contrary to preexisting practice, undesirable for creditors, and unsound as a matter of bankruptcy policy, but that should not be enough to deny the statutory language the meaning that both makes sense on its own and is consistent with the way the language is used elsewhere in the Code. Justice Scalia noted that the concept of the allowed secured claim is unique to the 1978 Act and has no statutory or case-law antecedents. These words are carefully defined and repeatedly and consistently used in other parts of the 1978 Act. Courts should assume that drafters knew what

[15] 502 U.S. 410 (1992).

they were doing, Justice Scalia argued. Competent drafters are unlikely to make such mistakes with stylized terms of art that are a fundamental part of the architecture of the statute. Although Justice Scalia failed to command a majority in *Dewsnup,* his concerns frequently surface both in majority opinions of the Court and in the bankruptcy courts. As a result, as a matter of good advocacy, one should avoid relying on legislative history as well as on pre-Code law in the absence of an invitation embedded in the statutory text itself.

Chapter Five

Property of the Estate and the Strong-Arm Powers

After establishing what claims creditors have, we need to know what assets are available to satisfy them. Outside of bankruptcy, creditors rely on assets that the debtor itself owns. Bankruptcy law ensures that creditors can look to these assets in bankruptcy as well. Through §541(a), creditors are able to enjoy whatever the debtor itself could enjoy, and all these assets become property of the estate. If we are dealing with a limited liability corporation, the creditors are entitled to whatever the debtor has, including future income. Section 541 lets the trustee sell the debtor's equipment, collect money owed the debtor, and bring the lawsuits the debtor has against third parties for the benefit of the general creditors. If we are dealing with a flesh-and-blood individual debtor, matters are slightly more complicated. The fresh start policy requires that we exclude future income from property of the estate and that we allow the debtor to share in property of the estate that is exempt. Section 541 is otherwise quite straightforward. The principal difficulty is ensuring that the bankruptcy process does not expand or contract the property rights the debtor enjoyed outside of bankruptcy.

Creditors outside of bankruptcy sometimes can reach assets that the debtor has attempted to transfer in whole or in part to someone else. Under the Bankruptcy Code, the trustee has analogous powers he can exercise on behalf of the creditors. The trustee can *avoid*—that is, nullify or undo—transfers that the debtor makes with the intent to delay, hinder, or defraud creditors. Similarly, the trustee can void security interests in assets that have not been properly perfected. These assets become part of the bankruptcy estate by virtue of the trustee's *strong-arm power*. This power is based on a sharing rule in which an unperfected secured creditor is treated the same as a general creditor who has not yet reduced its claim to judgment. The operation of the strong-arm power in §§544 and 545 is quite straightforward, as is its relationship with §541(a)(1). Whenever there is an asset that the creditors want, we ask first whether the asset is one that the debtor could enjoy outside of bankruptcy. If the answer is yes, the asset becomes property of the estate under §541(a)(1). If the answer is no, we ask next whether the trustee can bring the asset into the estate by virtue of the strong-arm power.

Using both §541 and §544 to identify the assets that creditors enjoy in bankruptcy, however, has created a trap for the unwary. The property brought into the estate through either section standing alone is necessarily less than our intuition tells us should be available to creditors. Judges must resist the temptation to distort the relatively simple tests each section sets out to reach assets that intuition suggests should be available to creditors. Reshaping the tests in this way undermines the operation of the Code in future cases. By remembering that the strong-arm power always works to supplement property of the estate, we avoid the dangers of expecting either §541 or §544 to produce an intuitively sensible result on its own.

Property of the Estate and the Scope of §541

Section 541(a)(1) ensures that in the case of the corporate debtor, creditors are able to reach all of the debtor's property in bankruptcy that they would be able to reach outside of bankruptcy. If a corporate debtor could enjoy a particular right outside of bankruptcy, the trustee enjoys it inside of bankruptcy. It is useful to see how §541 handles the easy cases. Suppose you take some clothes to the dry cleaner. Your dry cleaner also sells used clothing. The dry cleaner, much to your surprise, shuts down and files a Chapter 7 bankruptcy petition. It has thousands of creditors. You are not one of them. The debtor promised to clean your clothes for $5, the market price for cleaning them, due upon completion. The debtor has broken its promise, but if you have suffered no damages, you have no claim against it under nonbankruptcy law. Assume you have no immediate need for the clothes and you can easily find someone else to clean them for the same price. You go to the debtor and try to pick up your clothes and take them someplace else. The trustee tells you that you cannot have the clothes back.

Can the trustee wave §541 at you and say that your clothes are now property of the dry cleaner's bankruptcy estate? Section 541(a)(1) gives the trustee "all legal or equitable interests of the debtor in property as of the commencement of the case." Does the debtor have a right to your clothes that amounts to an interest in property? What are the debtor's rights with respect to the clothes? Under the Uniform Commercial Code, the debtor has the *power* (though not the *right*) to give good title to the clothes to a buyer in ordinary course of business. U.C.C. §2-403(2). The debtor is a merchant who deals in used clothes and you have entrusted your clothes to it.

Under §541(a)(1), we worry about only the debtor's rights. For purposes of this section, we focus on whether it is able to keep the clothes in the face of your assertion of ownership. If the dry cleaner has actually cleaned the clothes, it may have a mechanic's lien on the clothes that would give it a property interest in the clothes. The mechanic's lien would allow the trustee to keep the clothes until you paid for the cleaning, but let's assume the trustee has shut down operations and that the clothes have not been and will not be cleaned. In this case, the debtor cannot keep you from taking the clothes back outside of bankruptcy. Hence, the clothes do not become property of the estate under §541(a)(1). Because the debtor has no right to the clothes, the creditors do not have any rights to the clothes under §541(a)(1), either. The rights of the debtor define the outer limits of what the trustee can claim under §541(a)(1).

Cases can arise in which the debtor's ownership of a right is not clear. Consider, for example, an insurance policy. The policy itself belongs to the debtor and is property of the estate. The debtor, however, may not be entitled to the proceeds of the policy outside of bankruptcy. The policy, for example, may provide that the insurance company's obligation runs to the victim of an accident, not to the debtor. The debtor may have no ability to reach these proceeds under nonbankruptcy law. In this event, the proceeds of the insurance are not property of the estate. The victim of the accident, in addition to being a general creditor, may be entitled to pursue the insurance company during or after bankruptcy and to keep the proceeds of the policy rather than sharing them with the other creditors of the debtor.[16]

Section 541(a)(1) gives the creditors only those rights that the debtor itself enjoyed outside of bankruptcy. If a debtor owns a one-half interest in an oil well and files for bankruptcy, only the one-half interest becomes part of the estate, not the entire oil well. This rule is perfectly sensible. Suppose two corporations each have a one-half interest in the same well and both file bankruptcy petitions. We could not allow the trustees of both debtors to be entitled to the entire well.

Chicago Board of Trade v. Johnson is the old case that sets out this basic principle.[17] That case revolved around the question of how to allocate the proceeds of the sale of a seat on the Chicago Board of Trade. Its owner, a man named Henderson, went into bankruptcy owing money to lots of people, including members of the Board of Trade. At the time, the rules of the Board of Trade required a member to pay off any outstanding obligations to other members of the Board of Trade as a condition of selling the seat. The trustee wanted all the proceeds of the seat to come into the estate and the other Board members to be treated as ordinary creditors. The Supreme Court rejected this

---

[16] See Houston v. Edgeworth, 993 F.2d 51 (5th Cir. 1993); First Fidelity Bank v. McAteer, 985 F.2d 114 (3d Cir. 1993). Because the insurance policy (as opposed to the proceeds of the policy) is property of the estate, the accident victim should seek relief from the automatic stay. When the victim's right to the proceeds is clear, relief from the stay is routinely granted.

[17] 264 U.S. 1 (1924).

argument. The general creditors derived their rights from the debtor. If the debtor had the right to the proceeds only after the Board members were paid, then the general creditors had the right to the proceeds only after the Board members were paid. The general creditors could not do any better outside of bankruptcy, so they should not be able to do any better inside of bankruptcy.

Whether state law deemed the seat "property" was irrelevant (in fact, the Illinois Supreme Court had already held that state law did not); what mattered were the attributes of the seat. Outside of bankruptcy, the creditors had no right to reach the proceeds of the sale until the claims of Henderson's fellow Board members had been satisfied. Nonbankruptcy law has the effect of creating priority for one type of creditor over another, and such priorities are unobjectionable so long as they apply consistently outside of bankruptcy as well as inside. *Chicago Board of Trade* remains good law, both for its narrow point about the treatment of seats on exchanges in bankruptcy and for the broad principle it embraces.[18]

Some variations on the facts show how this principle works. Suppose Henderson chose not to sell the seat. Would it still have become property of the estate? Under state law, creditors could not levy on the seat or force an individual debtor to sell it. If Henderson decided not to sell the seat, then it would not become property of the estate. Consider the case, however, in which a corporation owns the seat. In this event, the debtor's *ability* to sell the seat is itself decisive. Outside of bankruptcy, the creditors of a corporation (unlike the creditors of an individual) could have a court appoint a receiver. The receiver would take control of the corporation and sell the asset. Anything left after the claims of the other Board members were satisfied would be distributed to the other creditors. If creditors could reach property outside of bankruptcy through this debt

---

[18] See In re Drexel Burnham Lambert Group Inc., 120 Bankr. 724 (Bankr. S.D.N.Y. 1990).

collection process, they should be able to reach it in bankruptcy as well.

Now consider a more difficult case. The debtor is again a corporation, but the rule of the Board of Trade is that seats cannot be sold at all. To say that the seat cannot be sold means in effect that the seat survives only so long as the corporation owning it survives as a distinct entity. You cannot sell the seat apart from the corporation's other assets. If, outside of bankruptcy, the seat can be sold only if it is bundled with the corporation's name, goodwill, furniture, and client lists, then it is subject to the same limitation inside of bankruptcy. The seat becomes property of the estate, but the trustee cannot sell the seat by itself. The nonbankruptcy limitation is recognized in bankruptcy. The most common example of an asset that can be sold only in connection with another is a trademark. It cannot be conveyed apart from the goodwill associated with the mark.[19]

Let's look at one more possibility. Suppose the seat on the Board is freely salable, but the Board's rules provide that the seat is forfeited if the debtor files a bankruptcy petition. Is this rule permissible? Although we generally respect rights as defined outside of bankruptcy, we do not allow anyone to opt out of bankruptcy altogether. Bankruptcy law respects restrictions that apply both inside of bankruptcy and out, but those that apply only in bankruptcy are ignored. This "ipso facto" principle is reflected in §541(c)(1) and in §545 with respect to statutory liens and in §365 with respect to executory contracts.

The principle of *Chicago Board of Trade* applies quite broadly. It is useful, for example, when we want to understand the rights that creditors enjoy by virtue of a license that their debtor enjoys. Courts have included in property of the estate everything from casino and racetrack licenses to broadcast li-

---

[19] See, e.g., Vittoria North America v. Euro-Asia Imports Inc., 278 F.3d 1076 (2001).

censes.[20] The *Chicago Board of Trade* principle ensures that debtors in bankruptcy enjoy the license on the same terms and subject to the same conditions as they did outside of bankruptcy. Suppose a failing airline files a Chapter 7 petition. It has a right to landing slots at a major airport, and another airline would pay a lot to have them. The airline's landing slots are, of course, property of the estate. The airline, however, needs to shut down its operations for a time, and FAA rules provide that an airline loses its licenses once it stops using them. This constraint on the right is one that applies outside of bankruptcy and hence inside of bankruptcy as well.[21] A debtor's property does not shrink by happenstance of bankruptcy, but it does not expand, either.

A more troublesome case arises when the issuer of the license is also a creditor. Suppose a town decides to auction off a taxi medallion. To encourage small entrepreneurs, the town agrees to finance much of the purchase price. One company makes a winning bid of $11,000 for the medallion. The company makes a down payment of $1,000 and promises to pay the balance over a number of years. The company borrows an additional $10,000 to pay for a used cab. The company's owner is confident that the taxi can generate enough money to pay back the town and the creditors and still leave the owner with a healthy profit. The local economy suffers a downturn, however, and the cab service is less popular than expected. As a result, the company cannot meet its obligations to the town and to the other creditors. It files a Chapter 11 petition. The company is

[20] See, e.g., Elsinore Shore Associates v. Casino Control Commission, 66 Bankr. 723 (Bankr. D.N.J. 1986); In re National Cattle Congress, Inc., 179 Bankr. 588 (Bankr. N.D. Iowa 1995), remanded on other grounds, 91 F.3d 1113 (8th Cir. 1996); Ramsay v. Dowden, 68 F.3d 213 (8th Cir. 1995).

[21] See Federal Aviation Administration v. Gull Air, Inc., 890 F.2d 1255, 1261 n.8 (1st Cir. 1989).

insolvent: it owes $20,000, but the business is worth only $15,000.

The taxi medallion is property of the estate under §541(a) and comes into the estate. Consistent with *Chicago Board of Trade*, however, it becomes part of the estate subject to all its nonbankruptcy limitations. If the company had no ability to sell the medallion outside of bankruptcy, it has no ability to do so inside.[22] At the same time, under §541(c)(1) the town could not cause the medallion to be forfeited in the event of bankruptcy. This rule vindicates again the principle that bankruptcy itself does not expand or limit a debtor's property rights.

As we shall see when we discuss the reach of the automatic stay in chapter 9 below, it is not always easy to draw the line between actions that the government takes by virtue of its position as postpetition regulator and those it takes as the holder of a prepetition claim. In the example above, nothing should prevent the license from becoming property of the estate. When the regulator is the federal government, however, the dispute may not even be adjudicated in the bankruptcy forum. Judicial oversight of federal administrative agencies may occur first through administrative tribunals and then through the court of appeals.[23] Nevertheless, the government cannot assert its rights as a creditor merely by asserting that it is wearing its regulatory hat. The Bankruptcy Code prevents the government from discriminating against debtors in bankruptcy with respect to the licenses or permits it issues. A governmental unit that attempts to exploit its ability to withhold licenses as a lever to enhance its rights as a creditor risks being hoisted by its own

[22] See, e.g., In re Tak Communications, Inc., 985 F.2d 916 (7th Cir. 1993).

[23] See In re Federal Communications Commission, 217 F.3d 125 (2d Cir. 2000).

petard, as such actions violate the antidiscrimination provision of §525.[24]

The Strong-Arm Power Under §544(a)

Outside of bankruptcy, a general creditor sometimes has greater rights than its debtor and can levy on assets to which the debtor does not enjoy paramount rights. The most common case arises when a debtor buys a machine from someone who retains a security interest in it but fails to perfect that interest by filing a financing statement. The debtor has no right to keep the machine vis-à-vis its seller if the debtor defaults on its payments. Under nonbankruptcy law, however, a creditor that reduces its claim to judgment can levy on the machine and take priority over the seller. To ensure that creditors can look to the same assets inside a bankruptcy proceeding as outside, the Bankruptcy Code must provide some mechanism to ensure that these assets become part of the estate as well. Section 544(a) serves this function.

Section 544(a) gives the trustee the right to that which the general creditors could have reached under nonbankruptcy law. The trustee has, in the case of personal property, the rights of a hypothetical lien creditor who comes into being and levies at the moment the petition is filed. In the case of real property, the trustee has the rights of a hypothetical bona fide purchaser for value. Section 544(b) enables the trustee to assert the rights that actual creditors would have had under state law, even if a creditor who came into being only at the time of the petition would have arrived too late to have a cause of action. Among the most important of these rights is the right of creditors to set aside transfers that a debtor makes, while insolvent, for less than reasonably equivalent value as well as any transfers that delay, hinder, or defraud creditors. These transfers, known as

---

[24] See F.C.C. v. NextWave Personal Communications, Inc., 537 U.S. 293 (2003).

fraudulent conveyances, are examined in chapter 7 below. Here we will focus on the general structure of §544 itself.

Section 544(a) gives us a measuring rod to determine who prevails in a contest between the trustee and adverse claimants: if an imaginary lien creditor (or bona fide purchaser) as defined in §544(a) would prevail against the adverse interest, the trustee wins. The person whose interest is avoided is reduced to the status of a general creditor. The property itself becomes property of the estate, and all the general creditors (including the erstwhile property claimant) share in it pro rata. There are two important points to keep in mind here: first, the trustee's rights are being measured by those of a *third party*, and second, this particular third party is a *hypothetical* one.

In the case of personal property, the trustee enjoys the powers of a lien creditor. The effect of granting the trustee this power is to preserve the relative positions of unperfected secured creditors and general creditors outside of bankruptcy. Article 9 of the Uniform Commercial Code provides that a secured creditor will win against a general creditor if the secured creditor perfects its interest, either by filing a financing statement or by seizing the collateral before the general creditor acquires a lien on it. If a general creditor brings a lawsuit against the debtor outside of bankruptcy, reduces its claim to judgment, and levies on the property before the unperfected secured creditor asserts its rights, the secured creditor will lose. Every general creditor is a potential lien creditor.

Article 9 embraces the principle that the unperfected secured creditor claims an interest in property that is invisible to third parties. Anglo-American law generally does not recognize such ownership interests vis-à-vis third parties unless public notice is given or some other step is taken to cure the ostensible ownership problem that arises from the separation of ownership and possession. Between two competing creditors, the one who is first to cure the ostensible ownership problem is typically the one who takes priority. A general creditor acquires its property interest and cures the ostensible ownership problem in one fell swoop, by levying on the property—by having it physically seized. Hence, outside of bankruptcy the general creditor prevails over the secured creditor if it levies before the secured creditor perfects, but not otherwise.

In short, outside of bankruptcy the unperfected secured creditor and the general creditor are in a race with each other. The outcome of this race is uncertain. The effect of giving the trustee the power to avoid the unperfected secured creditor's interest is to declare a tie. In bankruptcy, the trustee represents the interests of all the general creditors, and an unperfected secured creditor whose lien is avoided becomes a general creditor. (You are never worse off trying to get a security interest and failing than you would have been if you had never tried at all.) To say that the trustee wins is to say that all creditors share equally. The bankruptcy rule, in other words, preserves the nonbankruptcy rule in the sense that in the presence of uncertainty, the creditors share equally.

In the case of real property, the trustee has the rights of a bona fide purchaser for value, not only the rights of a lien creditor. This expanded power may be premised on the notion that the trustee should always win if the competing property owner (typically a mortgagee) has not done everything that it could have done to cure the ostensible ownership problem. Under some state laws, only a bona fide purchaser, not a lien creditor, prevails against unperfected secured creditors with respect to real property. But giving the trustee this right is not inconsistent with the idea that the trustee is simply vindicating the rights of the general creditors. Even though lien creditors may not be able to defeat unrecorded real property interests directly, they may be able to do so indirectly. (A purchaser at the sheriff's sale may take good title and the lien creditors may be able to keep the proceeds.)

The first responsibility of a lawyer representing a lender with a security interest is to ensure that the client has properly perfected its security interest. Under Revised Article 9, this is usually done at the secretary of state's office in the jurisdiction in which the debtor resides. When the debtor is a corporation, it is deemed to reside in the state in which it was incorporated.

Under the previous enactment of Article 9, the proper place to file was determined by the location of the collateral. If bankruptcy is already on the horizon, it may be too late, but often it is not. Moreover, mistakes are all too common, and lenders' interests can be unperfected for a number of reasons. Lenders might misspell the debtor's name and thus make the financing statement inaccessible. Moreover, Article 9 does not completely occupy the field. Federal law sometimes preempts Article 9. A prudent creditor who takes a security interest in a copyright, for example, will file both in the appropriate secretary of state's office and with the registrar of copyrights.[25]

Suppose a debtor borrows $100,000 from a finance company on January 1 and grants the company a security interest. The finance company fails to file the financing statement in the proper office. On March 1, the debtor files for bankruptcy. Under nonbankruptcy law, lien creditors prevail over (or, as many lawyers would say, *prime*) secured creditors if their lien arises before the security interest is perfected. To perfect its interest, the finance company must file a financing statement in the proper office. Because the company failed to do that, it will lose to a lien creditor on March 1, the date the debtor files for bankruptcy. The trustee has the powers of a lien creditor, so the finance company will lose to the trustee in bankruptcy. There is, however, a small hitch in the literal language of §544. Section 544(a) seems to require that the secured creditor have an interest that is "voidable" by a lien creditor. Under nonbankruptcy law, however, a lien creditor can only make the secured creditor's interest "subordinate" to its own.

---

[25] In all likelihood, the state filing is appropriate with respect to unregistered copyrights and the federal filing with respect to registered ones. See Aerocon Engineering, Inc. v. Silicon Valley Bank (In re World Auxiliary Power Co.), 303 F.3d 1120 (9th Cir. 2002). But one has to worry about copyrighted works, such as software programs, that are continually updated.

Suppose instead that the finance company realizes its mistake before it's too late and files its interest the day before the debtor files for bankruptcy. Under Article 9, the finance company's security interest is perfected on the date it filed. On March 1, could a lien creditor defeat the finance company's interest? The answer is no, it could not. A lien creditor needs to become a lien creditor *before* the security interest is perfected. Because a creditor cannot win if it levies after the security interest is perfected, the trustee cannot win under §544(a). So long as no other part of the Bankruptcy Code allows the trustee to set aside the finance company's property interest, the finance company's security interest will be respected in bankruptcy and it will be paid ahead any of the general creditors.

The finance company's last-minute grab is suspicious, but this kind of conduct is not something to which §544(a) is directed, just as §541(a)(1) is not directed at reaching assets that the debtor could not enjoy outside of bankruptcy. As we will see in chapter 8 below, the trustee will probably be able to avoid the finance company's interest as a preference under §547. Given that these sections work cumulatively, it is important to resist the temptation to assess the Bankruptcy Code's results prematurely.

The Trustee as Successor to Creditor Claims

Section 544(b) is quite different from §544(a). To use §544(b), the trustee must find a real, live creditor with an *allowable* and *unsecured* claim. Thus, the trustee must find an actual unsecured creditor of the debtor who, on the date of bankruptcy, is able to assert an interest in property that the debtor has transferred to a third party. If this creditor can reach that asset outside of bankruptcy notwithstanding the transfer (or, to use the language of the Bankruptcy Code, can avoid the debtor's transfer of that asset), the trustee can use §544(b) to step into the shoes of that creditor. The trustee recovers the asset from the third party. The trustee does not then turn over the asset to the creditor who would have reached it outside of bankruptcy. Instead, the asset is placed in the pile of assets that is divided pro rata among all the general creditors. This part of §544(b) is difficult to justify. One must explain why the creditor who had this right outside of bankruptcy must share it with other creditors inside bankruptcy.

The best justification for it is an entirely pragmatic one. Often when the trustee uses §544(b), nearly all the creditors have the right to avoid the transfer. To exclude from the distribution the creditors who would not have shared in the recovery under nonbankruptcy law may impose substantial administrative costs and have only a small effect on the distribution of the assets. Imagine, for example, that the debtor made a bulk sale of its inventory and did not follow the procedures set out in Article 6 of the Uniform Commercial Code. Article 6 allows only creditors of the debtor at the time of the bulk sale to avoid it.[26] There may be few creditors at the time of the petition who were not also creditors at the time of the bulk sale. Nevertheless, the trustee cannot set aside the transfer under §544(a). Under that section, the trustee asserts the rights of a hypothetical lien creditor who came into being only at the time of the filing of the bankruptcy petition. Section 544(b) is therefore needed to allow the creditors to act collectively. Because identifying the few creditors who were not creditors at the time of the bulk sale is difficult, distributing the recovery to everyone may sensibly approximate the nonbankruptcy regime.

A second feature of §544(b) is more troubling. Section 544(b) gives the trustee the power to avoid a transfer in its entirety, even if the party into whose shoes the trustee steps could have avoided only part of it. Consider a corporation that goes through a leveraged buyout. If the leveraged buyout leaves the

---

[26] As we discover in the next section, the revised version of Article 6 introduces a complication, ignored here, by characterizing the rights against buyers as damage actions rather than avoidance actions.

corporation insolvent, the buyout is a fraudulent conveyance.[27] Under state nonbankruptcy law, only creditors who had lent money to the corporation before the buyout would be able to bring a fraudulent conveyance action. The overwhelming majority of the creditors, however, appeared on the scene after the leveraged buyout, having lent with full knowledge of the leveraged buyout. Under state law, then, neither these creditors nor a hypothetical lien creditor who came into being at the time of the petition could bring a fraudulent conveyance action. Only one creditor was owed money at the time of the buyout and is still unpaid at the time of the petition. That creditor is a consumer who bought an oven under warranty and who now has a $1 claim because the oven's light bulb has burned out. This consumer is a creditor within the meaning of state fraudulent conveyance law both at the time of the petition and at the time of the buyout.[28]

Under nonbankruptcy law, this creditor could bring a fraudulent conveyance action at the time the bankruptcy petition is filed. Section 544(b) allows the trustee to step into the shoes of this single creditor. Under nonbankruptcy law, this creditor could never recover more than $1. The trustee, however, faces no such cap. The trustee can set aside a billion dollar transfer on the basis of a single creditor's $1 claim. All that matters is the existence of a single creditor at the time of the petition who has the power to bring an avoidance action against someone. The amount of that creditor's claim places no limit on

[27] This problem arose a number of times in the late 1980s and early 1990s. See Kupetz v. Wolf, 845 F.2d 842 (9th Cir. 1988). We examine the way fraudulent conveyances affect leveraged buyouts and other corporate transactions in greater detail in chapter 7 below.

[28] It does not matter whether the creditor's claim is matured or unmatured, liquidated or unliquidated, fixed or contingent, disputed or undisputed. See Unif. Fraudulent Transfer Act §1(3).

the extent of the trustee's power to avoid the transfer. This strange rule originated in *Moore v. Bay*.[29]

The Limits of the Trustee's Avoiding Power

Assume that many general creditors lend money to a corporation. The corporation's shareholders are so casual about maintaining the corporate form and separating their own assets from those of the corporation that the general creditors, under nonbankruptcy law, will be able to *pierce the corporate veil* that shields shareholders from the obligations of the corporation. When they are able to pierce the veil, creditors can sue the shareholders directly and recover what the creditors lent the corporation. If the corporation files for bankruptcy, should the trustee be able to bring the veil-piercing action on behalf of the general creditors? If the corporation itself has the power under nonbankruptcy law to sue its own shareholders and recover from them, the cause of action would be property of the estate under §541. The trustee would be able to assert it for the benefit of the creditors, just as the trustee can bring a contract or tort action that the debtor could have brought outside of bankruptcy. One never reaches the question whether the trustee could bring the action by using one of the avoiding powers.

But if the debtor could not itself bring the action, the trustee likely cannot bring it, either. In *Caplin v. Marine Midland Grace Trust Company*, the Supreme Court examined the trustee's ability to bring damage actions that the debtor itself could not have brought.[30] In that case, the Supreme Court held under the old Bankruptcy Act that the trustee could not bring a damage action on behalf of bondholders against the agent charged with representing their interests.[31] The agent may have failed to

[29] 284 U.S. 4 (1931). The opinion itself is opaque. For an analysis of it under the Bankruptcy Code, see Lippe v. Bairnco Corp., 225 Bankr. 846 (S.D.N.Y. 1998).

[30] 406 U.S. 416 (1972).

[31] The agent is usually called the *indenture trustee.*

monitor the debtor as it was charged to do, but the action the bondholders had against their agent was of no concern to the debtor's other creditors. The fiduciary duty breached in *Caplin* was owed to the bondholders, not to the debtor. A creditor of a debtor ordinarily cannot complain when a third party violates a duty owed to another creditor.

Section 544(b) allows the trustee only to avoid *transfers* that the debtor made or obligations the debtor incurred. It does not give the trustee the right to bring *damage actions*; rather, the trustee can bring damage actions only if the debtor itself would have been able to bring the action outside of bankruptcy. As noted, this issue commonly arises when the debtor has so disregarded its corporate form that its shareholders are liable for its obligations. Veil-piercing actions are in many respects identical to the avoiding actions that the trustee undoubtedly enjoys under §544(a). It is difficult to explain why the trustee should be able to avoid transfers of property that the creditors could have avoided, but not bring damage actions. The purpose of the trustee's strong-arm powers under §544 is to vindicate the rights of creditors as a group. Why the trustee may bring a fraudulent conveyance action against shareholders when the corporation transfers assets to them while it is insolvent, yet not bring a veil-piercing action when the shareholders fail to capitalize the business adequately initially, is a mystery. Nevertheless, as §544 has generally been interpreted, the trustee does not possess the power to bring such damage actions in her own right. She can bring them only if the debtor itself could.[32]

Some federal courts have found that the debtor can bring veil-piercing actions against its own shareholders, and hence the trustee can as well because of §541.[33] State law authority for this proposition, however, is not easy to find. Indeed, the

[32] See, e.g., Breeden v. Kirkpatrick & Lockhart LLP (In re The Bennett Funding Group, Inc.), 336 F.3d 94 (2d Cir. 2003).

[33] See, e.g., Steyr-Daimler-Puch of America Corp. v. Pappas, 852 F.2d 132 (4th Cir. 1988).

gravamen of the action—that the corporation and the share-holders are one and the same—is inconsistent with the idea that the company can sue the shareholders. At least one state supreme court has repudiated a federal circuit court's opinion that the debtor did possess such a cause of action against its shareholders.[34]

Because the debtor in possession has the same powers as the trustee, allowing the trustee to bring a veil-piercing action creates a conflict of interest in the typical Chapter 11 case. The debtor in possession is ordinarily the group of managers running the business; often the managers are substantial shareholders and thus unlikely to bring an action against themselves. In such cases, an individual creditor or the creditors committee can ask the court for leave to bring the action for and in the name of the debtor in possession.[35] To obtain permission to bring the action, a creditor or the creditors committee must establish both that the trustee or debtor in possession has unjustifiably refused a demand to pursue the action and that the cause of action is worth pursuing.[36] Alternatively, either can ask for the appointment of an examiner to bring the action.

There is another justification for limiting the trustee's ability to bring damage actions, quite apart from the conflict of interest that arises when we are in Chapter 11 and there is a debtor in possession. Recall the rule of *Moore v. Bay*. It requires the trustee to turn over any avoided transfer or damage recovery to creditors as a group, not those creditors who would have been able to avoid it under nonbankruptcy law. Given the rule in *Moore v. Bay*, *Caplin* serves to prevent general creditors from

---

[34] See In re Rehabilitation of Centaur Insurance Co., 632 N.E.2d 1015 (Ill. 1994).

[35] See Official Committee of Unsecured Creditors v. Chinery, 330 F.3d 548 (3d Cir. 2003).

[36] See In re Perkins, 902 F.2d 1254 (7th Cir. 1990).

sharing in a recovery that only a few creditors would enjoy under nonbankruptcy law.

Whenever such anomalies exist, we should expect related areas of the law to be affected as well. The sharp distinction that *Caplin* and its progeny have drawn between creditor avoidance actions and creditor damage actions led the drafters of Revised Article 6 of the Uniform Commercial Code to recharacterize as a damage action the right creditors have against a buyer who runs afoul of the bulk sales act. This change from prior law was made to take advantage of *Caplin* and limit the trustee's rights in bankruptcy.[37]

Statutory Liens and Constructive Trusts

The different roles that §§541 and 544 play becomes especially important when confronting cases involving statutory liens and constructive trusts. Take first the case in which some creditors benefit from a special state statute. Many states, for example, have statutes that protect special interests, such as those of liquor wholesalers. The state statute entitles these creditors to be paid in full before any of the general creditors.[38] Constructive trust cases involve victims of some egregious fraud. The debtor is still holding the money or other property it purloined from the victims, and the victims insist that they are entitled to it before any of the general creditors. The victims argue that the money or other property is held by the debtor in constructive trust.[39] We look at each situation in turn.

The case of the liquor wholesaler is the easier one. As already mentioned, a state statute that applies only when the debtor is in bankruptcy (or that is geared to the financial condi-

---

[37] See U.C.C. §6-107 (1988), Official Comment 2.

[38] See California v. Farmers Markets, Inc., 792 F.2d 1400 (9th Cir. 1986); Max Sobel Wholesale Liquors v. Nolden, 520 F.2d 761 (9th Cir. 1975).

[39] See Heyman v. Kemp (In re Teltronics, Ltd.), 649 F.2d 1236 (7th Cir. 1981).

tion of the debtor) should not be respected. States can establish generally applicable priorities, but they cannot dictate federal bankruptcy policy. The Bankruptcy Code tells us this explicitly in §§541(c)(1) and in 545(1). Let's assume, then, that the state statute in our case applies inside of bankruptcy and out. The assets that the trustee gathers under §541(a)(1) are subject to this priority claim, but this does not end the inquiry. To say that property of the estate under §541(a)(1) is subject to the claims of the liquor wholesalers is not to say that the liquor wholesalers prime the general creditors. The trustee, in addition to asserting the rights of the debtor vis-à-vis the wholesalers under §541(a)(1), also asserts the rights of the general creditors. Section 545 follows the same principle as §544(a). We need to ask how the liquor wholesalers would fare against the hypothetical person into whose shoes the trustee steps.

We saw in §544(a) that, against secured creditors and other transferees, the trustee asserts the rights of a hypothetical person, acting in good faith, who either levied on the property or purchased at the time of the petition. Section 545 tells us that against the holders of statutory liens, as against those with security interests in real property, the trustee exercises the rights of a bona fide purchaser for value. Hence, one must ask whether the debtor could have sold the liquor free of the claims of the wholesalers. The case law has invented distinctions between such things as "statutory liens" and illegitimate "statutory priorities." In the end, however, these distinctions do not focus on the two-step inquiry the Bankruptcy Code sets out. What matters is whether the wholesaler's priority right is good inside bankruptcy and out and whether that right gives the wholesaler priority under nonbankruptcy law over a bona fide purchaser for value.

The constructive trust cases are less clear. They typically arise when a general partner buys real property for the partnership. The property is recorded in the name of the general partner, not in the name of the partnership.[40] Under state law, the general partner is not the beneficial owner of the property and is deemed to hold it in constructive trust for the partnership. Nevertheless, a dishonest general partner can convey the property to a bona fide purchaser for value free of the interests of the limited partners. Because the debtor holds the property in constructive trust, the property does not become property of the estate under §541(a)(1). The question is whether the trustee can bring it into the estate by using §544(a). Remember that in the case of real property, the trustee has the rights of a hypothetical bona fide purchaser for value. We need to establish whether the limited partners' property interest takes priority over the bona fide purchaser whom the trustee represents. Can a bona fide purchaser reach and take the property free of the claims of the fraud victims? Outside of bankruptcy, the bona fide purchaser can indeed take the property free of such claims. Hence, even when state law treats the land as held in constructive trust, the trustee can pull all of it back into the estate for the benefit of all the creditors. These, of course, include (but are not limited to) the defrauded partners.[41]

This is a sensible result. Under state law, the general creditors of the debtor could sue, reduce their claim to judgment, force a judicial sale to a bona fide purchaser for value, and enjoy the proceeds free of the claims of the partnership. Similarly, the partnership could record its interest and prevail over a bona fide purchaser (and hence the trustee as well). Rather than guess who would have won this race outside of bankruptcy, §544(a) treats the partnership and the general creditors in the same manner. They share what there is pro rata.

---

[40] Belisle v. Plunkett, 877 F.2d 512 (7th Cir. 1989); City National Bank v. General Coffee Corp., 828 F.2d 699 (11th Cir. 1987).

[41] See Mullins v. Burtch (In re Paul J. Paradise & Assocs.), 249 Bankr. 360 (D. Del. 2000). But see Vineyard v. McKenzie, 752 F.2d 1009 (5th Cir. 1985).

In the case of personal property, the analysis applies except that we use the benchmark of the hypothetical lien creditor. We ask whether the fraud victims could prevail over a creditor who tried to levy on the property at the time of the bankruptcy petition. The case law here is unclear. Some courts hold that bankruptcy judges should not find that a constructive trust exists at all under these circumstances.[42] Under nonbankruptcy law, a constructive trust exists when fraud victims can trace the funds that the debtor took from them. Bankruptcy courts often rely on this test to conclude that when tracing is possible, the assets do not come into the estate under §541. Too often, however, these courts stop with their analysis of §541. They do not ask whether the trustee can nevertheless bring the assets into the estate using her strong-arm powers.[43] The victims should prevail only if beneficiaries of a constructive trust could prevent lien creditors from reaching assets outside of bankruptcy.

The relationship between property of the estate under §541 and the strong-arm powers of §§544 is one of the most important and least appreciated in all of bankruptcy law. The trustee enjoys the rights of the debtor under §541. In addition, the trustee can assert the rights that the creditors could assert against the debtor's property outside of bankruptcy under §544. Too often lawyers focus exclusively on §541 and forget that §544 does much of the work.

In this chapter and the one before it, we have seen how the Bankruptcy Code sensibly translates the rights and obligations of a debtor to the bankruptcy forum. In the next chapter, we examine how the Bankruptcy Code handles situations in which the rights and obligations are fused together. These issues— those associated with executory contracts—present a special set of challenges.

---

[42] See XL/Datacomp, Inc. v. Wilson (In re Omegas Group, Inc.), 16 F.3d 1443 (6th Cir. 1994).

[43] See, e.g., First American Title Insurance Co. v. Lett, 238 Bankr. 167 (Bankr. W.D. Mo. 1999).

Chapter Six

Executory Contracts

General Nature of Executory Contracts

The previous two chapters looked at a debtor's liabilities and assets—claims against the estate on one hand and property of the estate on the other. A tort action that a third party has against the debtor is a claim; a tort action that the debtor has against someone else is an asset. When the debtor has exchanged promises with a third party, the resulting contract is both a liability and an asset. The debtor's promise to a third party is a liability, while the third party's promise to the debtor is a claim. Section 365 of the Bankruptcy Code deals with such cases and sets out the rules governing them. The section is complicated—often unnecessarily so. Nevertheless, the basic principles at work are sound and can be demonstrated with a few variations on a single set of facts.

Let's start with the following case. I am Debtor Corporation. I pay you $5 and you agree to give me a bushel of wheat in a week. In the interim I file a bankruptcy petition. My trustee looks at this situation. The $5 I have paid out is gone forever. But the trustee does have a right to get a bushel of wheat from you. If you do not deliver, the trustee is going to sue you. What the trustee has is an asset under §541. All the creditors of the estate are better off with your promise to deliver a bushel of wheat than they would be without it.

Now suppose you give me a bushel of wheat and I promise to pay you in a week. In the interim I file a bankruptcy petition. What does the trustee find? Your right to get $5 from me is a garden-variety claim. You are one of many creditors, and your

126

claim, like the others, will receive just a few cents on the dollar when the trustee ratably distributes the property of the estate.

Let's combine the first two cases. You and I enter into a contract. You promise to give me a bushel of wheat in a week, and I promise to pay you $5 for it. Here there is both a liability (I have to pay you $5 in a week) and an asset (I have a right to get a bushel of wheat from you). We give the name *executory contract* to this kind of arrangement. It is one in which the debtor has an obligation to a third party and the third party owes the debtor an obligation in return. What matters, of course, is how we treat such a beast, not what we call it.

How does the trustee feel about this contract? It depends on what has happened to the market price of wheat in the interim. Assume that the market price of wheat has gone up, and a bushel of wheat now costs $10. In this case, the trustee is thrilled. The trustee can use $5 to get something in return that is worth $10 (the bushel of wheat). This is a good deal, and the trustee should be able to take advantage of it. You should be held to your bargain: You asked for $5, you will get $5. It is a losing deal for you, but it would have been a losing deal even if no bankruptcy petition had been filed. There is nothing about bankruptcy that should let you off the hook.

The trustee is simply new management.[1] There is nothing about the deal that we entered into that conditioned your obligation to give me a bushel of wheat in exchange for $5 upon the management's staying the same. We want to have a rule that says simply this: If the debtor has a good deal that new managers would have been able to enjoy outside of bankruptcy, the trustee should be able to take advantage of it inside of bankruptcy. At first cut, §365 does exactly this. As in the nonbankruptcy world, of course, the trustee has to keep the other side of the bargain. The trustee cannot get the wheat without parting with the $5. The formal process by which the trustee takes advantage of the favorable contract (and lives up

---

[1] See Commodity Futures Trading Commission v. Weintraub, 471 U.S. 343 (1985).

to the debtor's obligations under the contract) is called *assumption*. When the trustee assumes the contract and brings it into the bankruptcy estate, the estate enjoys all the benefits of the contract, but bears all its burdens as well.

But what happens if the price of wheat plummets? Now I could buy wheat for $1, and any wheat you have you will be able to sell for only $1. The deal does not look so great. I promised to pay $5 for something that is now worth only $1. It is making deals like this that drove me into bankruptcy. Ridding oneself of a burdensome contract and exposing oneself to a damage action is a power that everyone enjoys. We live in a Holmesian world.[2] The new managers of a corporation can break a contract that the old managers entered into, provided they are liable for damages. The trustee is new management and can breach a contract if it is in the interests of the estate. The trustee's ability to breach an executory contract (and trigger the third party's claim for damages) is, in the language of the Bankruptcy Code, the ability to *reject*. Rejection of an executory contract is not quite the same as breach of a contract outside of bankruptcy. Rejecting an unfavorable executory contract is akin to abandoning an asset.[3] Little of consequence turns on this distinction, however. For most purposes, you can safely assume that rejection of an executory contract in bankruptcy has the same consequences as breach of the same contract outside of bankruptcy.

Giving the trustee the ability to breach ensures equal treatment among those who are similarly situated. As far as their legal rights are concerned, a party who has a contract with the debtor is in the same situation as someone who has lent the debtor money. Both have the right to sue for damages if the

[2] See Oliver Wendell Holmes, The Path of the Law, 10 Harv. L. Rev. 457, 462 (1897) ("The duty to keep a contract at common law means a prediction that you must pay damages if you do not keep it—and nothing else.").

[3] See Brown v. O'Keefe, 300 U.S. 598 (1937); Sparhawk v. Yerkes, 142 U.S. 1 (1891).

debtor does not do what was promised. An insolvent debtor cannot keep all its promises. Rather than favor one group over another, the general rule of bankruptcy is one of pro rata sharing. Allowing the trustee to reject the debtor's contracts ensures that all those with damage actions against the debtor are treated the same way. At the end of the day, they all have a claim against the debtor and they all share pro rata in the bankruptcy estate.

This, as a very rough approximation, tells you what is at stake in §365. As illustrated above, an executory contract is something that is both an asset and a liability. When a contract is executory, the debtor is obliged to a party and that party is obliged to the debtor. The Bankruptcy Code itself does not define the term *executory contract*. The best-known and most widely accepted definition is Vern Countryman's. In his view, an executory contract is "a contract under which the obligation of both the [debtor] and the other party to the contract are so far unperformed that the failure of either to complete performance would constitute a material breach excusing the performance of the other."[4]

An executory contract is a good thing for the debtor if the debtor's obligation is less than what the other party owes the debtor in return. Section 365 ensures that the creditors (through the trustee) can enjoy the benefits of an executory contract that is favorable to the debtor. It also ensures that if the contract is unfavorable, the third party stands in the same position it would have been in had the debtor defaulted on a contract outside of bankruptcy. Painted with very broad strokes, the section makes sense. The particular details of §365, however, are harder to reconcile with one another. What we want to do now is look at the more complicated cases. The problems we face under this section fall into two categories. One is the problem that arises when the contract is a bad one and the trustee wants to breach. This is the problem of *rejection*. The other arises

[4] Vern Countryman, Executory Contracts in Bankruptcy (Part I), 57 Minn. L. Rev. 439 (1973).

when the contract is terrific and the trustee wants to keep a good thing going. This is the problem of *assumption*.

Rejection

Much of the difficulty in reconciling the case law on the rejection of executory contracts stems from the failure of a number of courts early on to distinguish the power of rejection from the consequences that flow from rejection. Some courts, for example, have held that the rejection of an executory contract not only triggers a prepetition claim for damages but also deprives the other party of any benefits of the contract. This result is unsound if the other party would have been entitled to these benefits had the breach occurred outside of bankruptcy. There is no bankruptcy policy in favor of "executoriness."[5] Section 365 is not an avoiding power designed to expand the assets of the estate and give creditors inside of bankruptcy something they would not have had outside. Several examples illustrate this point.

A corporation promises to sell you the Van Gogh that hangs in its lobby for $1 million. Before payment or delivery, the price of works by Van Gogh goes through the ceiling. The business goes broke in the meantime and files a bankruptcy petition. Its assets (apart from the Van Gogh) are worth $1 million. The business owes its creditors (not counting you) $5 million. The managers of the business have been spending too much time buying art and not enough time managing the business.

The trustee wants out of this deal because the Van Gogh can now be sold for $2 million. The trustee reasons that breaching the contract is in the interests of the general creditors because if the business performs on the contract and sells you the Van Gogh, there will be $2 million in assets ($1 million in other assets and the $1 million you fork over) and $5 million in claims. The general creditors will get 40 cents on the dollar. But if the trustee backs out of the deal, the Van Gogh can be sold for $2

---

[5] See Michael Andrew, Executory Contracts in Bankruptcy: Understanding "Rejection," 59 U. Colo. L. Rev. 845 (1988).

million. Then the assets of the corporation are $3 million ($1 million from other assets and $2 million from the sale of the painting). The liabilities are $6 million ($5 million in other claims and $1 million from you for damages for the breach of contract). The damages from the breach of contract is the $1 million difference between the current market price and the amount set in the contract ($2 million minus $1 million). Creditors will get 50 cents on the dollar.

To understand whether the trustee can in fact reject this contract and face only a damage action from you, we need to ask what would have happened if the business's managers had refused to turn over the Van Gogh outside of bankruptcy. You would be able to bring a specific performance action. Vis-à-vis the corporation, you have the right to the painting. Because the Van Gogh is unique, you do not simply get money damages. You get the painting. But you are in a race with the corporation's general creditors. You also need to ask whether you would be able to take the Van Gogh *in the face of their claims.*

We must go through the same process we went through in chapter 5 when we looked at rights that the creditors enjoyed by virtue of §541(a)(1) and those they enjoyed by virtue of the trustee's strong-arm power under §544 and §545. To measure your rights in bankruptcy, you have to worry about how well you would fare not only against the debtor but also against creditors of the debtor who reduced their claims to judgment and levied on the painting. If a lien creditor could prime your right to the painting outside of bankruptcy, you should not be able to insist on getting the painting when the corporation is in bankruptcy. Nonbankruptcy law generally gives priority to the lien creditor. Under U.C.C. §2-402, the property is subject to creditor levy so long as the seller retains possession. You might have a special buyer's lien on these goods if you had already paid for them, but you have not. The rule we have is that your rights to the picture are superior to those of corporation's creditors only after you cure the ostensible ownership problem. For this reason, you should have only a damage claim in the corporation's bankruptcy if you have not taken possession of the picture. Section 365 provides for this result.

Section 365 also applies to leases. Let's take some simple cases. Suppose I have rented a store on Rodeo Drive from you. I am paying $10,000 a month in rent, and I am bound to pay you this amount each year for five years, for a total of $600,000. The market for stores on Rodeo Drive collapses. The rental value of the store is now much lower. I file a bankruptcy petition. My trustee can break this lease, just as I was free to break the lease outside of bankruptcy. Outside of bankruptcy, you would have an action for the damages you have suffered as a result of my breach. In bankruptcy, the trustee can reject the lease and you are left with an action for damages.[6]

Let's look at the other side of this transaction. I own a piece of real property that you rent from me. You agreed to pay me $5,000 a month for six years. The lease obliges me to heat and cool the building, which costs me $2,000 a month. A year into the lease we find ourselves in the midst of a real estate boom. If you were to lease the property from me now, you would have to pay me $10,000 a month. I file a bankruptcy petition. What can my trustee do? More specifically, is there any way that the trustee can take advantage of the dramatic increase in the rental value of the property?

Outside of bankruptcy, I could cut off the heating and cooling of the building. In most jurisdictions, you could respond by either leaving the property and suing me for damages or by remaining in possession of the property and paying for the heating and cooling by deducting it from the rent. If we raise these questions in bankruptcy, we find much the same answers. The trustee can reject the lease and cease heating and cooling the building. Just as you could outside of bankruptcy, you can call off the whole deal and sue for damages. Alternatively, you can exercise your right to pay for heating and cooling out of the rental payments that would otherwise be owing.

---

[6] Recall, however, that there is a cap on damages from the breach of a lease under §502(b)(6).

Your right to stay in possession and offset such costs is given explicitly in §365(h). The trustee's rejection of my obligations under the lease, however, does nothing to dispossess you of the property. You have a right to stay in possession of the property. You have a leasehold interest. This property interest gives you a right to the asset that primes that of any of my creditors. Not even a bona fide purchaser of the property from the debtor can take it free of your right to enjoy the property for the remainder of the lease term. Although the general rule of *Chicago Board of Trade* would itself be sufficient to give us this result, §365(h) makes the point explicitly.

The drafters of the Bankruptcy Code created problems by providing such an explicit rule for real property but not for personal property. Should one infer that, notwithstanding *Chicago Board of Trade*, personal property is to be treated differently? Suppose I lease you a fancy computer. You pay $5,000 a month in rent. This computer now leases for $10,000 a month. I file a bankruptcy petition. The trustee can reject this lease, but what does it mean to reject it? Under nonbankruptcy law, I cannot force you to give the computer back by declaring that I am in breach. I have conveyed a property interest to you. It is a done deal. You are in possession. I can yell "I breach!" all I want, but I cannot force you to give me the computer back. In bankruptcy, the trustee can convert any service obligations I owed you into a general claim you have against my bankruptcy estate. It is just like the heating and cooling obligation in the case of real property. But does rejection mean anything more than that? Does it mean that the trustee can get the computer back? There is no §365(h) to which we can turn. There is nothing to say that you can keep the computer in the face of the rejection.

We could infer that the absence of an analog to §365(h) means, in our case, that when my trustee breaks a lease of personal property, you cannot remain in possession. Under the maxim of statutory interpretation of *expressio unius*, one infers from the inclusion of one thing the exclusion of another. One can infer that Congress, by providing explicitly that lessees of real property could remain in possession after rejection, implicitly found that lessees of personal property could not. One can also reach the opposite conclusion, however. An equally plausible view begins with the observation that few cases arise in which the trustee wants to reject a personal property lease. Rejection becomes attractive only when the property increases in value. This is unlikely to happen in the case of personal property. When Congress enacted §365(h), it merely confronted the case that was most likely to arise. Congress may have decided not to trust courts to rely on the principle of *Chicago Board of Trade* in the case of real property, but not have thought about the analogous case of personal property at all. Setting out the rule explicitly in the case of real property does not require the inference that Congress was repudiating the general principle elsewhere. Indeed, why would Congress repudiate so important a doctrine by indirection?

There is an important lesson here. It is one thing to say that the trustee can reject and free the estate from ongoing obligations with respect to a lease or an executory contract. It is quite another thing to identify the consequences that flow in the wake of such a rejection. Rejection does not necessarily return the parties to the position they were in before they entered into the deal. A trustee can reject a lease of property, but that does not mean that the leasehold is extinguished and that the estate regains ownership of the property. Nothing about the nature of "rejection" requires that the trustee be able to undo (or "avoid") what is tantamount to a consummated property transfer. We need to keep this lesson in mind as we look at the rejection of technology licensing agreements, covenants not to compete, and the like.

Let's look at the following problem. A business develops a new soft drink. Your client acquires the exclusive right to sell it in Kalamazoo, paying $10,000 up front and agreeing to pay an additional $1 for each case it sells. (Your client has the formula and manufactures the drink itself. The business, however, promises to run various local and national advertising campaigns.) The soft drink is a big hit in Kalamazoo, but it is a bust in the rest of the country. The business files a Chapter 11 petition. The trustee wants to take away your client's exclusive right to distribute the soft drink in Kalamazoo. If the trustee could do this, the trustee could then enter into a new licensing agreement with your client at a much higher fee. Alternatively, the trustee could sell the right to market the soft drink in Kalamazoo to someone else. The trustee argues that the exclusive distribution right is an executory contract. Moreover, the trustee contends that your client loses the right to sell the drink as soon as the contract is rejected and the business gains the ability to license others to sell it in Kalamazoo. Under the franchising arrangement, each party has obligations remaining that would, if breached under nonbankruptcy law, allow the other to call off the deal. The business has the obligation to provide some marketing support and to pay for some advertising. Your client, of course, has obligations because it has to pay the royalty of $1 per case.

One may be able to argue these obligations do not necessarily make the right to manufacture the soft drink in Kalamazoo part of an executory contract. Take the following example. A business sells you a machine and promises to service it. You promise to pay for the service. The trustee could not bundle this whole package together, call it an executory contract, take the machine back and sell it to someone else on that ground. This transaction may be no different. Your client bargained for the exclusive right to sell this soft drink in Kalamazoo. Your client already has this right. The business should no more be able to get this right back in its bankruptcy than it should be able to get back a machine it sold to you. The right to sell the soft drink in Kalamazoo does not belong to the business anymore. One can argue that it is not the paradigm case in which I promise to sell you wheat and you promise to pay for it, but rather the quite different case in which I have already sold the wheat. Once I have sold the wheat, it is not mine anymore.

But let's assume this is wrong. Assume that what we have in the Kalamazoo case is an executory contract. Even if the distribution right is an executory contract, we still need to identify the consequences of the rejection. The trustee refuses to go ahead with the debtor's obligations under the contract and to advertise the product. But that does not trouble your client much. The soft drink is so popular that no advertising is needed. In any event, your client has a claim for the value of the ads that the business promised and this claim can be offset against any royalties that are owed. But can your client keep on selling the soft drink? This seems to parallel the ability of a lessee to remain in possession. Under nonbankruptcy law, the business would not be able to stop your client from selling the soft drink. The business is the breaching party. It cannot go to court and get your client to stop, just as a lessor of real property on Rodeo Drive cannot file a bankruptcy petition, reject the lease, and evict its tenant. Your client is a licensee who is "in possession." Why should rejection under §365 give the trustee the right to dispossess your client?

What about the business's desire to give someone else the right to make and sell the drink in Kalamazoo? Outside of bankruptcy, if the business said it was breaking its contract and started giving others the right to sell the soft drink in Kalamazoo, you could get a negative injunction in a hurry. More to the point, the general creditors of the business cannot have a receiver appointed and assign to others your right to sell the soft drink in Kalamazoo. This case is crucially different from your right of specific performance when the trustee breached and refused to give you the Van Gogh. In that case, you had no right to the painting vis-à-vis a lien creditor. In this case, your rights are paramount. No matter how broadly we define the trustee's strong-arm powers under §544(a), they would not enable the trustee to defeat your client's right to market the soft drink. Outside of bankruptcy, neither the business nor its creditors would have the ability to stop your client from making the soft drink. Moreover, your client would be able to enjoin the business from marketing the drink. In addition, your client would also be able to enjoin any third party who acquired rights from the business, such as a buyer of the business or its assets. Before we conclude that your client should prevail, however, we need to ask whether any other bankruptcy policy enters into the picture. The principal question focuses on how the business's discharge will affect your client's rights.

Suppose a store sells you a computer with a warranty and you promise to pay for the computer in thirty days. The store delivers the computer. The store files a bankruptcy petition and rejects its contract with you. The computer is in short supply, and the store would like to reclaim it from you and sell it to someone else. If the trustee rejects the store's executory contract with you, you will have a claim against the store for breach of the warranty obligations. The store's discharge will extinguish your claim, but it will not change your right to keep the computer.

The strong-arm power does the trustee no good here. Using the strong-arm power, the trustee could reach the computer only if the store or a party claiming through the store could reach it. To be sure, nonbankruptcy law calls the rights you have in the machine a "property interest," but what matters is whether the trustee can assert a superior claim to it using §544(a), not whether the right is "property" under nonbankruptcy law. You have a "property interest" in the machine under nonbankruptcy law as soon as the computer is identified to the contract, but your paramount right to it does not arise until later. Given the trustee's strong-arm power, the "property interest" that arises on the identification of the goods to the contract does you no good if you have not paid for the computer and are not in possession of it.

The discharge does not affect your rights, either. Your claim against the store is discharged, but you still retain the computer and the ability to bring actions against the store to enforce the right. (The store could not seize the computer and resist your replevin action on the ground that bankruptcy had discharged your claim.) Discharge affects only general claims that third parties have against the store. Other rights that third parties enjoy pass through bankruptcy.

Similarly, in the case of the soft drink business, discharge affects your client's ability to reach the assets of the business after the bankruptcy is over. It does not give creditors the ability to control a valuable asset (like the right to sell the soft drink in Kalamazoo) that they could not have reached outside of bankruptcy. It should not matter whether the transaction involved a traditional property interest or an intangible right such as a right to distribute a soft drink. We should treat rights like those of the soft drink distributor in Kalamazoo in the same way we treat traditional property interests. So long as neither the debtor nor any hypothetical party claiming through the debtor can upset those rights under nonbankruptcy law, bankruptcy should leave them unaffected.[7]

The law in this area is clear when a traditional property right is in issue. Assume that Debtor sold Blackacre to Buyer. If Debtor later tries to move back onto Blackacre and then files a bankruptcy petition, everyone understands that Buyer's trespass action is a claim and that this claim is discharged. Everyone also understands that the discharge has no effect on Buyer's continuing ownership of Blackacre or on Buyer's ability to bring trespass actions in the future if Debtor tries to move back again. Buyer prevails because Debtor's creditors cannot bring Blackacre into the bankruptcy estate through the use of one of the avoiding powers. Discharge is itself irrelevant.

The case law, however, is less clear when the right is something like a covenant not to compete and the debtor is an individual. In such cases, some courts have found that the power to reject in §365 serves to protect the flesh-and-blood individual's right to a fresh start.[8] The debate over the effect of such a covenant on an individual, however, is better located in the doctrines that have grown around the fresh start policy and §541(a)(6). Discharge alone does not extinguish encumbrances or liens on the debtor's property or otherwise affect the rights that the debtor has conveyed to a third party. The fresh start for individuals, however, includes more than a simple discharge. As we discussed in chapter 2 above, the principle of *Local Loan*

---

[7] See In re Printronics, Inc., 189 Bankr. 995 (Bankr. N.D. Fla. 1995).

[8] See, e.g., Cloyd v. GRP Records, 238 Bank. 328 (Bankr. E.D. Mich. 1999).

Company v. Hunt gives individual debtors the right to free themselves from encumbrances on their future earnings.[9] Whether this principle should allow individual debtors to rid themselves of covenants not to compete is an interesting question, but it has nothing to do with §365. Grafting a fresh start policy onto §365 by insisting that rejection is something more than the ability to breach is inherently problematic, as §365 applies equally to corporations and to individuals.

Congress confronted the consequences that flow from rejection in the case of technology licenses, when the licensor is the debtor and it seeks to recapture a license it has already issued.[10] In the main, Congress embraced the idea that rejection itself should not allow the trustee to recapture rights that the debtor has already conveyed away. The specific rules governing technology licenses in §365(n) are analogous to the specific rules governing real property in §365(h). The effect of §365(n) on intellectual property it does not specifically cover (such as trademarks and franchise agreements) remains unclear. Courts may apply the maxim of *expressio unius*. Congress's decision to deny debtors the ability to recapture rights they have already conveyed in the case of technology licenses might be used to justify granting debtors this right in analogous cases that are not explicitly covered.[11]

Arguments that justify giving the trustee the power to recapture rights that could never be taken from a third party outside of bankruptcy should not, in principle, rest on the idea that there is a bankruptcy policy in favor of rehabilitating the debtor. The trustee's power to reject executory contracts under

[9] 292 U.S. 234 (1934).

[10] Congress acted in the wake of Lubrizol Enterprises v. Richmond Metal Finishers, 756 F.2d 1043 (4th Cir. 1985), an opinion that interpreted the power to reject too expansively.

[11] See, e.g., In re HQ Global Holdings, Inc., 290 Bankr. 50 (Bankr. D. Del. 2003). Not all courts have adopted this approach. See, e.g., In re Ron Matusalem & Matusa of Florida, Inc., 158 Bankr. 514 (Bankr. S.D. Fla. 1993).

§365 is the same in Chapter 7 as in Chapter 11. Nothing in the Bankruptcy Code or its antecedents suggests that the power to reject turns on whether the debtor is liquidating or reorganizing. If it does not, then the debtor's chances of reorganizing successfully should play no role in deciding the contours of §365. The company's ability to regain control of the soft drink franchise should be independent of whether it needs the money to stay in business or whether the trustee is simply distributing the proceeds to the general creditors.

Assumption and Limitations on the Power to Assume

We now turn to the *assumption* of an executory contract to look at deals that the debtor has made that are good. Let's recall what our basic problem is. There are some things that a debtor has that are mixed assets and liabilities. I can live in this apartment, which is great, but I have to pay rent, which is not so great. I have your promise to give me wheat next week, which is great. But I have to pay you $5 for it, which is not so great. We have been looking at cases in which the burdens outweigh the benefits. Now we want to look at cases in which the burdens are light and the benefits substantial. Can you keep this good deal even though you have filed a bankruptcy petition?

Section 541 tells us that states cannot dictate distributions in bankruptcy. Any priority scheme they create has to be one that applies generally inside of bankruptcy and out. The same principle applies to contracts that the debtor makes with others. A third party may ask for an *ipso facto clause*, which allows it to terminate the contract in the event that a bankruptcy petition is filed. The debtor may be quite willing to grant such a clause. Outside of bankruptcy, those who act on behalf of the debtor worry principally about the interests of the shareholders. The shareholders are the ones who ultimately hire and fire the managers of a corporation. Shareholders may have little incentive to resist clauses that will prove costly only when they are no longer in the picture, as is typically the case when the corporation is insolvent. For this reason, §365 makes ipso facto clauses unenforceable. As in the case of §541, this prohibition extends beyond termination clauses tied to the start of a bankruptcy case and applies to clauses tied to the insolvency or financial condition of the debtor as well. The net must be cast wide enough so that parties cannot do indirectly what they are forbidden from doing directly.

Parties are not made worse off by having unenforceable clauses in their contracts. Moreover, such clauses were enforceable under the 1898 Bankruptcy Act, even though case law watered them down to some extent.[12] For both these reasons, ipso facto clauses still abound in form books and preprinted contracts. Their pervasiveness should not lead you, however, to draw the inference that they are enforceable. They survive because no one has an incentive to remove them. (Indeed, they may give some contracting parties a false belief that they will not have to deal with their contracting opposite if it ever files a bankruptcy petition.) Nevertheless, the trustee's ability to assume executory contracts still presumes that the contract has not been terminated before the filing of the bankruptcy petition.[13]

Many of the issues involving the assumption of executory contracts could be handled easily if §365 did not exist at all. Courts would treat a favorable executory contract as property of the estate under §541 and apply the general principle of *Chicago Board of Trade v. Johnson*. Let's go through some examples. You run a Holiday Inn in Camden, New Jersey. You pay Holiday Inn a certain amount of money every month and you are obliged to run your hotel in a certain way. You must have ice machines on every floor. Outside of bankruptcy, your ability to keep the franchise will depend on whether you comply with these conditions. Courts will not second-guess their wisdom or

[12] See Queens Blvd. Wine & Liquor Corp. v. Blum, 503 F.2d 202 (2d Cir. 1974).

[13] Nemko, Inc. v. Motorola, Inc., 163 Bankr. 927 (Bankr. E.D.N.Y. 1994).

purpose. (This may be a good thing. Judges make for poor ho-teliers, and there is always the risk they will regard as unneces-sary requirements that are in fact forward-looking. Holiday Inn, for example, insisted on wheel chair accessibililty long before it was required to do so.)

The benefits of being a Holiday Inn are quite substantial. You have the benefit of the company's computerized reserva-tion system; you get a discount on credit card fees. (Credit card companies charge those who accept credit cards for reimburs-ing them.) You also get extra business from people who have never heard of your hotel before they came to Camden because they know what to expect. If you had exactly the same hotel, but did not have the Holiday Inn sign, your hotel would be worth much less.

Notwithstanding the Holiday Inn franchise, however, your hotel is a complete bust. The idea of a Holiday Inn in Camden seemed like a good one at the time, but not that many people who come to Camden want to spend the night there. You can get more money for the assets if you blow up the building and use the property as a parking lot rather than as a hotel. Let's assume that you have been religious in complying with the rules. You have never let an ice machine run out of ice. When you close up shop, can you sell your franchise to someone else? We have already talked about this question. The answer should hinge entirely on whether the right you have acquired can be transferred. Whether the franchise can be transferred, like the question that arose in *Chicago Board of Trade* over whether a seat could be sold, should turn on applicable nonbankruptcy rules.

Let's assume that each franchise is tied to a particular loca-tion. You are allowed to sell the franchise, only if you sell the hotel as a going concern. Note that any bankruptcy policy that justifies a different outcome has nothing to do with giving you a fresh start. You are out of the hotel business. The hotel itself is being converted into a parking lot. Your general creditors would like to sell the Holiday Inn franchise to some third party who operates a hotel at a different location. If they were able to do this, your creditors are better off and Holiday Inn is worse off. Your creditors would have the proceeds from the sale of the franchise instead of Holiday Inn. In addition, Holiday Inn would lose the ability to choose the new location and its operator. (For example, the new owner might not conform to Holiday Inn's efforts to make each Holiday Inn be like every other and thereby ensure that its guests will not face any unwelcome surprises in a strange place.)

The general creditors, however, should not be able to sell a franchise by itself inside of bankruptcy if they cannot sell it by itself outside of bankruptcy. There is no bankruptcy policy that suggests that we should deprive the Holiday Inns of this world of the revenue from the sale of franchises or control over their franchisees in order to put money into the hands of the general creditors. Giving general creditors more and third parties less, of course, has utterly no bearing on an individual's fresh start.

But consider a different case. Suppose you want to stay in the hotel business. The idea may have been bad, but given the investment you have already made, you are better off using the building as a hotel. Everyone would lose even more if the building were torn down and the land used as a parking lot. The hotel is generating a positive cash flow and cannot generate more in a different configuration. You decide to stay in the hotel business but restructure the debt by filing for Chapter 11. In this case, you should be able to continue to call yourself a Holiday Inn. At most, the filing of a bankruptcy petition brings about a change in management, but because you continue as the debtor in possession, even this change is small. The financial structure of the business changes when it is in Chapter 11, but its operations need not. Unless the guests of the hotel hang around bankruptcy court, they will not notice the slightest change. As far as the franchise is concerned, the bankruptcy case should not make any difference. If, in the course of the bankruptcy case, substantive changes are made, then the consequences should follow inside bankruptcy that would follow outside. Assume, for example, that you are an incompetent manager and the creditors want to replace you with someone else. The control that Holiday Inn would have over the selection of the new manager should be no different from the kind of control they could exert outside of bankruptcy.

We cannot, however, rely on §541 and the principle of *Chicago Board of Trade* to resolve these questions, as the Bankruptcy Code deals with them explicitly in §365. Unfortunately, §365 makes it difficult to deal with these issues consistently. The trouble begins with §365(c), which limits the kinds of contracts that may be assumed:

> The trustee may not assume ... any executory contract ... whether or not such contract ... prohibits or restricts assignment of rights or delegation of duties, if ... applicable law excuses a party, other than the debtor, to such contract ... from accepting performance from or rendering performance to an entity other than the debtor or the debtor in possession.

This limitation is inconsistent with §541(c)(1). The trustee should be able to assert control over the debtor's assets and ensure that the creditors can enjoy whatever assets they could enjoy outside of bankruptcy.

With respect to individuals in Chapter 7, §365(c) might seem to bring about a sensible result. An opera singer has a contract to sing with an opera house next year. The singer is slightly past his prime, and the opera house would not engage this singer if it were making the decision now. The singer is deeply in debt and files a Chapter 7 petition. In such a case, there are three players—the debtor, the debtor's contracting opposite, and the debtor's general creditors. Each views the situation differently. The singer wants to be able to sing at the opera house and enjoy the promised fee. The opera company would like the engagement cancelled. The creditors of the opera singer want to be able reach the lucrative fee to recover some of what they are owed.

This case is easy as a matter of first principle. The singer should be able to take advantage of the contract as it is part of his future earnings and therefore his fresh start. The creditors should not be able to reach the fee for the same reason. And *Butner* tells us that the opera house should not be excused from an unfavorable contract by the happenstance of the singer's financial problems.

It might seem that §365(c) exists to ensure that we reach this result. Under it, a trustee cannot assume such a contract, a contract that an individual debtor could not have delegated to anyone else outside of bankruptcy. Applying §365(c) to the opera singer's contract, however, does not mean that the opera singer can take advantage of the contract. Once one assumes that the singer's deal with the opera company is an executory contract that falls within the ambit of §365, the inability of the trustee to assume the contract means that it is rejected and §365(g) deems rejection a breach of the contract. The singer's bankruptcy filing released the opera house from an unfavorable contract. To avoid this outcome, a court might rule that the singer's contract with the opera house is personal to him, thus not subject to the trustee's assumption or rejection. Holding that §365(c) never applies in the case of an individual, however, takes away the only plausible justification for having the provision in the first place. To make §365 consistent with §541(c)(1) and the *Butner* principle, it would have to take on a radically different form. Contracts for future services by individual debtors should be beyond its reach altogether. Moreover, it would need to allow the trustee to assume every contract of a corporate debtor.

The law here remains in flux. The most important cases have involved patent licenses. Some courts have found ways to read the statute in a way that allows the debtor in possession to continue to use patent licenses even though nonbankruptcy law provides that they are not assumable. Other courts, invoking Supreme Court opinions that mandate fidelity to statutory text in bankruptcy, have refused to do so.[14]

While §365(c) inappropriately limits the trustee's ability to assume contracts, §365(f)(1) inappropriately expands the trus-

---

[14] Compare Institut Pasteur v. Cambridge Biotech Corp., 104 F.3d 489 (1st Cir. 1997), with Perlman v. Catapult Entertainment, Inc., 165 F.3d 747 (9th Cir. 1999), and RCI Technology Corp. v. Sunterra Corp. (In re Sunterra Corp.), 361 F.3d 257 (4th Cir. 2004).

tee's ability to assign whatever contracts the trustee can assume. On its face, it seems to allow the trustee to assign any contract that can be assumed. The power to assume and the power to assign, however, are quite different from each other. If the debtor is to remain intact as a going concern and if the effect of the bankruptcy proceeding is simply to rearrange its capital structure, the trustee's power to assume should not be limited in any way. A state law limitation on transfer should not matter because the appointment of a trustee is in substance merely the substitution of one manager for another.

Section 541(c)(1) provides that, in the case of ordinary assets, a limitation on transfer has no effect on the ability of a trustee to assert the rights of the debtor. In an executory contract, the right in question is linked with an obligation of some kind, but this should not make for a different result. If the debtor had fewer creditors, the debt might have been restructured in a nonbankruptcy workout. There is nothing about the existence of multiple creditors and the need for a collective proceeding to sort out these problems that should change the corporation's ability to enjoy the benefits of whatever contracts into which it has entered.

The power to assign the debtor's rights to some third party, however, is quite different in principle from the power to assume. Under *Chicago Board of Trade*, the trustee should be able to assign a contract to a third party only if it is assignable outside of bankruptcy. Under nonbankruptcy law, the question of assignability is one that is left up to the parties. If the parties specify in their contract that the duty is not delegable, their choice is ordinarily respected, even if the duty would be delegable if they had said nothing.[15] The nonbankruptcy rule presumes that most parties will not allow delegation when performance requires skills that are special or unique, and will allow delegation when they are not,[16] but this is only a presumption.

[15] See, e.g., U.C.C. §2-210.
[16] Taylor v. Palmer, 31 Cal. 240, 247–48 (1866).

Section 365(f) neglects the consequences that follow when the nonbankruptcy baseline is merely a presumption. In some environments, such as franchise agreements, parties by contract routinely agree that the franchise is not assignable when the background legal rule provides for the opposite. As with most contract rules, there a few costs when the law provides a default rule provided parties can contract around it easily. There may be some cases in which the legislature restricts freedom of contract, but in such cases the nonbankruptcy law is again written against a background of freedom of contract. State law, for example, often singles out automobile franchisees for special protection. Regardless of what the contract provides, franchisees are protected and they are able to transfer their franchisees provided specified conditions are met.

When applied in bankruptcy, however, the state law protecting automobile franchisees takes on a different meaning. All other franchisees are able to transfer their franchises freely because state law is silent and the contractual limits are made irrelevant. Automobile franchisees—the ones who were the most able to transfer their franchises out of bankruptcy—are not so lucky. The nonbankruptcy law that gave them the ability to transfer provided certain conditions were made is transformed in bankruptcy into a law that deprives them of the ability to make the transfer unless these conditions are met. The automobile dealers are more able to transfer their franchises outside of bankruptcy, but are less able inside. This shift in relative rights cannot be defended. More importantly, it shows how §365 lacks an internal coherence that we see in other parts of the Bankruptcy Code. We should not be surprised that some parts of the Bankruptcy Code do not make perfect sense. It is important, however, to know where a search for internal coherence will not be successful.

Curing Defaults

Section 365(b) provides that the trustee (or the debtor in possession) can assume a contract even if there have been defaults that would give rise to a right of termination. The trustee must cure past defaults, compensate the third party for losses from the breaches, and provide adequate assurance of future performance. In determining whether assurances are adequate, courts pay particular attention to the debtor's ability to meet its financial obligations going forward and to whether any defaults occurred since the petition was filed.[17]

In some cases, the defaults may not be curable. A franchise agreement may give the franchisor the right to terminate if the franchisee has failed to operate the business for some period of time. Sometimes the same condition that ultimately pushed the debtor in Chapter 11 forced the debtor to suspend its operations just before the bankruptcy. Even if the debtor subsequently reopens, its failure to remain open triggers a default under the "going-dark" clause that is inherently incapable of being cured. Section 365(b)(1) responds to this problem. It excuses curing nonmonetary defaults with respect to real estate leases "if it is impossible for the trustee to cure such default by performing nonmonetary acts at and after the time of assumption." The trustee, of course, must comply with such provisions on a going-forward basis.[18]

If the debtor assumes an executory contract, it must assume the entire contract with all its burdens. It cannot pick and choose those parts that are to its liking.[19] Adequate assurance of future performance, however, is a term of art. In *In re U.L. Radio*, the court authorized the assignment of a lease of a television sales and service store to someone who wanted to convert it into a bistro on a budget of $50,000 notwithstanding a use

---

[17] See, e.g., In re Texas Health Enterprises, Inc., 246 Bankr. 832 (Bankr. E.D. Tex. 2000).

[18] The language quoted here was added to resolve an ambiguity. Compare Eagle Insurance Co. v. BankVest Capital Corp., 360 F.3d 291 (1st Cir. 2004), with Worthington v. General Motors Corp. (In re Claremont Acquisition Corp.), 113 F.3d 1029 (9th Cir. 1997).

[19] See In re Crippin, 877 F.2d 594 (7th Cir. 1989).

restriction in the lease.[20] The court observed that the primary focus of adequate assurance is the assignee's ability to satisfy financial obligations under the lease. In another case, the court authorized a debtor, whose lease limited it to selling paint and hardware, to assign its lease to a store that sold woman's clothing, even though the landlord had promised another lessee not to let another woman's clothing store operate in the building. The court again found that the landlord was not worse off financially and the bankruptcy proceeding itself insulated the landlord from contractual liability to the other tenant because of the doctrine of impossibility.[21] One may doubt whether $50,000 is in fact enough to convert an appliance store into a bistro in New York City or whether the doctrine of impossibility protects the lessor from actions from a third party. More importantly, however, one needs to ask again what bankruptcy policy justifies ignoring use restrictions in a lease. Courts, however, do not to set down hard-and-fast rules in these cases.[22]

Timing and Consequences of Rejection and Assumption

Section 365(d) requires that the trustee make the decision to assume or reject leases of nonresidential real property within 120 days, subject to a single extension of 90 days. Further extensions require the lessor's consent. This strict time limit was introduced into the Bankruptcy Code in 2005 and will likely change the dynamics of Chapter 11 cases involving large retailers, whose stores usually occupy leased land. While a seven-month period is long enough for simple cases, it may present significant challenges for debtors that have hundreds of such leases.

Upon assumption, the obligation becomes one of the estate, and the debtor is required to perform. Any subsequent breach

[20] 19 Bankr. 537 (Bankr. S.D.N.Y. 1982).

[21] See In re Martin Paint Stores, 199 Bankr. 258 (Bankr. S.D.N.Y. 1996), aff'd, 207 Bankr. 57 (S.D.N.Y. 1997).

[22] See, e.g., In re Tama Beef Packing, Inc., 277 Bankr. 407 (Bankr. N.D. Iowa 2002).

will no longer be a prepetition breach. §365(g). Damages will be entitled to administrative expense priority (if it occurs during bankruptcy), or to ordinary damage rules if breached subsequent to the termination of the bankruptcy proceeding. By contrast, upon rejection, the resulting damage action (if any) is treated as a prepetition claim. The debtor, however, does not make the decision to assume or reject immediately and in most cases the debtor continues to enjoy the benefits of the contract or lease. If the debtor ultimately assumes, it presumably has to pay all its obligations at the contract rate, as well as cure any defaults. On the other hand, if the debtor ultimately rejects, the outcome is less clear.

Section 365(d) requires ongoing performance of obligations before assumption or rejection for leases of nonresidential real property and provides more limited protection for personal property lessors as well. The case law suggests that with respect to executory contracts and other leases, the third party is entitled to administrative expense priority, not under the terms of the lease or contract, but "under an objective worth standard that measures the fair and reasonable value" of the contract or lease.[23]

If the benefits the debtor receives correspond to the costs the other party incurs, this rule would seem to make sense. The trustee would have a chance to assess the situation and the third party would not bear the costs of the delay. The existing rule, however, does not necessarily make the third party whole. Some courts have found that the option value inherent in the right to use the asset does not count as a benefit for which compensation is required.[24] Paying for benefits received is not the same as compensating the third party for all the costs it incurs between the filing of the petition and the rejection. The starkest case arises when the third party is supplying insurance. Assume that debtor fails to make payments on its fire in-

---

[23] See, e.g., In re Thompson, 788 F.2d 560, 563 (9th Cir. 1986); In re Patient Education Media, Inc., 221 Bankr. 97 (Bankr. S.D.N.Y. 1998).

[24] In re Enron Corp., 279 Bankr. 79 (Bankr. S.D.N.Y. 2002).

surance for the first six months of the bankruptcy. It then decides to reject the contract. What is the benefit that the debtor has received? Can the debtor argue that, given that its building did not burn down, it did not receive any benefit? One would not think so, but exactly this problem can arise in more subtle guises. Assume a software producer has agreed to write the operating system for a new computer Debtor is developing. The operating system is due on July 1 and the computer cannot work without it. Debtor files a bankruptcy petition on January 1. In order to finish the program on time, the software producer must spend $10,000 each month. The trustee rejects the contract on June 1 after deciding that the new computer is not worth developing. The software producer seeks $50,000 in damages for all it spent on the program between the filing of the petition and the time of the rejection. The trustee will argue that because the debtor never used the program (and indeed the program was never finished), the debtor never received any benefit and hence does not owe any damages that deserve administrative priority under §503(b).

There is a second and much more common limitation on the protection that third parties receive before assumption or rejection. Many businesses in bankruptcy have a single secured creditor with a security interest in the debtor's assets. The trustee is entitled to incur expenses and charge them against the secured creditor's secured claim. Third parties, however, cannot do this.[25] For this reason, those in the position of the software producer or the insurer should negotiate with the secured party at the start of the case to ensure that they are paid. It should immediately ask the court to give the trustee a deadline. §365(d).

A negative implication of §365's decision to give the trustee the power to assume is that the third party cannot terminate the contract on the ground of the debtor's breach, as it would typically be able to do outside of bankruptcy. An effort to ter-

[25] See Hartford Underwriters Insurance Co. v. Union Planters Bank, 530 U.S. 1 (2000).

minate is simply a nonevent. Section 362 stays everyone from "any act . . . to exercise control over property of the estate." An attempt to terminate might be seen as not merely as a breach, but as an effort to exercise control over property of the debtor (the "property" being the right of the debtor to the performance of the third party) that violates the automatic stay and may expose the producer to sanctions from the court.[26] When one is in doubt, one should always petition the court for a declaratory order that the proposed action does not violate the automatic stay. If the automatic stay applies, one can ask for relief from it or, in the alternative, one can ask for adequate protection. §362(d).

---

[26] See Computer Communications v. Codex Corp., 824 F.2d 725 (9th Cir. 1987) (holding an effort to terminate violated the automatic stay, the court awarded $4,750,000 in general damages and $250,000 in punitive damages).

Chapter Seven

Fraudulent Conveyances and Related Doctrines

In this chapter, we examine the protections enjoyed by creditors both inside and outside of bankruptcy. These protections, embodied in fraudulent conveyance law and related doctrines, are best understood as protections that most creditors would bargain for when making their loans.[1] In chapter 8, we look at voidable preferences. This bankruptcy-specific policy ensures that when bankruptcy is on the horizon, no creditor engages in gun-jumping.

Fraudulent conveyance law is a feature of state law that the trustee can use by invoking §544(b). Most states have adopted the Uniform Fraudulent Transfer Act; some still follow its predecessor, the Uniform Fraudulent Conveyance Act, and a few, such as New York, have their own versions of fraudulent conveyance law. The Bankruptcy Code has its own version of fraudulent conveyance law as well, in §548. When transactions span a number of different jurisdictions, the trustee is able to invoke bankruptcy's fraudulent conveyance rules without having to identify which state's fraudulent conveyance law governs. The reach of these laws is largely the same, except that §548 reaches back only two years, while its state law counterparts reach back as long as the relevant statute of limitations permits.

Fraudulent conveyance doctrine encompasses actions that are fraudulent at common law, but its reach is much broader. It is a flexible principle that looks to substance, rather than form, and protects creditors from any transactions the debtor engages in that have the effect of impairing their rights, while ensuring

---

[1] See Robert Charles Clark, The Duties of the Corporate Debtor to its Creditors, 90 Harv. L. Rev. 505 (1977).

that the debtor can continue to do business and assuring third parties that transactions done with the debtor at arm's length will not be second-guessed.

Some carelessly written opinions leave the impression that fraudulent conveyance law reaches only those transactions in which the debtor makes a transfer while insolvent for less than reasonably equivalent value or engages in actual fraud. More than 400 years of history teaches, however, that this is emphatically not the case, as we will see below. Fraudulent conveyance law gives the trustee a broad power to void transfers tainted by "badges of fraud" and ensures that debtors and their confederates suffer the consequences of being too clever by half.

Fraudulent conveyance law first took statutory form in 1571. Transfers made and obligations incurred with the intent to delay, hinder, or defraud creditors were deemed fraudulent and void as against creditors. The statute underwent a dramatic expansion just a few years after it was enacted. In 1600 or thereabouts a Hampshire farmer named Pierce conveyed his sheep to a man named Twyne. Twyne allowed Pierce to remain in possession of the sheep, to shear them, and to mark them as his own. A creditor of Pierce's reduced his claim to judgment and had the sheriff try to levy on the sheep that were still in Pierce's hands even though they had been sold to Twyne.

A fight of some kind ensued, and Edward Coke, then the Queen's attorney general, brought a criminal action against Twyne, the buyer of the sheep, in the Star Chamber.[2] The Star Chamber was a court largely reserved for treason trials and other crimes against the state. The Elizabethan fraudulent conveyance statute provided that a share of any assets recovered went to the Crown. The Crown had always enjoyed substantial revenue from those convicted of treason and felony, and fraudulent conveyance law was a useful tool in preventing traitors and felons from putting their property beyond its reach.

---

[2] Twyne's Case, 3 Coke 80b, 76 Eng. Rep. 809 (Star Chamber 1601).

These concerns may explain why a case involving a creditor levying on sheep was litigated here.[3]

The court in *Twyne's Case* found the transfer of the sheep voidable, not because one could prove that Pierce acted with actual fraudulent intent but because *badges of fraud* were associated with the transaction. A transfer of ownership without a simultaneous transfer of possession was inherently suspect. As the doctrine developed, the badges of fraud ceased to be merely proxies for fraud that was hard to prove and instead covered transactions that, although perhaps not fraudulent, were ones to which creditors would object nevertheless.

Transfers by Insolvents for Less Than Reasonably Equivalent Value

The principal badge of fraud, the one that covers the vast majority of cases and the one embodied in explicit statutory language, is a transfer a debtor makes while insolvent and for which the debtor receives nothing, or too little, in return. The paradigm here is a gift. An insolvent debtor gives a birthday present to a parent. Under fraudulent conveyance law, the creditors can reach the gift that is now in the parent's hands. This transaction may or may not be part of a scheme to defraud creditors, but making these sorts of transactions voidable may nevertheless make sense. First, it is possible that so many of the transactions in which an insolvent debtor gives away something and receives nothing or too little in return are fraudulent that one is better off voiding them all rather than engaging in elaborate case-by-case inquiries into fraud. Second, even if most of these transfers are not fraudulent, so many may be transfers that creditors would want banned that we are well off banning all of them.

Fraudulent conveyance law applies to corporations as well as individuals. In the corporate context, "reasonably equivalent value" is given in almost any arm's-length transaction in the

---

[3] See Garrard Glenn, Fraudulent Conveyances and Preferences §§61–61e (rev. ed. 1940).

marketplace, but transactions with insiders are subject to scrutiny. *Any* transaction that takes assets out of an insolvent corporation and puts them into the hands of shareholders is a fraudulent conveyance. Dividends, stock repurchases, and corporate restructurings that have the same effect all reduce the pool of assets available to creditors without bringing anything of value to the corporation in return. Hence, when the corporation is insolvent, such transactions are voidable.

We focus first on the badge of fraud covering transfers for less than reasonably equivalent value while insolvent, as it is the one most commonly encountered and easiest to apply. UFTA §5(a) and Bankruptcy Code §548(a)(2) reflect the idea that a solvent debtor can do what it pleases with its assets, but one that is insolvent (or becomes insolvent as a result of the transfer) cannot incur obligations or convey assets for less than reasonably equivalent value. Section 4 of the UFCA uses "fair consideration" instead of reasonably equivalent value but operates in the same way.

The way in which these terms are defined determines the scope of fraudulent conveyance laws. Trading one asset for another is an exchange in which there is fair consideration or reasonably equivalent value. Hence, such a transaction is not a fraudulent conveyance, even if the debtor is insolvent. Creditors are stuck with the business decisions its debtor makes so long as the debtor remains in control. Moreover, creditors are powerless to reach assets once they have been placed in the hands of a good faith purchaser for value.

Debtors in financial trouble often try to pay one creditor rather than others. That creditor may be an important supplier or simply a particularly aggressive lender. A transfer to that creditor (called a *preference*) makes the other creditors worse off, but that does not make it a fraudulent conveyance. The UFCA, the UFTA, and §548 ensure this outcome by providing that a transfer on account of an antecedent debt is conclusively presumed to be one for which fair consideration or reasonably equivalent value is given.

This result makes sense. Outside of bankruptcy, every creditor must rely on its own efforts to obtain repayment. Obtaining payment on a debt is simply the nature of the game when a collective proceeding is not on the horizon. Such transfers on account of an antecedent debt may affect how assets are distributed among the different creditors, but they do not affect the pool of assets available to the creditors. Creditors as a group are not worse off when one is paid and others are not. A creditor can challenge a payment to another creditor under the fraudulent conveyance laws only if the payment was made with actual fraudulent intent. Such cases arise most frequently when the creditor is an insider.[4] To challenge a payment to a creditor, one ordinarily must show that it is a preference, a transfer made on the eve of bankruptcy that violates the collective norms of bankruptcy. We will examine preferences at length in chapter 8.

Creditors are always worse off when the debtor takes assets whose value is certain (such as cash) and exchanges assets whose value is uncertain. A new machine may or may not increase earnings sufficient to offset its costs. Creditors must choose debtors whom they believe able to make competent decisions about how to run their businesses. Lenders know that their debtors will take risks. It is possible that the debtors will not succeed, but creditors are compensated for that risk. Fraudulent conveyance law is limited to actions that we are confident most creditors would forbid if they could. For example, all creditors would agree that the debtor should not hide assets from them when they try to collect. Nor should the debtor be able to give away money when the debtor already lacks the money to pay off creditors in full.

The concept of reasonably equivalent value must be interpreted sensibly to ensure that fraudulent conveyance law does not extend too far. Suppose a creditor forecloses on property, and the property is sold at a properly run foreclosure sale. The

---

[4] See, e.g., Bullard v. Aluminum Co. of America, 468 F.2d 11 (7th Cir. 1972).

debtor is insolvent and allows its right to redeem the property to lapse. The debtor's loss of this equity of redemption is itself a transfer of property as defined in §101 of the Bankruptcy Code. A court, however, does not inquire into whether the foreclosure yielded a reasonable price in this particular case. A regularly conducted, noncollusive foreclosure sale necessarily yields reasonably equivalent value.[5]

Determining whether a corporate debtor is solvent at a given time requires answering a simple question: Would a solvent buyer at the relevant moment be willing to pay a positive price to take on all the debtor's assets and all the debtor's liabilities?[6] Assume that a debtor has guaranteed a $10 million debt of its parent corporation and otherwise has no other obligations. The debtor's assets are worth $1 million. If you were solvent, whether you would pay to acquire the debtor's assets and liabilities would turn on whether the chance that you will be called upon to honor the guarantee was greater or less than one in ten. No one would agree to acquire an asset worth $1 million if it came with a 50–50 chance of having to pay $10 million. But a buyer might acquire the asset if the chance that it would have to pay $10 million were, say, only one in twenty. Hence, the debtor is insolvent in the first instance and solvent in the second.

The insolvency test is based on the idea that when a corporation's assets are greater than its liabilities, the shareholders are the residual claimants. They enjoy each additional dollar the corporation brings in, and they lose each additional dollar the corporation loses. Because they are the residual owners, they internalize the benefit of making the right decisions and the cost of the wrong ones. When a corporation is insolvent, the shareholders enjoy some of the upside if the corporation's fortunes improve enough, but they bear none of the downside risk. By adding an insolvency requirement, we ensure that

---

[5] See BFP v. Resolution Trust Corp., 511 U.S. 531 (1994).

[6] See Covey v. Commercial National Bank, 960 F.2d 657 (7th Cir. 1992).

creditors are able to upset only those transactions where the shareholders do not internalize the costs of their decisions. Creditors are assumed to trust the shareholders to make decisions when the shareholders themselves are the first to lose when they make bad decisions. If they want to limit the shareholders further, they must bargain for such protections in their loan agreement.

The insolvency requirement, however, is underinclusive. A corporation can be solvent and the shareholders can still have the incentive to engage in transactions that run contrary to the creditors' interest. Assume that a corporation owes its creditors $10. One asset is $10 in cash and the other is a lottery ticket that has a one-in-ten chance of paying $101. If the corporation decides to use the cash to make a dividend of $10, the corporation would still be solvent. Its remaining asset—a lottery ticket worth a little more than $10—is greater than its $10 in liabilities. But the dividend would dramatically change the creditors' chances of being repaid. The insolvency test is not sensitive to lenders' concerns about both the magnitude of a debtor's assets and liabilities and the chances that each might change. If a creditor wants to be able to object because the value of the debtor's assets was subject to variance, it has to bargain for such a right. The off-the-rack protection of fraudulent conveyance law cannot be carefully fitted to every debtor.

Whether a company is insolvent at any given moment depends on what is known at that time, not on what is known in hindsight. Consider the case in which a corporation's sole asset is an oil-drilling venture. Its only creditor is owed $100. At the time the corporation declares a dividend, the corporation is drilling ten wells. There is a 90 percent chance that at least one of them will strike oil. If any of the wells is successful, the company will be worth at least $1,000. There is, however, a 10 percent chance that none of the wells will produce. In this event, the corporation will be worthless. A year passes and all the wells prove to be dry holes. Can the creditor attack the dividend on the ground that the corporation was insolvent at the time of the dividend? No. The determination of insolvency must be tied to what was known at the time the dividend was made. At that time, a solvent buyer would have paid a positive price for the oil wells. This is sufficient. To work effectively, fraudulent conveyance law must focus on the position of the parties at the time of the initial transaction.[7]

As noted in chapter 5, fraudulent conveyance law, working in conjunction with §544(b) and the doctrine of *Moore v. Bay*, is conspicuously defective in one respect. Existing law may not sufficiently distinguish present and future creditors. Suppose a corporation issues a huge dividend to its shareholders, and the dividend leaves the corporation insolvent. Anyone who was a creditor at the time of the dividend should, of course, have a fraudulent conveyance action against the shareholders. But what about the creditors who came on the scene after the dividend? Unless they lent because they were misled by the past financial health of the corporation, they are no different from creditors who lend to a corporation that has become insolvent through a market reverse. Ordinarily, those who lend to thinly capitalized corporations have no right to reach that corporation's shareholders in the event it fails. Such a right typically exists only when the corporate form has been abused. If creditors want shareholders to become liable for the corporation's obligations, they must insist on a guarantee, as indeed many do.

Fraudulent Conveyance Law and Badges of Fraud

Fraudulent conveyance law extends beyond transfers by insolvent debtors for less than reasonably equivalent value. Consider the case of OfficeCo, a company that builds and manages office buildings. It has shown impressive growth and consistent earnings in a highly volatile real estate market. Much of OfficeCo's success is attributed to its ingenious and creative CFO. One of OfficeCo's recent projects was carried out by its wholly owned subsidiary, White Elephant Enterprises. The

---

[7] See Lippe v. Bairnco Corp., 249 F. Supp. 2d 357 (S.D.N.Y. 2003).

subsidiary's sole asset is White Elephant Plaza, a large office building that cost $800 to build, much more than anyone expected. OfficeCo manages the building. The managers of OfficeCo believe that the Plaza is worth at least $1,000, but they fear it may decline in value. To protect OfficeCo's track record, they decide to sell the Plaza. To their surprise, they cannot find anyone willing to buy the property for $1,000. Indeed, they cannot find anyone willing to buy it from them for $800.

The CFO, however, finds a way to ensure that the uncertain fortunes of the Plaza do not jeopardize OfficeCo's solid reputation among investors. With the approval of the board of directors, the CFO creates CFOPartners, a limited partnership. The general partner of CFOPartners is the CFO and the limited partners are a group of outside investors. The CFO contributes $2 and the limited partners put in $198.

CFOPartners then forms WhiteElephantCo, a wholly owned subsidiary of CFOPartners. WhiteElephantCo buys OfficeCo's equity stake in White Elephant Enterprises for $1,000 ($200 in cash and a long-term unsecured note for $800). WhiteElephantCo also enters into a long-term contract with OfficeCo that gives OfficeCo the right to manage the building. Soon after the purchase of the Plaza, WhiteElephantCo borrows $250 from Bank and gives it a first mortgage on the Plaza. A little while later, WhiteElephantCo declares a dividend of $250. CFOPartners distributes the cash to the partners.

OfficeCo reports record profits for the year, and its CFO continues to be highly praised for his astute and aggressive management. Three years pass, but then OfficeCo's fortunes take a turn for the worse. OfficeCo defaults on its loans. The CEO and CFO are fired. The company files for bankruptcy. The assets of OfficeCo are only enough to give its general creditors a return of ten cents on the dollar. The creditors of OfficeCo would like to bring White Elephant Plaza into the bankruptcy estate free of Bank's security interest. They would also like to recoup the $250 paid to the investors in CFOPartners.

It might seem that the creditors could attack the transfer of the Plaza (or, more precisely, OfficeCo's transfer of its equity interest in White Elephant Enterprises, the company that owned the Plaza) on the ground that it is not a true sale. Such an approach, however, is off the mark. As we discuss in chapter 9, the true sale jurisprudence that developed in bankruptcy courts focuses on the question whether someone who purports to be a third party insulated from the bankruptcy process is in fact a secured creditor who must comply with the automatic stay and other restrictions imposed on secured creditors even while their priority rights are respected. The OfficeCo problem is radically different. The creditors want to recover White Elephant Plaza free of Bank's security interest. Even if true sale doctrine led to the conclusion that the Plaza was part of the bankruptcy estate, it would do nothing to change Bank's priority right. Determining whether a transaction is voidable requires going considerably further. The principles available, however denominated, must be derived from fraudulent conveyance law.

Turning to badges of fraud, we see that the most familiar one (transfers by insolvent debtors for less than reasonably equivalent value) may not work here. CFOPartners may be able to argue that White Elephant Plaza was worth more than what they paid for it and that the dividend did not leave it insolvent. The more volatile the value of the underlying asset, the harder it will be to show insolvency at the moment the dividend is made. The creditors of OfficeCo, however, may be able to show that other badges of fraud are present.

"Badge of fraud" is a term of art. It identifies behavior that reasonable creditors would prohibit if they could, regardless of whether the behavior would be considered fraudulent at common law. A transaction is not voidable merely because it contains a single badge of fraud, but transactions that contain a sufficient number of badges of fraud are voidable. A transfer can be found to hinder, delay, or defraud within the meaning of fraudulent conveyance law if it there is a close relationship between the parties, the transfer is not in the usual course of business, the debtor retains control after the conveyance, and the transfer is concealed.[8] Fraudulent conveyance law does not require more than that the transfer was part of a plan designed to lull creditors into inactivity.

Taking several steps back from OfficeCo's transaction, we can see that it does exhibit badges of fraud. The transaction took the form of a sale of stock. There was no public record of the transfer. The acquiring entity was controlled by an insider of OfficeCo. From the perspective of creditors, nothing changed. The day-to-day operations of White Elephant Plaza continued. The owner of record (White Elephant Enterprises) remained unchanged. Debtors, of course, routinely engage in transactions that have the side effect of making its balance sheet look healthy and robust. But these transactions offer some collateral benefit, such as favorable tax treatment. The transaction here served no purpose other than to make OfficeCo's earnings appear more stable than they were and to prevent creditors from seeing that the capital spent on Plaza was at greater risk than it appeared. Here we have a transaction that unambiguously took resources out of corporate solution and served no purpose other than to make it hard for creditors to understand what its debtor was doing.

The absence of a business justification has long been a common hallmark of transactions that are ultimately found to have sufficient badges of fraud to make them fraudulent conveyances,[9] and we continue to see state courts invoke the idea of badges of fraud even when actual fraud has not been proved and reasonably equivalent value exists. That the other badges of fraud are invoked so rarely stems not from their underlying soundness, but from the fact that insolvency and lack of reasonably equivalent value cover so much of the terrain. Only in transactions in which the debtor spends considerable creativity in making life hard for creditors is it necessary to look to other badges of fraud, but when such cases arise—and Enron is a

---

[8] See Wall Street Associates v. Brodsky, 684 N.Y.S.2d 244 (App. Div. 1999); Citibank v. Benedict, 2000 WL 322785 (S.D.N.Y. 2000).

[9] See, e.g., Clow v. Woods, 5 Sergeant & Rawle 275 (Pa. 1819).

conspicuous recent example—the other badges of fraud become useful.[10]

The Step-Transaction Doctrine

Perhaps the most difficult part of modern fraudulent conveyance doctrine concerns not whether a fraudulent conveyance exists but rather the person against whom the fraudulent conveyance remedy should apply.[11] Consider the following case. A debtor goes to a jewelry store, gives the store $100, and asks it to give a gold ring to one of his parents. In this case, $100 is transferred from the debtor to the jewelry store and the ring is transferred from the store to the parent. If a creditor tries to recover the ring from the parent, can the parent argue that the creditor has no right to the ring because the debtor never owned it? Under this view, the only transaction that can be challenged is the one between the debtor and the jeweler. The debtor gave the jeweler $100 and received nothing back. Most of us would reject this argument. In form, there might have been a transfer between the insolvent debtor and the jeweler and then a second transfer between the jeweler and the parent, but the substance of this transaction was quite different: an insolvent debtor bought the ring and then gave it to the parent. A fraudulent conveyance action should lie against the parent but not the jeweler.

Fraudulent conveyance problems involving multiple parties usually arise in corporate transactions, and here it can be much harder to identify the true substance of the transaction. We might begin with each party's knowledge or good faith.[12] This approach may be misguided, however, because it strains the traditional meaning of good faith; ordinarily, the honesty of the

---

[10] Indeed, the OfficeCo example presented here is modeled after the "Raptor" transactions in Enron. Those transactions were far more complicated, but their basic structure was the same.

[11] Lippi v. City Bank, 955 F.2d 599 (9th Cir. 1992).

[12] See, e.g., United States v. Tabor Court Realty Corp., 803 F.2d 1288 (3d Cir. 1986).

lender or any other person against whom the action is brought is not an issue. We need to ask whether, under all the circumstances, the transaction, as a matter of substance and not merely form, was one in which a party gave fair consideration or reasonably equivalent value to another. Answering this question requires determining whether the transaction was at arm's length. We also need to decide the extent to which one creditor should be required to monitor its debtor for the benefit of other creditors. Reducing everything to the procrustean inquiry of whether the party exercised good faith is unlikely to illuminate matters. The alternative standard that some have proposed—asking whether the party had knowledge of the overall transaction—rewards ignorance and stupidity, something that the law should not do.

The step-transaction doctrine is indispensable in a case such as OfficeCo.[13] When we look at the various discrete transactions as a single deal, we can see that the principal beneficiary of this transaction is CFOPartners. It put nothing at risk and ended up with $50 in cash and all the gains in the event that Plaza ever is worth more than $1,000. Though not couched in these terms, CFOPartners ended up with not only cash but also the equivalent of an option to buy Plaza for $1,000.

The OfficeCo transaction involved a number of steps, but in a sense these do not matter. Our hypothetical would be no different if, instead of equity in a company that owned an office building, the debtor had transferred sheep to some third party, but continued to possess the sheep, shear them, and mark them as his own. If such a transaction falls within the reach of fraudulent conveyance law even in the absence of actual fraud, then OfficeCo's transaction should as well. And as *Twyne's Case* is still good law, there is no doubt about the outcome of the case involving sheep.

It might seem that Bank's security interest should be respected. It parted with $250 and hence gave value in turn for its security interest. All is not so simple, however. We can rechar-

---

[13] See, e.g., Orr v. Kinderhill Corp., 991 F.2d 31 (2d Cir. 1993).

acterize Bank's transaction as a transfer to CFOPartners for which Bank received a security interest from WhiteElephantCo. Bank's security interest is vulnerable in exactly the same way it would have been had it facilitated a leveraged buyout. Bank will undoubtedly argue that its lien on White Elephant Plaza should be respected at least to the extent that it gave value. The trustee can argue that, in substance, though not in form, the transaction was one in which Bank made a transfer to the investors in CFOPartners and gave nothing to WhiteElephantCo itself. Bank might be able to resist this argument on the ground that it acted in good faith and engaged in an arm's-length transaction according to ordinary business terms.

Courts, however, have been quick to question the bona fides of Bank in a case such as this. While a leveraged buyout can serve important aims, a transaction such as OfficeCo's has no legitimate purpose. In any event, there are few cases in which court found a fraudulent conveyance but still refused to void the security interest of the party in the position of Bank. Bank's position would be even less tenable if it or an entity related to it also participated as an investor in CFOPartners, as in some of the Enron transactions.

Only a few courts have explicitly recognized the step-transaction doctrine as part of fraudulent conveyance law. Lenders who enter into such transactions are well advised to create a record that shows that the borrowing corporation was solvent at the time of the transaction. It is usually easier for the lender to show that the transaction was a sensible deal than that even though it was not, someone else should be held responsible.

Section 550 of the Bankruptcy Code empowers the trustee to recover the value of the transferred property from either the initial transferee or from the entity for whose benefit the transfer was made. The breadth of the phrase "for whose benefit the transfer was made" allows considerable flexibility to reach various parties to this transaction. The absence of any safe harbor for initial transferees may subject them to liability when others are unavailable. Banks or financial intermediaries acting on behalf of clients can argue, however, when they are mere conduits, they are not transferees within the meaning of §550. In other cases, the debtor may be directed to pay a third party. The third party may argue that the person who directed the funds was the transferee and that thus it is entitled to the benefit of the safe harbor for subsequent transferees in §550(b). But courts may be reluctant to insulate them from responsibility.[14]

Equitable Subordination and Deepening Insolvency

Sometimes a creditor may acquire a great deal of control over the debtor and may use this control to benefit itself at the expense of other creditors. At some point this creditor may go too far and thereby forfeit its right to take priority over others (if it is secured) or even lose its ability to share with them pro rata. When all the debtor's assets go to one secured creditor, the only chance that the general creditors have to recover anything is to find some defect in the claim of the secured creditor. If the secured creditor's interest has been properly perfected and cannot be avoided under the strong-arm powers, the trustee will sometimes examine that creditor's conduct to see whether a claim of *equitable subordination* can be made out.

The origins of the equitable subordination doctrine can be found in *Pepper v. Litton*:

> In the exercise of its equitable jurisdiction the bankruptcy court has the power to sift the circumstances surrounding any claim to see that injustice or unfairness is not done in administration of the bankrupt estate.[15]

In *Pepper v. Litton* the dominant shareholder of a corporation had caused the corporation, before the bankruptcy, to confess judgment on a long-dormant wage claim he had against it. Justice William O. Douglas noted that the dominant shareholder

[14] See, e.g., Schafer v. Las Vegas Hilton Corp., 127 F.3d 1195 (9th Cir. 1997); Leonard v. First Commercial Mortgage Co., 228 Bankr. 225 (Bankr. D. Minn. 1998).

[15] 308 U.S. 295, 307–8 (1939).

had manipulated the corporation's affairs so that an unsecured creditor would receive nothing. For this reason, he found that the debtor's action failed the test of "whether or not under all the circumstances the transaction carries the earmarks of an arm's length bargain."[16]

There is nothing inherently wrong with insiders or shareholders also being creditors of the corporation. Indeed, they are among the ones most likely to be willing to extend credit to the corporation, particularly when it is in trouble. But if they want to enjoy the status of creditors or secured creditors, they must cut square corners.[17] A creditor who enjoys the benefit of an insider guarantee or who otherwise is in a position to exercise control over the debtor is also at risk. As the Fifth Circuit noted in *Smith v. Associates Commercial Corporation*, however, creditors acting within the scope of the ordinary powers given to them in their original loan agreements are safe:

> [A] creditor is under no fiduciary obligation to its debtor or to other creditors of the debtor in the collection of its claim. . . . The permissible parameters of a creditor's efforts to seek collection from a debtor are generally those with respect to voidable preferences and fraudulent conveyances proscribed by the Bankruptcy Act; apart from these there is generally no objection to a creditor's using his bargaining position, including his ability to refuse to make further loans needed by the debtor, to improve the status of his existing claims.[18]

---

[16] Id. at 306–7.

[17] See Stoumbos v. Kilimnik, 988 F.2d 949 (9th Cir. 1993).

[18] 893 F.2d 693, 702 (5th Cir. 1990), quoting Cosoff v. Rodman, 699 F.2d 599, 609–10 (2d Cir. 1983). See also Sloan v. Zions First National Bank, 990 F.2d 551 (10th Cir. 1993); Kham & Nate's Shoes No. 2 v. First Bank of Whiting, 908 F.2d 1351, 1358 (7th Cir. 1990) ("Although Debtor contends . . . that Bank's termination of advances frustrated Debtor's efforts to secure credit from other sources, and so propelled it down hill, this is legally irrelevant so long as Bank kept its promises.").

Yet the course of this case through the Fifth Circuit illustrates the uncertainty in applying the equitable subordination doctrine. In its first opinion, the same panel unanimously held that the secured creditor's claim should be subordinated. In this opinion, the court emphasized the amount of control that the lender exercised over the debtor's affairs and the way the lender took advantage of this control to ensure that in the end it was paid in full. The trustee used to good advantage the testimony of one of the lender's former employees, who took great delight in explaining how his one goal in life had been to ensure his employer was paid in full "by hook or crook." The panel, however, subsequently reassessed the substance of the employee's testimony, vacated its opinion, and held that the lender's security interest should be respected. The court recognized that every lender "effectively exercises 'control' over its borrower to some degree." It distinguished the ability to control the debtor from "the exercise of such total control over the debtor as to have essentially replaced its decision-making capacity." The Fifth Circuit relied heavily on the fact that the loan agreement itself authorized all the actions that the lender took to enforce its rights.

Asset-based lenders often deal with troubled debtors, and they must walk a fine line. They must keep on top of their debtors while avoiding any action that would trigger equitable subordination. Worse yet, a trustee may bring a lender liability action in which the trustee alleges that the lender broke its duty of good faith or its promises (such as an implied promise not to cut off a credit line without warning). As a result, the lender may be exposed to a substantial damage action. One cannot be sure that exercising only the powers set out in the loan agreement will give lenders a safe harbor, even though some cases suggest as much. Courts possess some leeway in shaping equitable subordination doctrine under §510(c)(1), but they cannot go so far that they effectively alter the priorities that Congress has provided for different kinds of claims.[19] That courts some-

---

[19] United States v. Noland, 517 U.S. 535 (1996).

times view their mandate broadly should not obscure the basic lesson of these cases for creditors: The lender who does more than it was authorized to do in the original loan agreement or who fails to fire the requisite warning shots is asking for trouble. A lender who is also an insider faces more considerable risks.[20]

While a creditor faces risks by shutting down a debtor prematurely, the same creditor faces risks from doing the opposite as well. A creditor can exercise so much control over the debtor, in effect propping it up, that other creditors are worse off than they would have been if the creditor with control had simply shut down the debtor's operations. In some recent cases, creditors have argued that such a creditor violates a duty to them and is liable under the tort of "deepening insolvency."[21] Whether such a cause of action becomes important in the dynamics of bankruptcy remains to be seen. A bank that extends credit to a failing business or fails to exercise default rights may show bad judgment, but that alone does not constitute the violation of a duty that gives rise to a tort action.[22]

Substantive Consolidation

When the debtor is part of a larger corporate group, the trustee may have an additional place to turn to enhance the bankruptcy estate. The trustee may be able to combine the assets and liabilities of the debtor with those of a related corporation. A subsidiary's parent, for example, may have fewer liabilities and more assets than the subsidiary. If the assets and liabilities of both corporations were combined, the creditors of the subsidiary would enjoy a larger pro rata share. Putting the assets

[20] In re Mid-American Waste Systems, Inc., 284 Bankr. 53 (Bankr. D. Del. 2002).

[21] See Official Committee of Unsecured Creditors v. Credit Suisse First Boston (In re Exide Technologies, Inc.), 299 Bankr. 732, 750–52 (Bankr. D. Del. 2003).

[22] See In re Global Service Group, LLC, 316 Bankr. 451 (Bankr. S.D.N.Y. 2004).

and liabilities of two related corporations into a single pool is known as *substantive consolidation*. Substantive consolidation must be distinguished from cases that are jointly administered. Related corporations frequently file bankruptcy petitions at the same time, and the different bankruptcy cases can be administered together. Assuming conflicts of interest do not stand in the way, these separate corporations can pool their resources by hiring the same professionals and the like.

Substantive consolidation is quite a different affair. To the extent that the creditors of one corporate entity benefit from substantive consolidation, the creditors of the other are made correspondingly worse off. To justify substantive consolidation, one must justify not only the benefit that one set of creditors receives but also the harm that other creditors suffer as a result. When a corporate group files for bankruptcy, however, substantive consolidation simplifies matters considerably. The creditors among themselves might willingly consent to a plan in which the different entities were lumped together. But hard questions arise when some creditors resist.

The following hypothetical reflects the common pattern. Premium Paint is one of the largest manufacturers, distributors, and retailers of paint and paint-related merchandise in the Midwest.[23] It consists of six separate corporations. Premium Paint Co., Inc., is a publicly traded Delaware corporation. Its only function is to serve as a holding company for its various subsidiaries. With some overlap, the remaining corporations work as follows: RetailCo operates most of the retail paint and paint-related stores. NewRetailCo operates the balance. Formerly owned by a competitor, Premium acquired NewRetailCo several years ago and assumed all of its debt, including a number of long-term unsecured notes. Putting intercorporate obligations to one side (of which there are many), NewRetailCo is in the best financial shape of any of the subsidiaries.

---

[23] These facts are loosely based on In re Standard Brands Paint Co., 154 Bankr. 563 (Bankr. C.D. Cal. 1993) and, to a lesser extent, those in Flora Mir Corp. v. Dickson & Co., 432 F.2d 1060, 1062 (2d Cir. 1970).

ManufacturerCo manufactures paint and paint-related items. DistributorCo is the distribution subsidiary for paint manufactured by ManufacturerCo. RealtyCo owns or manages real estate holdings, including those where RetailCo and NewRetailCo operate the retail paint stores.

The six corporations operate as a consolidated entity, with the subsidiaries and parent all being dependent on one another to make a functional whole. Separate books and records are kept for internal purposes, but the debtors have always done their reporting to the SEC on a consolidated basis. The institutional creditors that lend to any entity typically secure cross-guarantees from the others. Cash from each entity is swept every day into the same account. Intercompany accounts are kept, but no cash changes hands and no accounts are ever closed out. Assets such as computer software are shared, as is office space. Employees of the different entities work together in planning new products and advertising campaigns. Overhead costs are divided among the different entities according to a formula that was established years ago.

Invoices do indicate the separate corporate status of the different entities in fine print, but other communications are less clear. All the entities use the Premium Paint logo on their stationery, on their advertising, and on press releases. They usually also include their own names. RetailCo's letterhead, for example, says, beneath the Premium Paint logo, "RetailCo, a member of the Premium Paint Group." DistributorCo's letterhead says, beneath the same logo, "DistributorCo, a division of Premium Paint." "Divisions" at Premium Paint, however, do not always correspond with discrete legal entities. ManufacturerCo is divided into several product lines (such as Premium Outdoor and Premium Metallic), and occasionally these have identified themselves as "divisions" of Premium Paint, even though they are part of ManufacturerCo and not separate legal entities.

The boards of directors of each subsidiary consist entirely of officers of the parent. The debtors, however, have always paid meticulous attention to corporate formalities, such as holding meetings and keeping minutes. Institutional lenders know they are dealing with different legal entities, as do the largest trade vendors. There is disclosure of the corporate structure in an exhibit to Premium Paint's 10-K and some discussion of some of the entities in the body of the 10-K and footnotes to the company's financial statements. Nevertheless, most trade vendors and the public at large are not aware of the different corporate entities. On-the-ground employees are not always completely aware of them either and sometimes blur the lines in accounting for costs and recording intercompany transactions.

When such a corporate group files for Chapter 11, the plan that emerges often consolidates the claims against all the entities, while the separate entities themselves are preserved (often for tax reasons). Consolidation for the purposes of distribution avoids the complications that arise from sorting out the many intercorporate balances and the rights that various creditors have against the different entities. Competing groups often reach agreement with one another, and the court approves what is, for practical purposes, a consensual plan.

But what happens if the negotiations fail? Can the plan still be confirmed even if what is proposed is only a "deemed" consolidation in which the entities are to retain their separate identities after the Chapter 11 is over? Someone who wants to argue that substantive consolidation is appropriate in a case such as Premium Paint usually begins with *Auto-Train*.[24] That case, at least as read by lower courts, suggests that substantive consolidation requires a three-part inquiry. First, those proposing substantive consolidation have to show "a substantial identity between the entities to be consolidated." The consolidated financial statements and a seamless interaction between the

---

[24] Drabkin v. Midland-Ross Corp. (In re Auto-Train Corp.), 810 F.2d 270, 276 (D.C. Cir. 1987). *Auto-Train* itself discusses substantive consolidation only in dictum and purports to follow the cases in the Second Circuit. Teasing out of it a test for substantive consolidation that is distinctly different from that of the Second Circuit, as lower courts have done, may be a mistake.

various entities that we see in Premium Paint may be sufficient to make such a showing. Second, the proponent needs to show that "consolidation is necessary to avoid some harm or to realize some benefit." Here again, sorting out the messy intercorporate transactions and protecting the vast majority of creditors who thought they were dealing with a single business seem to satisfy this test.

At this point, the burden shifts to the opponent of consolidation to show that "it relied on the separate credit of one of the entities and that it will be prejudiced by the consolidation." Under our facts, only the noteholders of NewRetailCo will be able to argue that they relied on the separate form of NewRetailCo. So long as these creditors consent to the plan, there may be no one around to rebut the presumption of consolidation. Even if a few of these noteholders do dissent, they may not be able to show that the harm to them outweighs the benefits that everyone as a group enjoys from the consolidation.

The old noteholders of NewRetailCo may have to contend with two additional arguments as well. First, the typical case today does not involve substantive consolidation in the traditional sense. The entities still retain their separate identity after the reorganization. (Indeed, the failure to do this will trigger tax liabilities.) What we have instead is substantive consolidation for distributional purposes only. The proposed plan pays out different claims as if the entities were consolidated, but the entities are not actually consolidated. If the premerger noteholders of NewRetailCo as a class approve the plan, an unhappy noteholder holding a claim in that class may be out of luck. Given that other members of its class accepted their distribution under the plan, the dissenter can insist only on receiving what it would receive in a Chapter 7 liquidation, which may be little or nothing.

A second avenue of defense exists, and it is available even if the dissenting noteholders as a class reject the plan. Assume that NewRetailCo has assets of $100. The old noteholders are its only creditors, and they are owed $100. The plan proposes paying everyone 40 cents on the dollar. The noteholders are worse off in the absence of intercorporate liabilities, for if NewRetailCo were in Chapter 11 by itself, they would be paid in full. But intercorporate liabilities cloud the issue considerably. NewRetailCo owes for the paint it has bought from ManufacturerCo. There is the back rent owed RealtyCo. NewRetailCo owes DistributorCo for advertising and other expenses. There are disputes about whether the formula used to apportion overhead still makes sense. Workers paid by other divisions may have worked for NewRetailCo. If NewRetailCo and the other entities enter into a comprehensive settlement of intercorporate obligations in which NewRetailCo has net obligations of $60 or more, the dissenting creditors will be unable to show that substantive consolidation prejudices them.[25]

The *Auto-Train* test, as received in other courts, has morphed into long laundry lists. Such lists are too often messy and confusing affairs put together with too little thought. But one can take the array of tests and factors and argue that substantive consolidation is plausible in a case such as Premium Paint, where everything, including cash, is centrally managed and controlled and where the different legal entities function as a single whole rather than being merely a collection of discrete businesses under one corporate umbrella. We have substantial identity, benefits from consolidation, and relatively few who can show reliance on corporate separateness. The harm that creditors suffer from the plan may be modest relative to the benefits of a fast and efficient reorganization, especially if intercorporate transfers make their payout under a stand-alone plan uncertain.

When the goal is to confirm a plan and see a business's rapid exit from Chapter 11, there is a natural tendency to gloss over the legal niceties involving the corporate form of related entities.[26] *Auto-Train* and its progeny have now evolved into a doc-

[25] See In re Genesis Health Ventures, 266 Bankr. 591 (Bankr. D. Del. 2001).

[26] See, e.g., In re Worldcom, Inc., 2003 WL 23861928 (Bankr. S.D.N.Y. 2003).

trine that is altogether different both from veil piercing, sub-stantive consolidation's first cousin outside of bankruptcy, and from the doctrine long articulated in the Second Circuit.

The Second and Third Circuits, however, have put forward a much different approach.[27] They have held that substantive consolidation is appropriate in only two circumstances. One is that the affairs of the entities are so closely entwined that each lacks a separate existence for all practical purposes. Substantive consolidation in this context is simply the bankruptcy analog for piercing the corporate veil. The two doctrines are not quite the same,[29] but both apply when the debtor has disregarded separateness so significantly that creditors treated the different corporations as one legal entity.[30] The second circumstance is that keeping the entities' affairs separate is impractical. Here we need to look at the costs of sorting out the affairs of related corporations if they are treated as one entity and if they are treated as several. Even though the corporations are sufficiently separate that we would not pierce the corporate veil outside of bankruptcy, their affairs may be so entangled and their assets

[27] Union Savings Bank v. Augie/Restivo Baking Company, Ltd., 860 F.2d 515, 518–19 (2d Cir. 1988); In re Owens Corning, 419 F.3d 195 (3d Cir. 2005).

[29] Veil piercing allows the creditors of a subsidiary to reach the as-sets of the parent, but does not at the same time allow creditors of the parent to reach the assets of the subsidiary. By contrast, substantive consolidation puts all the assets are put in a common pool and credi-tors of the various entities share in it pro rata.

[30] Substantive consolidation is not limited to combining the assets of corporate entities, nor do both need to be in bankruptcy. See, e.g., Alexander v. Compton (In re Bonham), 229 F.3d 750 (9th Cir. 2000) (consolidating assets of a debtor individual and a nondebtor corpora-tion).

so meager that unscrambling the mess may simply not be worth the cost. When the administrative costs of sorting out the obligations of the various corporations dwarf the benefits to any group of creditors from keeping the corporations separate, it is in everyone's interest to consolidate them.[31]

In one Second Circuit case, the court confronted a situation in which there were multiple subsidiaries and "a multitude of intercompany transactions, many without apparent business purpose."[32] The court found these alone "grossly insufficient" to allow substantive consolidation, especially when the objecting creditor, like the noteholders of NewRetailCo in our example, came into being before their debtor became part of the corporate group.

A court that follows *Augio/Restivo* and *Owens Corning* is not likely to allow substantive consolidation under the facts of Premium Paint. Under the first test, such factors as common control, consolidated financials, and modern cash management would not be enough trigger corporate law veil-piercing and alter-ego actions outside of bankruptcy. Indeed, the court in *Owens Corning* questioned whether there could ever be such a thing as "deemed" substantive consolidation. The entities cannot be both so intertangled as to justify consolidation and yet so distinct that it was both possible and desirable to keep them separate after bankruptcy.

The Supreme Court or an appellate court such as the Seventh Circuit might even reject the doctrine of substantive consolidation outright. The power of the court to order substantive consolidation is not well grounded in the statute.[33] Substantive

[31] See In re The Leslie Fay Companies, 207 Bankr. 764 (Bankr. S.D.N.Y. 1997).

[32] Flora Mir Corp. v. Dickson & Co., 432 F.2d 1060, 1062 (2d Cir. 1970).

[33] Section 1123(a)(5)(C) suggests a plan can provide for the "consolidation of the debtor with one or more persons," but this cannot sensibly be read as a grant of power. It cannot, for example, give the debtor the ability to merge itself with any third party it pleases,

consolidation emerged through a series of judicial opinions under the Bankruptcy Act. In the view of some, such substantive powers continue under the Bankruptcy Code only to the extent that they grow out of particular provisions of the Bankruptcy Code. Substantive consolidation is, as the words suggest, a *substantive* power. Courts have told us again and again that we cannot derive substantive powers from §105. Whatever powers exist must come from substantive provisions of the Bankruptcy Code itself.

There is still another reason to question the continued viability of substantive consolidation. In *Grupo Mexicano de Desarrollo v. Alliance Bond Fund, Inc.*, the Supreme Court found that in the absence of explicit congressional authorization, district courts lack the power to issue preliminary injunctions to protect the rights of general creditors.[34] The reasoning of *Grupo Mexicano* reaches beyond its narrow holding and suggests that federal courts cannot create new powers as courts of equity. Courts lack the power to "create remedies previously unknown to equity jurisprudence." Equitable powers are limited to those that have a long history. New rules can "radically alter the balance between debtor's and creditor's rights which has been developed over centuries through many laws—including those relating to bankruptcy, fraudulent conveyances, and preferences."

Substantive consolidation did not develop over "centuries." Substantive consolidation emerged as a distinct power of the bankruptcy judge only in the 1960s and 1970s. Earlier cases involved either fraudulent conveyances or other nonbankruptcy principles such as veil piercing, none of which is sufficient in a case such as Premium Paint. The first use of the term "substantive consolidation" in a reported opinion was not until 1975— the same year in which the remedy at issue in *Grupo Mexicano*

---

whether that party wants the merger or not. The source of such a power must come from elsewhere.

[34] 527 U.S. 308, 330–31 (1999). See, e.g., J. Maxwell Tucker, *Grupo Mexicano* and the Death of Substantive Consolidation, 8 Am. Bankr. Inst. L. Rev. 427 (2000).

emerged.[35] Substantive consolidation stands distinct from the preference, fraudulent conveyance, and other bankruptcy powers that existed in 1789.

Nevertheless, substantive consolidation may have more traction than this discussion seems to suggest. On a set of facts much like those in our hypothetical, the court in *WorldCom* allowed substantive consolidation even though it purported to follow *Augie/Restivo*. Two factors proved decisive. First, as often happens in bankruptcy practice, the major parties reached a deal with each other. The court did not face the concerted opposition that would lead, among other things, to a strongly contested appeal of the decision. Second, and much more important, was the sheer size and number of intercorporate transfers. In a single month, there were over 600,000 transactions. Millions of transactions flowed through intercompany accounts, and these aggregated a *trillion* dollars. When a corporate group merely functions as a single whole, courts may be quick to find "substantial identity." They may be easily persuaded that creditors relied on the debtor as a single legal entity.[36] Such reasoning is hard to resist in a case such as *WorldCom* when confirmation will lead to a quick exit from bankruptcy and the creditors overwhelmingly support the plan. For this reason, the prudent lender should document reliance on corporate separateness as part of every extension of credit.

[35] See In re Continental Vending Machine Corp., 517 F.2d 997 (2d Cir. 1975).

[36] See, e.g., In re Standard Brands Paint Co., 154 Bankr. 563, 573 (Bankr. C.D. Cal. 1993).

Chapter Eight

Preferences

Preferences Under §547: The Basic Elements

The descent of a healthy business into insolvency and then bankruptcy is usually a long, slow process. Bankruptcy law has a set of rules to prevent creditors from trying to grab assets when bankruptcy is on the horizon. The rules that prevent creditors from receiving *preferences*—eve-of-bankruptcy transfers to creditors that distort bankruptcy's pro rata sharing rule—are embodied in §547 of the Bankruptcy Code.

A creditor would much rather be paid off in full than work things out with everyone else and ultimately take fewer than 100 cents on the dollar. If we allowed creditors to keep payments they extracted when they knew bankruptcy was imminent, bankruptcy might do more harm than good. The prospect of a bankruptcy proceeding might have the effect of accelerating and exacerbating the creditors' race to the assets. To guard against this prospect, we need a bankruptcy rule that has the effect of turning back the clock and returning people to the positions they were in before bankruptcy was on the horizon.

Although its rules are complicated, the basic purpose of preference law is quite straightforward and quite different from the role of fraudulent conveyance law. Recall that a transfer to a creditor on account of an antecedent debt is typically not a fraudulent conveyance. The antecedent debt counts as fair consideration or reasonably equivalent value. Preferences to creditors are themselves unobjectionable so long as a collective proceeding is not in the works. Every creditor is "preferred" when it is paid, and paying a creditor is an ordinary part of commercial life. Section 547 is designed to root out only preferences that are made on the eve of bankruptcy and hence interfere with the collective norms of bankruptcy law.

Section 547(b) defines a transfer as presumptively preferential if it is made by an insolvent debtor to or for the benefit of a creditor on account of an antecedent debt within ninety days of filing a bankruptcy petition, provided the transfer leaves the creditor better off than if the transfer had not been made. Such a transfer is presumptively preferential (and therefore voidable by the trustee) because it is likely to be a "last-minute grab." It is probably the result of opt-out behavior. Because an insider is likely to know more about the debtor and be able to see the prospect of bankruptcy before others, transfers made on account of antecedent debts while the debtor was insolvent are suspect for the entire year before the filing of the petition, provided again that the transfer makes the insider better off.

Like any other bright-line rule, §547(b) is both under- and overinclusive. Some creditors will see bankruptcy coming and act outside the ninety-day preference period; others will be paid within the ninety-day period knowing nothing of the imminent bankruptcy petition. Section 547(c) cuts back on the breadth of the rule by excepting some transfers, but nothing is done to reach deliberate opt-out behavior that takes place outside the ninety-day preference window. As a result, §547 is subject to manipulation. A big creditor can twist the debtor's arm, bleed it dry, and then prop it up for ninety days. A review of the case law reveals a large number of filings ninety days after a big transfer to a major creditor. This does not seem a coincidence.

Let's look at how §547(b) plays itself out. The most obvious preference is that of a debtor who pays cash to a creditor a few days before filing a bankruptcy petition. A preference also exists if the debtor gives a general creditor a security interest in its assets just before it files a petition. Even though the trustee cannot strike down the last-minute transfer of a properly perfected security interest using the strong-arm power of §544(a), the trustee can void such a transfer under §547. The security interest gives the creditor priority over other general creditors and, assuming the debtor is insolvent, makes it better off. Section 547, however, covers more than transfers of cash or security interests. For example, assume that a business buys a season's worth of fuel oil from a supplier and pays in advance. The supplier delivers the fuel on schedule. Spring comes and the supplier files a bankruptcy petition. The supplier's trustee may have a preference attack. The business became a creditor of the supplier when it paid for the oil in advance. The supplier had an obligation it owed the business. Each shipment of fuel discharged some of that obligation and was therefore a transfer on account of an antecedent debt owed the business. So long as the supplier was insolvent at the time it shipped the fuel, each shipment is a preference. There are exceptions to §547(b) in §547(c), but none apply here. There is an exception for payments in ordinary course transactions in §547(c)(2), but here the "transfer" was a shipment of fuel, not a "payment."

There cannot be a preference unless the transfer to or for the benefit of a creditor is made on account of an *antecedent* debt. In every case involving a potential preference, we must ask two questions: When was the debt incurred and when was the transfer made? We do not have a voidable preference unless the first event took place before the second. A lender who makes a loan just before the filing of the bankruptcy petition and simultaneously takes and perfects a security interest in the debtor's property does not receive a preference. The transfer of the security interest to the creditor is on account of a debt, but it is not on account of an *antecedent* debt. Consider another example. You are about to file a bankruptcy petition. You go to a lawyer and ask her to handle your bankruptcy. The lawyer asks for a retainer of $10,000. There are rules in the Bankruptcy Code (such as §329) dealing with compensation of a debtor's lawyer, but is this transaction objectionable so far as preference law is concerned? Isn't the lawyer grabbing assets while bankruptcy is on the horizon? The lawyer is, but this does not matter. Before a lawyer agrees to represent you, the lawyer is not your creditor. When you pay the retainer, you are paying for future services. You are a creditor, not a debtor, in this transaction. You have not made a transfer *on account of an antecedent debt*, the sine qua non of a preference.

If the debtor has enough money to pay everyone in full, there is typically not going to be a race to the assets. All the creditors believe they will be paid in full. Hence §547(b) applies only if the debtor is insolvent at the time of the transfer. Under §547(f), a debtor is presumed insolvent during the ninety days before the filing of the petition. Most debtors are in such bad shape at the time of the petition that they became insolvent well outside the ninety-day period. Bankruptcy petitions are more often filed too late than too early, and insolvency is rarely litigated in preference cases. There is, however, no presumption of insolvency between ninety days and one year before the filing of the petition in the case of an insider. In this situation the trustee carries the burden of showing that the debtor was insolvent at the time of the transfer, and whether the debtor was insolvent a full year before the filing of the petition may not always be evident.

Section 547(b)(5) requires that the transfer make the creditor better off than it would be in a Chapter 7 liquidation. Imagine that you are a fully secured creditor. You have lent Jones $1,000 and you have a fully perfected security interest in Jones's red Porsche. Jones pays you in full ten days before filing for bankruptcy. Is the repayment a voidable preference? Jones was insolvent at the time he paid you, and his payment is a transfer on account of an antecedent debt to you, a creditor, within ninety days of the filing of the bankruptcy petition. The payment, however, does not make you any better off. In bankruptcy, you would, in theory, be paid in full because your security interest in the Porsche would entitle you to priority. We are going to look at this idea more closely later. A secured creditor would much rather be paid in full before the start of the petition than have a fully secured claim in bankruptcy. Nevertheless, the common understanding of §547(b)(5) ensures that transfers to fully secured creditors are not voidable preferences.

The extent to which we apply §547(b)(5) to other transactions is unclear. If the debtor had not made the transfer, the creditor might have behaved differently. For example, it might not have made the debtor another loan or shipped it new supplies. We do not know the extent to which a creditor can make such arguments about what the world would have looked like if the transfer had not been made. The exceptions to the preference power in §547(c) protect the creditor in those cases that matter the most (such as an additional extension of credit after a payment that, in hindsight, turns out to be preferential). Courts, however, may point to these exceptions as a rationale for interpreting §547(b)(5) narrowly.

Let's recap §547(b). The six requirements that must be met before a preference is voidable are that (1) a transfer is made (2) on account of an antecedent debt (3) to or for the benefit of a creditor (4) while the debtor was insolvent (5) within ninety days of the filing of the petition (6) that left the creditor better off than it would have been if the transfer had not been made and it had asserted its claim in a Chapter 7 liquidation. If a transfer is preferential, §550 tells us that the trustee can recover the amount transferred from either the initial transferee or the party for whose benefit the transfer was made.

Section 547 provides only a weak deterrent against opt-out behavior. The trustee can recover the amount of the transfer and interest on the amount of the transfer, but interest generally runs only from the time that the trustee asks for the transfer back, not from the time of the transfer. The person who receives the transfer enjoys the time value of the transfer from the time it receives the preference until the trustee demands its return. If you see the debtor sinking, why not grab while the grabbing is good? The debtor may survive for ninety days, in which case you are in the clear. Even if the debtor does not survive that long, the trustee may not find you. Even if the trustee does find you, you need only give the property back. You suffer no penalty for having received a preference.

With these basic principles in mind, most preference problems are straightforward. You lend Jones $1,000. The loan is payable on demand. You leave the country for six months. You return, completely unaware that Jones's financial situation has deteriorated substantially. You ask for repayment. Jones obliges you even though Jones is now hopelessly insolvent. A week later Jones files a bankruptcy petition. Is this a voidable preference? Section 547(b) is a per se rule: although it is aimed at opt-out behavior, it does not require us to ask whether there was opt-out behavior in any given case. Hence, the transfer from Jones to you is a voidable preference. It does not matter what your motives were or that you were completely unaware of Jones's financial straits.

In making intent irrelevant, the Bankruptcy Code differs from its antecedents. Under the 1898 Act, a transfer was a preference only if the creditor receiving the transfer knew, or had reason to know, of the debtor's insolvency. This intent-based test generated a huge amount of litigation. Under the Bankruptcy Code, some creditors are subjected to a voidable preference attack even though there is no opt-out behavior. It may be better to pick up the few creditors who were genuinely unwitting, however, than to litigate the many cases of creditors who tried to grab assets but deny it after the fact with wide-eyed innocence.

Let's look at a variation on the facts above. You return from your trip and ask for your money back. Jones refuses. You sue, reduce your claim to judgment, and have the sheriff levy on the Porsche. You get your $1,000 back, but only with Jones kicking and screaming all the way. The sheriff seizes and sells the Porsche ten days before the filing of the petition. What do we do about this case? In the past, preferences were thought objectionable because the debtor was picking and choosing among its creditors, and the debtor should not be allowed to favor some creditors over others. From this perspective, the transfer should not be voidable. You simply won the race to the assets fair and square. If another creditor did not like it, it could have joined the race or it could have filed a bankruptcy petition and put a stop to it. Modern preference law, however, focuses on the behavior of creditors and asks whether they were trying to opt out of an impending bankruptcy. It does not matter that the property was taken from the debtor involuntarily. There was still a transfer within the meaning of §101.

Let's focus on another requirement of §547(b), the requirement that there be a transfer of an "interest of the debtor in property." Suppose you take your $1,000 watch to a jeweler to be repaired. You pay the jeweler in advance for the work. Three weeks later, you pick up your watch. The jeweler files a bankruptcy petition a month later. Can the trustee argue that the jeweler's return of the watch was a voidable preference? The jeweler transferred the watch to you within ninety days of the filing of the petition, while insolvent, and on account of an obligation previously incurred. The transfer, however, is a preference only if the watch is property of the debtor within the meaning of §547(b). It might seem obvious that the watch does not belong to the jeweler, but we have to be careful. While in the possession of the watch, the jeweler had the power to convey it to a buyer in ordinary course. To reject the argument that the watch is not the jeweler's, we have to be able to explain why this power is insufficient to make the watch the jeweler's property for purposes of §547.

The answer ultimately lies in the trustee's powers under §§541 and 544(a). We can first ask what would have happened if the jeweler had still possessed the watch at the time of the bankruptcy petition. The watch would not become property of the estate under §541(a)(1) because the jeweler has no right to keep the watch in the face of your claim. Moreover, the trustee could not bring the watch into the estate under §544(a) because a hypothetical lien creditor would have no ability to levy on the watch while it is in the jeweler's hands. That the jeweler could have conveyed good title to a buyer in ordinary course should not matter. The trustee should be able to avoid the transfer only if the transfer took assets out of the reach of creditors.

Other cases can arise in which the answer is not so intuitive. Consider a retailer who is shipped goods on consignment.[1] A consignee holds goods under the authority of others in order to sell them, at specified prices, to third parties. Title—ownership—remains in the hands of the consignor. A consignee typically has the right to return goods without any obligation because it is an agent and not a buyer. If the goods are sold, the consignee has the obligation to remit the proceeds to the seller. This case is different from the one involving the watch in one crucial respect: the jeweler's creditors have no ability to levy on the watch while it is in the jeweler's hands, whereas if the consignor fails to jump through a number of hoops, creditors of the consignee can levy on the assets outside of bankruptcy. By returning the assets, the consignee removes them from the creditors' reach on the eve of bankruptcy. The consigned goods should therefore be considered property of the debtor for purposes of §547. The general principle was well stated in *Danning v. Bozek*: "[P]roperty belongs to the debtor for purposes of §547 if its transfer will deprive the bankruptcy estate of something which could otherwise be used to satisfy the claims of creditors."[2] If a debtor holds an asset in trust, its creditors cannot reach it.[3] But if the item at issue is money in an account from which the debtor's creditors could have sought payment, it is property of the debtor. It does not matter that, for example, the funds are in an account held not by the debtor but by a related entity.[4]

Let's look at one more case dealing with the meaning of "interest of the debtor in property." A parent corporation owes money to a lender. The parent is insolvent, but one of its assets is its stock in a subsidiary and the subsidiary is solvent. The lender presses the parent for payment. Rather than use its own

---

[1] See, e.g., Loeb v. G. A. Gertmenian & Sons (In re A.J. Nichols), 21 Bankr. 612 (Bankr. N.D. Ga. 1982).

[2] 836 F.2d 1214, 1217 (9th Cir. 1988).

[3] Begier v. Internal Revenue Service, 496 U.S. 53 (1990).

[4] See Southmark Corp. v. Grosz, 49 F.3d 1111 (5th Cir. 1995).

money, the parent has the subsidiary pay the lender. The subsidiary owes the lender nothing, so its transfer to the lender is for less than fair consideration. The subsidiary, however, is solvent and it is able to pay all *its* creditors in full. The transfer, therefore, is not a fraudulent conveyance so far as the subsidiary's creditors are concerned. Moreover, the transfer cannot be a fraudulent conveyance so far as the parent's creditors are concerned, either. The transfer is on account of an antecedent debt and thus, from the parent's perspective, is supported by fair consideration.

The transfer might appear to be a preference. It is a transfer to the lender, on account of an antecedent debt, made while the parent is insolvent, within ninety days of the filing of the bankruptcy petition, and the transfer makes the lender much better off. The parent's other creditors are made worse off. If the transfer had not taken place, the subsidiary would have more assets and the parent's equity interest in the subsidiary would be worth much more. Nevertheless, bringing a preference attack and recovering the money from the lender will not be easy. The trustee can assert that the transfer from the subsidiary to the lender is voidable and can be brought into the *parent's* bankruptcy estate only by showing that the parent transferred *its* property when it had the subsidiary make the transfer. If one looks only at form, the *parent* made no transfer. The parent's creditors were injured only because the value of one of its assets (its equity interest in the subsidiary) went down. No assets, however, actually left the parent's hands.

If one looks to substance rather than form, the transaction does amount to a transfer of property. If the parent had given some of its shares in the subsidiary to the lender and if the subsidiary had then repurchased the shares, there would have undoubtedly been a preference. Transfer of the shares is a transfer of property of the debtor within the meaning of §547. The transaction in which the subsidiary pays the lender directly is identical in substance, though not in form, to this one. The transfer from the subsidiary to the lender is therefore a preference to the extent that one can recharacterize the transaction and treat it like one that is economically the same in substance but different in form.[5]

Secured Creditors and Voidable Preferences

You lend Jones $1,000. Jones's fortunes take a turn for the worse. You come to Jones and ask to be paid ahead of everyone else before Jones goes into bankruptcy. Jones does not have the money and so turns you down. Besides, if Jones granted your request and then entered bankruptcy, any cash you received would be on account of an antecedent debt and would thus be a voidable preference. Suppose Jones offers instead to give you a security interest. Can you take him up on it and not worry about the impending bankruptcy?

No. When bankruptcy is on the horizon, changing your status from general creditor to a secured creditor is itself a form of opt-out behavior. One can argue that taking a security interest should not be treated the same way as a naked seizure of assets because taking a security interest affects only how the pie is divided among creditors. It does not actually destroy value in the same way that seizure of assets does. Existing law, however, treats them the same. You are improving your position in anticipation of bankruptcy in the same way (although not to the same extent) that you would if you were paid off. In both cases, you are receiving an interest in property within the ninety-day period, while Jones is insolvent, on account of an antecedent debt. By receiving the transfer you are ensuring that you get paid in full, which puts you in a much better position than if you had not tried to improve your place in line. This transaction is, of course, a voidable preference. The two of you cannot use a security interest to circumvent bankruptcy's pro rata sharing rule.

Suppose Jones needs additional money to keep his unincorporated business alive. Jones's existing creditors, however, re-

---

[5] See Harry M. Flechtner, Preferences, Postpetition Transfers, and Transactions Involving a Debtor's Downstream Affiliate, 5 Bankr. Devs. J. 1 (1987).

fuse to throw good money after bad. Jones comes to you. You agree to lend, but only if Jones agrees to give you a security interest in his machine, the only piece of equipment his business owns. Is this a voidable preference? Of course not. No gun-jumping has taken place. Jones transferred an interest in the machine to you, but did not make the transfer on account of an *antecedent* debt. Jones did it in order to get the money in the first place. You were not opting out at the time you took the security interest; you were opting *in*. Jones gave up something (an interest in the machine) but got something in return at the same time (cash). Jones's creditors cannot complain. If they think that Jones is so far gone that they should take control, they should throw Jones into bankruptcy. Until they do, Jones is free to borrow money in arm's-length transactions and encumber assets that would otherwise go to the general creditors.

A secured creditor avoids a preference attack by ensuring that the security interest is transferred to it within the meaning of §547(e) at the same time it extends value to the debtor. Remember our discussion of §544(a). If you are a secured creditor but have not perfected your interest, you are at risk. All you have done is bargain for the ability to repossess without having to go to court, provided you can repossess without a breach of the peace. Vis-à-vis other creditors, you are no better than a general creditor. You are still in a race to get a priority right. The relevant time is not the moment that you enter into a security agreement with the debtor, but rather the moment that you perfect your interest (typically through a public filing) and acquire priority over a lien creditor. So far as other creditors are concerned, a preexisting but unperfected secured creditor who perfects on the eve of bankruptcy has grabbed assets just as much as an unsecured creditor who takes a security interest and perfects on the eve of bankruptcy. The crucial factor is not the existence or the nonexistence of the security interest, but rather the existence of the priority right. If we are measuring your rights against the rights of the other creditors, it makes sense to date the time of the transfer from the time that you acquired the priority right. You should be able to enjoy your security interest only if you acquired your priority right a long time ago, or only if you acquired your priority right at the same time you extended credit.

The plight of the secured creditor who wakes up and discovers that its security interest is not perfected is a common one. A bank will make a loan and everyone will shake hands and pass out cigars. The loan documentation will be filed away and forgotten. Only when the deal starts to go sour does anyone look at it again. Indeed, the lawyers handling the workout may not even come into the deal until after it has gone sour. At this point, their first job is to check out the paperwork. Should they be able to correct the paperwork without having to worry about a voidable preference attack? Of course not. The workout lawyers have been called in because the debtor is sinking fast and bankruptcy is on the horizon. They are in the picture because the race to the assets has begun and they are trying to win it. It is exactly this kind of opt-out behavior that §547 tries to prevent.

Section 547 does allow a short grace period for perfecting the security interest. Assume that Jones is in big trouble and borrows $1,000 from you. Jones gives you a security interest in his machine, but you take five days to file the financing statement. You were not trying to opt out; it just took some time to get all the paperwork in order. In §547(e), the Bankruptcy Code tries to distinguish between the case in which you wake up and discover that your interest is not properly perfected and the case in which the filing in the ordinary course comes a little while after the security interest attaches. Section 547(e) provides for a grace period of thirty days. A transfer takes place at the time it is effective between the parties, provided that you perfect within thirty days. The grace period collapses only the time of perfection and the time of attachment. You still have to ask when the debt was incurred. If the debt was incurred before the security interest attached, there is a presumptive voidable preference, regardless of whether perfection took place at the same time.

Suppose Jones borrows $1,000 from you on January 1. On that day, you take a security interest in his machine, and Jones signs a written security agreement. Five days later you file your financing statement. A month later Jones files a bankruptcy petition. There is no voidable preference. The debt was incurred on January 1. Because the filing was made within ten days, §547(e) provides that the transfer of the security interest from Jones to you took place on that day as well. If you had waited until January 15 to file, there would be a voidable preference, because the act that makes the transfer good as against lien creditors took place outside the ten-day grace period. Problems also would arise if you lent the money on January 1 and filed on January 1 but Jones did not sign the security agreement until January 5. A transfer does not take place for purposes of §547(e) until it is effective between the parties and, under Article 9 of the Uniform Commercial Code, a security interest is not effective between the parties until the debtor signs a written security agreement. The transfer in this case took place on January 5, after the debt was incurred. To survive a preference attack, you would have to show that you fit under one of the exceptions to the trustee's preference power. These are in §547(c), and it is to them that we now turn.

The Safe Harbors of §547(c)

The Net Result Rule. Section 547(c)(4) protects lenders who make a new loan after an old one is paid off. The typical case is a revolving credit arrangement. Suppose you lend Jones $1,000 for thirty days, and Jones pays you back at the end of thirty days. You lend Jones $1,000 again for another thirty days, and so on. At the time Jones files a bankruptcy petition, you have been repaid a $1,000 loan three times during the ninety days before the filing of the petition. Under §547(b) each of the transfers would be preferential. Each of the repayments was on account of an antecedent debt and each made you better off than you would have been if you had not been repaid and everything else remained the same. It would not make sense, however, to allow recovery of all three $1,000 payments. The purpose of the credit arrangement was to limit your risk to $1,000 at any one time. You made the subsequent loans only because Jones paid off the earlier ones. The transfers made you better off only to the extent of $1,000, the most you would have lost if any of the transfers had not been made. You might argue that two of the $1,000 transfers are not preferential because of §547(b)(5). These two payments did not make you better off than you would have been if the payments had not been made. If the payments had not been made, you would not have extended new credit. In other words, §547(b)(5) forces us to ask what the picture would look like if Jones had not made the transfer. This is not necessarily a picture in which everything else looks the same. If Jones had not repaid the old loans, you would not have made the new loans. Thus, $2,000 of the $3,000 you received did not make you better off, because these payments induced you to extend $2,000 in new credit. You need not, however, rely on §547(b)(5) here. This case is specifically covered in §547(c)(4). One looks at the *net result*—the extent to which you were preferred, taking account of the new value you extended to Jones *after* repayments on old loans.

Section 547(c)(2). Section 547(c)(2) excepts from preference attack routine payments to creditors. These are payments that are made in ordinary course on debts incurred in ordinary course or according to ordinary business terms. Without §547(c)(2), the trustee would have the power to avoid many routine transactions. You receive your phone bill on the fifth day of the month and you regularly pay it on the twentieth day of the month. Without §547(c)(2), there might be a preference action against the phone company. The transfer occurs on the day you make the payment. The debt, however, is incurred when you use the phone service, which is during the prior month. It is a transfer on account of an antecedent debt, but there is no opt-out behavior. It is the ordinary way you go about paying bills. Section 547(c)(2) serves to except these sorts of payments from the trustee's avoiding powers. Section

547(c)(2), however, deals only with *payments*. It does not apply to any transfers of property.

The §547(c)(2) exception is designed to limit the trustee's avoiding powers under the preference section to actions that, at least presumptively, are the result of conscious opt-out behavior. Section 547(c)(2) replaces the reason-to-know-of-the-insolvency test under the 1898 Act, and it may work better because it uses an objective standard and does not require an inquiry into the transferee's state of mind. Whether debts were incurred in the ordinary course and whether payments were made in the ordinary course are necessarily questions involving a number of facts, and it is easy to find cases that fall on either side of the line. Our previous example involving a telephone bill paid at the same time in the same way as the debtor and others in the same business usually pay such bills does fall within §547(c)(2). A late payment by certified check after several dunning phone calls is not made in ordinary course.

Determining whether a loan is made in the ordinary course of business, however, is not always so simple. Consider a corporation with a large, long-term operating loan. Was this loan incurred in the ordinary course of business? We know that we cannot exclude the loan from the reach of §547(c)(2) simply because it is long term.[6] Nevertheless, one can argue that when the corporation incurs such a loan only once in its life, the loan is not incurred in the ordinary course. This interpretation of "ordinary course"—focusing on whether obtaining such a loan is an everyday event for this debtor—is consistent with the way the term is understood in §364. That section requires court approval of a postpetition loan that is not made in ordinary course, and no one thinks that the trustee could enter into such a loan without first obtaining court approval. But there is a completely different way of interpreting §547(c)(2). One can argue that "ordinary course" in the context of §547 (as opposed to §364) requires us to identify particular features of the trans-

---

[6] See Union Bank v. Wolas, 502 U.S. 151 (1991).

action that make it suspect. So long as similar companies typically have such a loan, §547(c)(2) should apply.

Once it is established that the debt itself was incurred in the ordinary course of business, the creditor must show either that the payment was made in the ordinary course or according to ordinary business terms. Fitting into the second category may often be easier than the first. When a business is in trouble, few decisions may be made in the ordinary course. For example, a decision to make timely payments to a business's largest and most important creditor may cease to be ordinary if an implicit decision is made at the same time not to pay others, especially if the debtor's president guarantees the loan and must pay it out of pocket if the debtor defaults.

The Contemporaneous Exchange for New Value. Section 547(c)(1) introduces another grace period. Suppose you buy supplies from a supplier and pay by check. You take the supplies back to your store, and the supplier deposits the check the same day. The check clears the next day. Two months later you file a bankruptcy petition. Can the trustee recapture the payment you made to the supplier? Under §547(b), the supplier did not make a transfer to you until its bank honored your check.[7] Only at this point are assets removed from the reach of the other creditors. This transfer was on account of the debt incurred when the supplier gave you the goods several days before. At that time, you already had been using the supplies for a day. For the interval between the time you took the goods and the time the check cleared, the supplier was your creditor. The supplier, however, was not engaged in opt-out behavior. There was a gap between the time the debt was incurred and the time the transfer was made, but it was too short to be opt-out behavior. We exempt an exchange that is substantially contemporaneous from voidable preference attack.

Secured creditors who make a loan to enable the debtor to acquire collateral enjoy their own safe harbor under §547(c)(3). They may also be able to take advantage of the contemporane-

---

[7] Barnhill v. Johnson, 503 U.S. 393 (1992).

ous exchange exception in §547(c)(1). Consider a case where it might matter. At a time when Jones is solvent, you lend Jones money and take a security interest in Jones's machine. Later, when Jones is insolvent and trying to turn the business around, Jones asks for your permission to trade in the machine in which you have a security interest for a new machine. You agree to give up your security interest in Jones's old machine in exchange for a security interest in the new one. Is that a substantially contemporaneous exchange for new value? You are giving new value because you are giving up something that is yours. Your security interest in the old machine is valuable. It would survive the sale, and if you did not give up the interest, you could still seize the old machine even though it was in the hands of the new buyer. Think of it this way: if Jones repaid the loan in full, you would not be receiving a preference. Assume that Jones sold the machine and gave you the proceeds. Jones then asked for a new loan for a new machine. You make the loan on the condition that you get a security interest in this machine as well and Jones agrees. Even if Jones is insolvent and a few weeks away from filing, the transfer of the security interest in the new machine in this case would not be preferential. Because this transaction is not a voidable preference, why should we not allow the substitution of collateral? You are giving up a security interest instead of cash, but the economic effect is the same. The case law on this point is not clear. The less the secured creditor is involved in the details of the replacement of one machine with the other, the less likely a court is to find that the exception applies.

The Floating Lien. A creditor will commonly take a security interest in a debtor's inventory or accounts. These turn over constantly. The supplies the debtor has this month in its store are not the same supplies the debtor will have next month. When is the security interest in the debtor's new inventory transferred to the secured creditor for purposes of §547? You could make an argument that a security interest is like a Heraclitean river. There are no new transfers. The secured creditor has a continuous interest in the inventory, even though the inventory itself is constantly changing. But there is a potential for manipulation. A debtor could favor a secured creditor who was undersecured by acquiring new inventory just before going under. The Bankruptcy Code confronts this problem in §547(c)(5) and §547(e)(3). Section 547(e)(3) provides that transfers cannot take place until the debtor acquires the property, but §547(c)(5) goes on to protect the secured creditor to the extent that it did not improve its position during the preference period. We take two snapshots, one at the start of the ninety-day period (or the time of the loan if the loan was made during the ninety-day period) and one at the time of the petition. The secured creditor is protected to the extent that it has not improved its position in inventory or accounts between the first snapshot and the second.

Consider the following problem. A florist buys flowers every day from many different vendors in a wholesale market. It gives a bank a security interest in all its inventory, existing and thereafter acquired, to cover a $12,000 loan. On January 1 the loan is made, the florist signs a security agreement, and the bank files its financing statement. On February 1 the inventory is worth $5,000. Ninety days later, the florist files a petition in bankruptcy. During those ninety days, the inventory has completely turned over and the amount of the inventory has increased. When the petition is filed, the inventory is worth $15,000 and the florist still owes the bank $12,000. To what extent does the bank have a security interest that will survive the attack of the trustee?

If §547 did not exist, the bank would have a perfected security interest in the flowers that the florist has when the petition is filed. Article 9 of the Uniform Commercial Code warmly embraces the idea of the *floating lien*. The bank can take a security interest in a pool of assets and date priority back to the time it files its financing statement, even though the things in this pool are constantly changing. So long as the bank's filing is proper, the world is on notice that the bank may be claiming a security interest in the flowers. But what happens under §547? We need to determine if there has been a transfer on account of an antecedent debt, and we have to go through §547(b) before looking to §547(c). When was the debt incurred? The debt was incurred on January 1. When did the transfer of the security interest from the florist to the bank take place? We have to look at the language of §547(e)(3). It tells us that the transfer did not take place until the florist had rights in the collateral. When did this happen? We are not sure, but we know that the property changed over completely between February 1 and the date on which the petition was filed. It follows necessarily that the florist did not acquire any rights in the inventory it now has until after February 1.

Therefore, we have a transfer that took place *after* the debt was incurred (on January 1) and within ninety days of the filing of the petition. Providing that the other conditions of §547(b) are met and providing that nothing in §547(c) calls it off, we have a voidable preference. Has the bank engaged in opt-out behavior here? It may well have. The bank's position improved during the relevant time period. At the start of the ninety-day period, the flowers were worth only $5,000. Bank was undersecured to the extent of $7,000. At the time of the filing of the petition, however, the bank was comfortably oversecured. It is possible that there was some kind of side deal. It may not have been mere coincidence that the inventory increased in value. The florist could have been filling its shop with flowers because the bank threatened to pull the rug out from under it even sooner if it did not. Or the florist might have had more flowers on hand for some innocent reason. Perhaps flower shops typically have more stock on hand in May than in February. Without knowing more facts, we cannot determine whether the bank has engaged in opt-out behavior.

The Bankruptcy Code does not engage in such a case-by-case inquiry, however. Instead, it provides for a limited exception to floating liens in inventory or accounts and the proceeds of either. Section 547(b) starts by striking down all new acquisitions of inventory within the preference period, but then §547(c)(5) provides a partial safe harbor. A creditor's security interest is recognized in bankruptcy, but only to the extent that the creditor does not improve its position during the ninety days before the filing of the bankruptcy petition. In our case, the bank was undersecured to the extent of $7,000 at the start of the preference period. Section 547(c)(5) tells us that the bank is going to be an unsecured creditor to that extent, even if the value of the inventory happens to increase during the ninety-day period. The bank will therefore have a secured claim in bankruptcy for only $5,000. The bank should be no better off than it would have been before it knew that bankruptcy was on the horizon, and this date is arbitrarily set at ninety days before the filing of the petition (or the time of the loan itself if later). Section 547(c)(5) embraces what is called the *two-point net improvement test*.

To apply the two-point net improvement test, let's look at the extent to which the bank is undersecured ninety days before the filing of the petition or on the date that the loan was made, whichever is later. (The language focuses on the extent to which the creditor is undersecured rather than on the amount the creditor is owed because the debtor could opt out by increasing the amount of inventory or decreasing the amount of the debt.) If the bank is no better off on the date of bankruptcy than it was ninety days before, §547(c)(5) will protect the bank with a floating lien on inventory or accounts. The section even allows for the bank to improve its position, if the improvement is not "to the prejudice of other creditors holding unsecured claims." This language is typically interpreted narrowly, however, and applies only when the increase in inventory is attributable to changes, such as harvest cycles, that affect the whole industry and not just the debtor.

Working through the basics is essential to solving any §547 problem. Consider the following case. An automobile dealership has fifty foreign cars. On January 1 the bank lends the dealer $500,000 and simultaneously takes a security interest in the cars. The bank makes a proper Article 9 filing. The dealer sells only five cars and acquires no new ones. Exactly ninety days before bankruptcy, the dealer's inventory of foreign cars is worth $450,000. Thereafter the dealer acquires no new cars, but those the dealer already carries happen to be in short supply, and their value rises unexpectedly. As a result, the inventory is worth $500,000 on the date the bankruptcy petition is filed. The bank's position has improved by $50,000 during the ninety days before bankruptcy. Is there a voidable preference to this extent?

We should begin with the two basic questions of any preference analysis. When was the debt incurred? On January 1. When did the transfer occur? All the inventory that is at issue was in the dealer's hands on January 1. The bank's security interest was both attached and perfected on that date. Therefore, under §547(e)(2), the transfer took place on January 1. There is a transfer on account of a debt, but not a transfer on account of an *antecedent* debt. Under normal definitions of *transfer*, increases in the value of an item attributable solely to market forces are not transfers. Such a definition also fits well with the purpose behind voidable preferences—after all, no opt-out behavior is at issue if the increases are due solely to market forces. The trustee therefore lacks the power to set aside the bank's security interest under §547(b). Whether the bank could assert an exception under §547(c) is therefore irrelevant. Section 547(c)(5) applies only when inventory has turned over.

As the following example illustrates, §547(c)(5) is straightforward in its application, but at the cost of glossing over some activity that might be opt-out behavior. Suppose a bank lends a debtor $20,000 on January 1 and takes and perfects a security interest in the debtor's inventory. At that time, the inventory is worth $15,000. The value of the inventory remains at that level through January, although the inventory turns over several times, but by the middle of February, the value of the inventory plummets to $8,000. The debtor files for bankruptcy on April 1, ninety days after taking out the loan. At that time, the inventory has regained value and is worth $14,000. Because of the turnover in inventory, the bank's interest in the inventory on April 1 was "transferred" to it within ninety days of the filing of the petition. Section 547(e)(3) compels this conclusion. We turn next to the two-point test to determine whether the bank falls within the §547(c)(5) exception. That section requires us to focus on whether the transfers to the bank improved its position. Did they reduce the unsecured portion of its claim against the debtor, the portion that would not be paid in full? In this case, $5,000 of the bank's claim was unsecured ninety days before the filing of the petition. The bank, however, was in even worse shape at the time of the petition. Its loan was undercollateralized by $6,000 on the date of bankruptcy. The bank's position improved dramatically between the middle of February 10 and the filing of the petition on April 1, as the bank went from being undersecured to the extent of $12,000 to being undersecured by only $6,000. But the value of the inventory in February is irrelevant. Under the two-point test we look only at the two end points, not at what happens in the meantime. We sacrifice actual inquiries into preference-type behavior for a rule that establishes rough but cheap justice.

The floating lien is no longer litigated as much as it was under earlier law. Section 547(c)(5) eliminated some of the provisions that had generated litigation under the 1898 Act. Careful inventory financers can avoid preference attacks by ensuring that the debtor's inventory and the proceeds from the sale of inventory are always worth more than what they are owed. Moreover, inventory and accounts financing is not as large a part of the secured credit picture as it once was. The limitations that §547 places on security interests in after-acquired property matter largely with those who claim interests in types of collateral, such as equipment, that fall outside the ambit of §547(c)(5). A secured creditor faces a preference attack with respect to any equipment the debtor acquires during the ninety days before the filing of the petition, unless the secured creditor gives new value or falls within the exceptions in §547(c)(1) or §547(c)(3) for substantially contemporaneous exchanges and purchase money security interests.

The Scope of §547

The knottiest preference problems arise when there are three parties in the picture. Consider the following situation. A debtor has a long-standing relationship with a bank, and it has a credit line that it can draw on. Any obligations that the debtor owes the bank are secured by interest in all the debtor's assets. The debtor obtains most of its raw materials from one supplier. On January 1, the debtor owes the supplier $100,000. The supplier, sensing that the debtor will likely file for bankruptcy, wants to extricate itself. Rather than demanding payment, something that would subject it to a preference attack, the supplier persuades the debtor to go to the bank and have the bank issue a standby letter of credit, naming the supplier as the beneficiary. The supplier can draw on the letter of credit on March 1 to the extent of any obligations the debtor owes it. The bank knows nothing of the supplier's relationship with the debtor. It is willing to issue the standby letter of credit, however, because, under letter-of-credit doctrine, the debtor is obliged to reimburse it in the event the letter is drawn on, and this obligation, like all the debtor's other obligations to the bank, is fully secured. When March 1 arrives, the supplier draws on the letter of credit. On March 2, the debtor files a bankruptcy petition. The trustee discovers the transaction and seeks either to recover $100,000 from the supplier or reduce the bank's security interest by the same amount.

The trustee's task here is not easy. The supplier will argue that the letter-of-credit relationship between it and the bank is independent of its relationship with the debtor. The transfer of $100,000 of the bank's money under the draw on the letter of credit did not affect any of the debtor's general creditors. When the letter of credit was issued, there was the transfer of a security interest from the debtor to the bank supporting the bank's contingent obligation under the letter of credit, but this transfer took place because of the relationship between the debtor and the bank. It was independent of the relationship between the supplier and the bank.

The bank, for its part, will argue that the transfer of the security interest supporting its contingent obligation under the letter of credit was in return for issuing the letter of credit, not on account of the antecedent debt owed the supplier. In short, the supplier argues it never received anything from the debtor, while the bank argues that it never received a transfer on account of an antecedent debt.

Our instincts, however, should tell us that something is amiss here. We should not allow the bank and the supplier to fragment this transaction into its separate pieces and find that no preference took place when, if we step the various transactions together, there has been a transfer on account of the antecedent debt owed the supplier that left the general creditors worse off.

Courts have allowed preference actions against the supplier in such cases.[8] These courts reason that the transfer of the security interest to the bank was a transfer on account of the antecedent debt owed the supplier. It was not a transfer directly to the supplier, but the language in §547(b) allows preference actions when a transfer is made either to or for the benefit of a creditor on account of an antecedent debt. Section 550 allows the trustee to recover from the supplier the value of the transfer made for the supplier's benefit.

These cases, however, lead us to two additional inquiries. First, can the trustee recover from the bank instead of the supplier? The bank did not itself receive a transfer on account of an antecedent debt owed it, but it was the initial transferee, and §550 allows the trustee to recover from transferees even if they were not themselves creditors who were preferred.[9] Sections 547(i) and 550(c) limit the trustee's power to recover from initial transferees, but only in one kind of three-party case. Suppose a corporate debtor repays a general creditor that has a

[8] See Kellogg v. Blue Quail Energy, Inc., 831 F.2d 586 (1987), rehearing granted, 835 F.2d 584 (5th Cir. 1988).

[9] See Levit v. Ingersoll Rand Financial Corp. (In re DePrizio), 874 F.2d 1186 (7th Cir. 1989).

guarantee from an insider, such as the debtor's principal share-holder. The debtor files for bankruptcy more than ninety days after but within a year of the transfer. The transfer is a preference because it relieved the insider of her liability on the guarantee within a year of the bankruptcy petition. In this three-party case, the trustee's only recourse is against the insider. Given the unequivocal language of §550(a), however, the trustee has unfettered rights to pursue initial transferees that were not themselves preferred in other kinds of transactions.

The example shows how preference law ensures substance prevails over form by stepping discrete transactions together to allow a preference recovery. Our second inquiry asks whether the converse is also true: Can we step transactions together to *prevent* a preference attack when the transaction as a whole is not preferential? On occasion, the proceeds of a new loan are paid directly to an existing creditor. Sometimes the debtor has discretion over the use of the proceeds and asks the new lender to direct them to the existing creditor. Other times it is the new lender who insists that the new loan be used to repay an earlier obligation. The lender's reasons vary. The new lender may, for example, want to ensure the earlier creditor's release of collateral that the debtor has pledged to the new lender. In any case, when a new lender directly pays an antecedent debt, or the debtor is obligated to use the proceeds of a new loan to repay such debt, the new loan is called an *earmarked loan*. The transaction is one in which one lender leaves the picture and another stands in its place. It is the same as if the old lender had traded its claim against the debtor to the new lender.

The trustee would like to argue that nothing requires the two transactions to be stepped together. The new lender's decision to extend credit is one transaction. The repayment to the old lender is a separate one. It should not matter that the new loan was intended or earmarked for the old lender. Although there is no explicit statutory basis for an earmarked loan exception to the voidable preference rules, courts have established such an exception, known as the *earmarking doctrine*. The doctrine applies when the amount of the new loan is no greater, and of no higher priority, than the loan to be repaid. First, one can argue that the proceeds of an earmarked loan do not constitute an interest of the debtor in property and thus are not subject to §547(b) preference rules. Second, one can argue that unpaid creditors are not injured by an earmarked loan transaction. When one creditor replaces another, the whole of the transaction does not look like the last-minute grab that preference law is designed to prevent. Thus, courts conclude, no purpose would be served by requiring reimbursement from the recipient of an earmarked loan's proceeds. Nevertheless, even if the first creditor is secured, the second creditor is itself subject to a preference attack with respect to its security interest if it fails to perfect it in a timely fashion.[10]

The way in which transactions are linked together, however, is not always clear. Consider the following case. A retailer engages a supplier to buy clothes for it from abroad. To ensure that it is paid, the supplier requires the retailer to have its bank issue a letter of credit in the supplier's favor. The supplier is entitled to draw upon the letter up to $1 million whenever it has reasonable grounds for insecurity. First Bank issues the letter, and the retailer promises First Bank that it will cover the total amount of the draw on the letter of credit on the same day it is made. The retailer can make such a promise, because it enjoys a $1 million credit line with Second Bank.

The supplier, reasonably fearing that the retailer is in trouble, draws on the letter of credit on August 1. At this point, the supplier has not purchased any goods on the retailer's behalf and it has no claim against retailer. First Bank honors the letter of credit on August 1 and gives the supplier $1 million. Within a few minutes, the retailer transfers $1 million from Second Bank to First Bank. Two months later, before the supplier has given the retailer any goods, the retailer files a Chapter 11 petition. The retailer continues to stay in business. During the next

[10] See Shapiro v. Homecomings Financial Network (In re Davis), 319 Bankr. 532 (Bankr. E.D. Mich. 2005); Vieira v. Anna National Bank (In re Messamore), 250 Bankr. 913 (Bankr. S.D. Ill. 2000).

two months, the supplier delivers $1 million worth of goods. The supplier charges the cost of each shipment against the $1 million it received as a result of the draw on the letter of credit.

In March, the case is converted to Chapter 7 and a trustee is appointed. The trustee brings a preference action against First Bank to recover the $1 million it was paid on August 1. The trustee argues that this payment was on account of the retailer's obligation to reimburse First Bank if First Bank was forced to pay on the letter of credit. First Bank will argue that the transfer of $1 million it received should be linked to the $1 million it had given the supplier a few minutes before. If the two transactions are linked, there is no preference. Before the draw on the letter of credit, the retailer had a $1 million credit line with Second Bank. Five minutes later, the retailer had a right to receive $1 million in goods from the supplier. The retailer has converted a credit line from a bank into an obligation from a third party to ship goods of equal value. Such a transaction does not make the creditors worse off.

If the retailer had simply transferred the money from Second Bank to the supplier directly, there would have been no preference. This transaction is arguably no different. A preference exists only if a transfer diminished the estate.[11] Finding in First Bank's favor, however, depends on the court's willingness to step the transactions together. Letter-of-credit doctrine insists on the independence of the supplier's right to draw on its letter of creditor from whatever rights First Bank might have against the retailer.[12] But whether multiple transactions should be joined together to establish whether a preference has taken place is a question of bankruptcy law, not of the law governing letters of credit.[13]

---

[11] See Kapela v. Newman, 649 F.2d 887 (1st Cir. 1981) (Breyer, J.).

[12] See Sabratek Corp. v. LaSalle Bank, 257 Bankr. 732 (Bankr. D. Del. 2000).

[13] For a case in which the court declined to step the transactions together under these facts, see P.A. Bergner & Co. v. Bank One, 140 F.3d 1111 (7th Cir. 1998).

Chapter Nine

The Automatic Stay

The Scope of the Automatic Stay

In a perfect world, a corporate bankruptcy proceeding would be over in an instant (assuming that in a perfect world you would still have bankruptcy). The world we live in, however, is not so simple. Even a straight sale of the business for cash takes time. We need a mechanism to preserve the status quo while we sort out the affairs of the debtor. This is the purpose of §362 and the automatic stay. Section 362 stops individual creditors from taking actions that would thwart the reorganization and, at the same time, allows the debtor to continue doing business with the rest of the world on ordinary terms.

The general creditors of an insolvent debtor must wait until the entire proceeding is over. They will receive only a fraction of what they are owed, and we will not know until the bankruptcy proceeding is over how large that fraction will be. Allowing creditors to take action during the bankruptcy proceeding would undermine bankruptcy's pro rata sharing rule. The justification for continuing the automatic stay against a secured party is, however, different from the one for general creditors. Someone with a property interest that prevails against both the debtor and the trustee will be paid in full at the end of the day. We still need to stay the secured creditor's hand, however. Even though we know how much the secured creditor will be paid, allowing the secured creditor to exercise its rights before the end of the case is likely to interfere with the debtor's attempt to reorganize. But if a secured creditor will receive the property in any event and if the property is not needed for the reorganization, the court will grant a motion to lift the stay.

The automatic stay extends beyond actions of creditors to ensure that the bankruptcy court retains control over the assets of the estate. Bailors, for example, cannot retrieve property from the debtor, but in these cases the stay is short-lived. Return to the case we considered in chapter 5, in which a dry cleaner files a Chapter 7 petition after you have given it your clothes to clean. In such a case, the automatic stay should preserve the status quo, but only for as long as it takes to sort out whether there is a true bailment. We need to be sure that the clothes are yours and not the dry cleaner's. Once that is determined, you should be able to recover your clothes.

The automatic stay, however, does not alter the debtor's interactions with the rest of the world going forward. A business outside of bankruptcy cannot force others to transact with it. A supplier can refuse to ship goods to it for any reason or for no reason at all. In bankruptcy, it is no different. A business in bankruptcy has no right to go to those with whom it has never dealt and insist upon a special deal or, indeed, any deal at all.

Section 362 for the most part does an effective job of ensuring that rights of prepetition creditors remain frozen in place while ongoing relations with others remain unaffected. You will never see a reported decision in which a general creditor asserts the right to levy on its debtor's assets once the bankruptcy begins. Everyone understands that this action is forbidden. So it is with many other easy cases. As we look the hard cases, do not forget that §362 does most of its work without great controversy.

Section 362(a) prevents a prepetition general creditor from enforcing a claim. The automatic stay also applies to other actions to further the pursuit of a prepetition claim. Even if one does not touch property of the estate, §362 forbids one from going ahead in another forum on a prepetition claim. The bankruptcy proceeding is designed give the debtor's assets a safe harbor. The trustee is supposed to have time to take stock of where things stand. Moreover, the trustee (or, more typically, the debtor in possession) is supposed to be able to deal with all the creditors in a single forum. The bankruptcy court is in charge of determining the size and validity of a claim. The stay allows the bankruptcy court to control where the claim is heard—in the nonbankruptcy forum, or in bankruptcy under either a §502(b) notice and hearing action or under a §502(c) estimation hearing. In addition, §362(a)(4) ensures that attempts to perfect or create liens against property also violate the automatic stay.

Section 362 does not stay all debt collection. Pursuit of post-petition claims is not stayed. For example, you can sue a debtor in a nonbankruptcy forum for a postpetition tort. The automatic stay, however, prevents you from actually levying on the debtor's property. The bankruptcy judge has to be in control of the property of the estate to ensure order. This distinction is reflected in the differences between §362(a)(4) and (a)(6). The automatic stay does not prevent prepetition creditors from going against third parties or exercising control over their assets. Prepetition creditors may pursue guarantors or codefendants. Indeed, they are subject to the statute of limitations if they fail to do so.[1] Some courts have found that in unusual circumstances, the automatic stay will apply to actions against third parties. Courts take this extraordinary step only when there is such an identity between the debtor and the third party that a judgment against the third-party defendant will in effect be a judgment against the debtor, such as when a judgment against a third party will trigger indemnification obligations on the part of the debtor.[2] A similar problem arises when the same insurance policy covers the debtor and codefendants. Actions against codefendants could reduce the total obligations of the insurer under the policy.[3] Allowing such actions would adversely affect the property of the estate. Cases also arise in

[1] See C.H. Robinson Co. v. Paris & Sons, Inc., 180 F. Supp. 2d 1002 (N.D. Iowa 2001).

[2] See, e.g., W.R. Grace & Co. v. Chakarian, 2004 WL 954772 (Bankr. D. Del. 2004); McCartney v. Integra National Bank North, 106 F.3d 506 (3d Cir. 1997).

[3] See A.H. Robins Co. v. Piccinin, 788 F.2d 994 (4th Cir. 1986).

which a court stays actions against officers of the debtor under §105 on the ground that they need to devote their attention to the affairs of the debtor.[4] Such cases, however, are rare.[5]

There is one more important point about §362(a) that should be remembered. One can always ask to have the automatic stay lifted. For example, if it makes sense for the government to litigate an environmental claim against the debtor in another forum because the litigation in that forum is well under way, the government can always go to court to ask to have the stay lifted. When a policy embedded in some provision of the Bankruptcy Code requires an action to be stayed, the court has the power to issue a stay under §105 even if the action is not automatically stayed under §362(a). In the end, the automatic stay simply establishes a presumption. If one finds an action that ought to be stayed that is not within the scope of §362(a), it does not necessarily mean there is anything wrong with the way §362(a) is written. Rather, the stay is designed to cover actions so common and easy to describe that they can be stayed automatically without requiring a court to review the particulars.

We can see how the automatic stay works by considering a third party that seeks to terminate an ongoing relationship with the debtor after the debtor files for bankruptcy. If the right to terminate exists only when the debtor files a bankruptcy petition or becomes insolvent, then it violates the automatic stay. Section 363(*l*) parallels other provisions of the Bankruptcy Code, such as those in §§541, 545, and 365, that refuse to give effect to ipso facto clauses. Bankruptcy does not respect rights that are effective in bankruptcy but not outside. A much harder case arises when the third party has a general right to terminate, but exercises it only because of the bankruptcy petition.

---

[4] See, e.g., Lazarus Burman Associates v. National Westminster Bank, 161 Bankr. 891 (Bankr. E.D.N.Y. 1993).

[5] In re Mid-Atlantic Handling Systems, LLC, 304 Bankr. 111 (Bankr. D. N.J. 2003).

Cahokia Downs operated a racetrack and had a prepaid fire insurance policy.[6] The racing commission denied racing dates for the season, and Cahokia Downs was pushed into bankruptcy. The insurance policy entitled the insurer to cancel for any reason on thirty days' notice. A week after the bankruptcy filing, the insurance company exercised its right to terminate.

We must decide whether, when the insurance company asks for relief from the stay, the court should grant its motion. The racetrack will be worse off if the insurance company can cancel the policy, but this seems neither here nor there. The racetrack would be better off if we all agreed to go there every day (assuming its racing season had not been canceled), but the court will not make us go to the track just because it will make the debtor better off. The insurance company may be in the same position. The insurance company is not a creditor of the racetrack. It is not owed any money. It is not trying to grab assets or opt out of the collective proceeding. Before we reach any firm conclusion, however, we need to focus more closely on the insurance company's motives and ask if, in light of them, relief from the stay is appropriate.

There are at least two explanations for what the insurance company is doing. The first (and less likely) is that the insurance company—independent of the bankruptcy filing—reevaluated the risk of fire and decided to terminate the policy. The racing season has been canceled and the track is deserted. A stray spark is likely to have greater consequences. In addition, the closing of the track and the presence of the insurance policy may combine to make fire an attractive option to people whose scruples are not what they should be. The insurance company would terminate the policy even if no bankruptcy petition had been filed. If the bankruptcy filing were utterly unconnected with the termination of the policy, we should let the insurance company terminate. The debtor did not pay the extra premium the insurance company would have demanded for a

---

[6] Holland American Insurance Co. v. Sportservice, Inc. (In re Cahokia Downs, Inc.), 5 Bankr. 529 (Bankr. S.D. Ill. 1980).

policy that was not terminable. No coherent bankruptcy policy suggests that the debtor should be able to obtain this kind of policy without paying for it.

The termination and the bankruptcy filing, however, may not be independent events. The insurance company may have canceled the policy only because the bankruptcy petition alerted it to the poor condition of the racetrack. In the absence of the bankruptcy petition, it would never have found out about the problem. The question we face here is the extent to which we should prevent the insurance company from taking advantage of the informational signal that bankruptcy conveys.[7]

Most courts would agree that the trustee has no right to extend a policy beyond its term.[8] Moreover, most courts would allow parties to terminate when they are able to show that they would exercise the right apart from the bankruptcy filing.[9] In these cases, however, parties must first obtain relief from the automatic stay. A third party that terminates is taking an action that "obtains possession . . . of property from the estate" within the meaning of §362(a)(3). The automatic stay needs to last long enough to establish that, given the third party's right to terminate, the debtor has no right to the property. Even if their ability to cancel at will is "cause" that justifies relief from the stay under §362(d), when they act unilaterally, they act at their peril.[10] Some bankruptcy judges may take an inappropriately expansive view of the automatic stay. When they do, relief must be obtained through appeal of the bankruptcy court's decision. It cannot be collaterally attacked.[11]

---

[7] In re National Hydro-Vac Indus. Services, LLC, 262 Bankr. 781 (Bankr. E.D. Ark. 2001).

[8] See Heaven Sent Ltd. v. Commercial Union Insurance Co., 37 Bankr. 597 (Bankr. E.D. Penn. 1984).

[9] See In re M.J. & K. Co., 161 Bankr. 586 (Bankr. S.D.N.Y. 1993).

[10] See In re Elber Beerman Stores Corp., 195 Bankr. 1012 (Bankr. S.D. Ohio 1996).

[11] See Celotex Corp. v. Edwards, 514 U.S. 300 (1995).

Government Regulations and §362(b)(4)

Bankruptcy is not an occasion to give debtors special breaks from the operation of substantive nonbankruptcy law. Consider a debtor that produces silicon chips. Let us assume that the debtor's assets are worth $2 million if they are used to make these chips. In other words, a buyer would pay $2 million for the assets free of prebankruptcy liabilities. The buyer who buys the assets at a certain price is willing to pay that price only after concluding that the net income of the project offers a sufficient return on $2 million. In calculating the business's net income, the buyer will take into account, among many other things, the costs that various legal rules impose. A law may require, for example, the installation of environmental equipment at a cost of $500,000. In arriving at a value of $2 million, the buyer has already taken this cost into account.

If the assets could be used to produce silicon chips without complying with this regulation (and assuming that pollution victims otherwise had no legal recourse), a buyer would pay $2.5 million for the assets rather than $2 million. Hence, relieving a party from the duty of complying with such a rule increases the value of the assets. Again, no bankruptcy policy suggests that the debtor in possession be able to obtain such relief. The need to free an individual from the burdens of past debt or the need to give a business a new capital structure provides no justification for allowing the debtor to play by a different set of rules. We find the same idea at work in 28 U.S.C. §959(b):

> [A] trustee . . . appointed in any cause . . . including a debtor in possession, shall manage and operate the property in his possession . . . according to the requirements of the valid laws of the State in which such property is situated, in the same manner that the owner or possessor thereof would be bound to do if in possession thereof.

This principle is embraced in §362(b)(4), which provides that the automatic stay does not apply to "the commencement or continuation of an action or proceeding by a governmental unit . . . to enforce such governmental unit's police or regulatory power." Debtors in bankruptcy have to play by the same rules as everyone else. For example, they cannot pollute. If a debtor is operating in violation of a state or federal statute, the government should be able to tell it to stop regardless of whether it is in bankruptcy. Spending money to comply with governmental orders is not one of the things that a business should be able to avoid simply because it is in a collective proceeding. Section 362(b)(4) ensures that the government retains this power notwithstanding the automatic stay. This power remains even when the action will have irreversible consequences for property of the debtor, such as a city's demolition of a debtor's building after it has been condemned.[12]

Section 362(b)(4) requires that we draw a line between the actions a governmental unit takes in the exercise of its police or regulatory power and those it takes as an ordinary prepetition creditor.[13] An action does not cease to be regulatory simply because it forces the debtor to spend money. But because the government can always assert that it is advancing a police or regulatory purpose with respect to any action it takes, drawing the line is not easy. The government can argue, for example, that a debtor's obligation to clean up property it did not own at the time of the petition serves a regulatory purpose, even though the obligation predated the bankruptcy petition and even though meeting the obligation requires only paying the agency money.[14]

Consider the extreme case in which an agency auctions off a license but lends qualified buyers part of the purchase price. The agency argues that the purpose of the auction was to identify those who value the license most and it can ensure that this happens only by collecting its loans in full. One of the buyers files for bankruptcy at a time when it is current on its payments to the agency. The debtor believes that, for purposes of collect-

[12] Javens v. City of Hazel Park, 107 F.3d 359 (6th Cir. 1997).

[13] In re McMullen, 386 F.3d 320 (1st Cir. 2004).

[14] See Torwico Electronics, Inc. v. New Jersey Department of Environmental Protection, 8 F.3d 146 (3d Cir. 1993).

ing the money, the agency is a prepetition creditor rather than a regulator. The debtor ceases its payments to the agency while in bankruptcy. Can the agency cancel the license and then seek to sell the license to someone else?[15] The answer is that it should not. Section 362(b)(4) was not intended to allow the government to act when it is merely vindicating its rights as a creditor. Even if the government is not acting as a creditor, §525 prevents the government from taking actions (such as canceling a license) in response to a bankruptcy petition.[16]

When the regulator is the federal government, the power of the bankruptcy court may be limited in another way. The agency can argue that even when its actions violate the automatic stay, the bankruptcy court may still not be able to do anything about it because it has no subject matter jurisdiction over the actions of federal administrative agencies.[17] Review must be conducted through administrative law judges and then the court of appeals.

When the government acts as a postpetition regulator, it is not engaging in any of the acts prohibited by the automatic stay in §362(a), at least so long as it does not assert control over the debtor's assets. One can argue that the exceptions carved out for actions of the government in §362(b) go beyond simply those actions that the government takes as a postpetition regulator. Under this view, the purpose that §362(b) serves is largely jurisdictional. The government is not obliged to resolve its prepetition disputes against the debtor in the bankruptcy forum when the dispute arises by virtue of the government's exercise of its police or regulatory power. The government, acting in this capacity, is presumptively entitled to pursue the debtor in the forum of its own choosing. In the absence of any

[15] See In re Kansas Personal Communications Services, Ltd., 252 Bankr. 179 (Bankr. D. Kan. 2000).

[16] F.C.C. v. NextWave Personal Communications, Inc., 537 U.S. 293 (2003).

[17] See In re Federal Communications Commission, 217 F.3d 125 (2d Cir. 2000).

order issued under §105, the government can pursue its claim in the nonbankruptcy forum.[18]

The Supreme Court confronted a similar problem in *Board of Governors v. MCorp Financial*.[19] Before filing for bankruptcy, MCorp caused two of its subsidiary banks to extend credit to an affiliate and engaged in other transactions that may have violated federal banking law. The Board of the Federal Reserve commenced one administrative proceeding before the bankruptcy began and then another after MCorp entered bankruptcy. The Supreme Court rejected MCorp's argument that the board was trying to enforce a prepetition claim and therefore violated the automatic stay. In the Court's view, the board's actions fell under §362(b)(4). The proceedings might culminate in a final order that would interfere with the bankruptcy court's exclusive jurisdiction over property of the estate under 28 U.S.C. §1334(d), but until that time, the board's actions did not violate the automatic stay. The Court was not persuaded that "the automatic stay provisions of the Bankruptcy Code have any application to ongoing, nonfinal administrative proceedings."[20]

MCorp and similar cases suggest that in the case of government regulations, some policies conflict with bankruptcy's goal of resolving all claims against a debtor in a single forum. One might also take the view that both §362 and nonbankruptcy federal law give the government a privileged place among those to whom the debtor owes obligations. One provision of §362(b), for example, exempts Housing and Urban Development foreclosure actions from the automatic stay.

[18] See United States v. Nicolet, Inc., 857 F.2d 202 (3d Cir. 1988). The argument in text is set out in Robert K. Rasmussen, Bankruptcy and the Administrative State, 42 Hastings L.J. 1567 (1991).

[19] 502 U.S. 32 (1991).

[20] Id. at 41.

The Automatic Stay and the Secured Creditor

Bankruptcy provides the secured creditor with the value of its secured claim, but it does not allow the secured creditor to exercise the default rights it has under nonbankruptcy law. It cannot physically seize its collateral. To take such an action, the secured creditor must ask for relief from the stay. When is such relief granted? And when it is not granted, what must the trustee do to protect the secured creditor's collateral? As elsewhere in bankruptcy, there are a few basic guideposts that resolve many of the cases we are likely to encounter.

The secured creditor is entitled to have the stay lifted if its collateral is at risk. Section 362(d) provides that the stay can be lifted for cause. If the debtor is damaging the collateral or has stopped insuring it, a creditor will be able to lift the stay. If the collateral is not at risk, the secured creditor has no right to have the stay lifted when the collateral is worth more than the amount the secured creditor is owed. The debtor is the one who stands to gain or lose when the property is sold. The secured creditor is the wrong person to conduct the sale. The secured creditor has nothing to gain from getting more than the amount it is owed. Hence, it will be unlikely to sell it in a way that maximizes its value. We do have rules that require the secured creditor to act reasonably, but we are going to be better off if the person conducting the sale has the incentive to get the best price. The Bankruptcy Code recognizes this idea in §362(d)(2). In the absence of cause, the secured creditor cannot lift the stay if the debtor has any equity in the property. Sometimes a secured creditor's collateral is worth more than it is owed, but other creditors also have security interests in the property, and all these interests together exceed the value of the property. One needs to ask whether the debtor lacks equity in the property within the meaning of §362(d)(2). Most courts have concluded that the debtor has no equity in the property in such a case.[21] This seems a defensible interpretation of the language of the Bankruptcy Code, but it may not make sense as a matter of first principle. If the property is worth more than the secured creditor is owed, the secured creditor may not have the right incentives to obtain the best price for it.

When the debtor lacks equity in the property, it can keep the collateral only if the collateral is necessary for an effective reorganization. A secured creditor has the right to lift the stay where there is no "reasonable possibility of a successful reorganization within a reasonable time."[22] The lift-stay motion forces the debtor to set up a timetable. To persuade a court to deny a lift-stay motion, the debtor has to show how it will reorganize itself and why the amount of time it will take is reasonable. The court can then use the debtor's own timetable to hold it to account at the next juncture in the case, which might be another lift-stay motion, a request to extend the exclusivity period, or a motion to convert the case to Chapter 7. Lift-stay motions, like these others, are the discrete points in a case when the court must decide whether to continue the business or shut it down. Just as the venture capitalist tells the entrepreneur that a new round of funding is assured only if the prototype works by a certain date, the bankruptcy judge will demand that the debtor present objective indicia of the business's prospects.

While the automatic stay is in force, the secured creditor is protected in a number of ways. Often the secured creditor asserts an interest not only in an asset such as a piece of real property but also in the revenue stream that the property generates. Section 552 relieves the secured creditor of the burden of showing that its interest in rents is perfected under nonbankruptcy law. Unlike a security interest in after-acquired personal

---

[21] Nantucket Investors II v. California Federal Bank (In re Indian Palms Associates, Ltd.), 61 F.3d 197 (3d Cir. 1995); Viper Mining Co. v. Diversified Energy Venture, 311 Bankr. 712 (Bankr. W.D. Pa. 2004).

[22] United Savings Association v. Timbers of Inwood Forest Associates, 484 U.S. 365, 376 (1988).

property, state law sometimes does not allow for automatic perfection of rents (and analogous income streams from hotels). Section 552 reflects the judgment that the notice the bankruptcy process provides obviates the need to demand simultaneous compliance with perfection requirements under state law.

More generally, we require the trustee to ensure that the value of the secured creditor's rights are adequately protected throughout the bankruptcy process. Failure to offer adequate protection is itself cause that requires lifting the automatic stay under §362(d)(1). The meaning of *adequate protection* is illustrated (although not quite defined) in §361. First, the debtor may periodically make cash payments to the creditor, to the extent that the stay decreases the value of the secured creditor's interest in the property. Second, the debtor may provide an additional or replacement lien under the same circumstances. Finally, the debtor may give some other kind of protection (other than giving administrative expense priority) that will result in the "indubitable equivalent" of the right that the secured creditor is asserting.[23]

Even though adequate protection cannot be in the form of an administrative priority, the secured creditor is entitled to an administrative expense claim that trumps others if what is offered as adequate protection turns out to be inadequate. Assume that the secured creditor is entitled to $100 at the end of the bankruptcy proceeding but is given a lien on an asset that proves to be worth only $80 at that time. The secured creditor is entitled to be paid the $20 shortfall before any other administrative expenses are paid, including fees for the trustee and the debtor's lawyers. §507(b). The value of this super-administrative priority lies largely in the incentives it gives those who run the case. They will ensure that the secured creditor's protection is adequate, because they will not be paid until

---

[23] The idea of the indubitable equivalent is repeated in §1129 and comes from Learned Hand's opinion in In re Murel Holding Corp., 75 F.2d 941 (2d Cir. 1935).

after the secured creditor's right to adequate protection is vindicated.

Secured creditors enjoy more protection in single-asset real estate cases. These are cases (other than residential property with fewer than four units) in which a single piece of real property generates substantially all the income of the debtor and on which the debtor conducts no substantial business other than operating the property. As of 2005, these cases include all types of buildings, including large office buildings that formerly were thought too large to be treated under expedited procedures. Section 362(d)(3) requires that in such cases the debtor file within ninety days a reorganization plan that has a reasonable possibility of being confirmed within a reasonable time. If it does not do so, it must make monthly interest payments at the nondefault contract rate to secured creditors equal to the value of its interest in the real estate. Even if a bank is undersecured (its mortgage on Blackacre secures a $100 loan, but Blackacre is worth only $60), the debtor must make payments that protect the time value of the bank's secured claim (that is, to the extent of $60). Imposing this requirement on the debtor in the single-asset real estate case is reasonable. There are no jobs at risk and there is no going-concern value to be protected.

Other secured creditors are not entitled to adequate protection for the time value of their claims.[24] Assume a bank has lent $100 and has a security interest in a machine that is worth $60 at the time the bankruptcy petition is filed. The bankruptcy will take several years. The bank is entitled to insist only on receiving protection on account of its $60 secured claim sufficient to ensure that, two years hence, it will receive $60 in nominal dollars. Receiving $60 in two years is not the same as receiving $60 today. The effect of interpreting adequate protection in this fashion is to require the bank to make a forced, interest-free loan for the duration of the bankruptcy.

---

[24] United Savings Association v. Timbers of Inwood Forest Association, 484 U.S. 365 (1988).

This rule creates a number of inconsistencies. As noted, a single-asset real estate lender does enjoy protection for the time value of its secured claim. The rule also treats different secured creditors differently depending on how their collateral is used. If a debtor owns a machine and leases it out, the secured creditor gets the rental payments under §552 so long as it would have received them under applicable law or under its contract. If the debtor owns a machine and uses it in its business, the secured creditor receives nothing on account of the debtor's use of the property. The streams of income a capital asset produces are economically identical.

Sometimes, the secured creditor repossesses before the bankruptcy petition is filed. Suppose a solvent debtor takes out a loan to buy a drill press, but falls behind on its payments to the bank. The bank repossesses the press and sells it before the debtor files for bankruptcy. In this case, the debtor is simply out of luck. It cannot bring a voidable preference action against the bank because a preference action does not lie against a fully secured creditor who repossesses or is paid off. (Recall that the transfer does not make the bank better off within the meaning of §547(b)(5), another anomaly given the treatment of time value in the bankruptcy case.) Nor can the debtor recover the property from a third-party buyer. Because the buyer is a bona fide purchaser for value, the trustee cannot retrieve the machine. The debtor no longer has any cognizable interest in the drill press, nor do any of the creditors. The person who now owns the drill press is a stranger to the process.

What if the bank repossesses but does not sell the drill press before the debtor files the petition? In this case, we do not have a bona fide purchaser for value in the picture. Let's look first at how this situation is handled outside of bankruptcy. Normally the debtor could recover the machine provided it pays the entire amount of the debt, not simply the value of the machine. The debtor continues to have a property interest in the machine, but its only interest is its right to redeem the property upon payment of the debt, not a right to the machine itself. Now let's examine how the situation is handled inside bankruptcy. Section 542 requires those holding property that the trustee can use, sell, or lease to turn it over. Under §363 the trustee can sell, use, or lease property of the estate, which is defined in §541 as the debtor's interest in the property. It might seem that §542 does not apply to the case in which a secured creditor has repossessed before the petition, because after the repossession the debtor's interest in the machine is only its right to redeem the property by forking over the full amount that the bank is owed. The trustee can use, sell, or lease that right of redemption, but not the collateral itself. The Supreme Court, however, interpreted this problem more broadly in *United States v. Whiting Pools, Inc.*:

> Although these statutes could be read to limit the estate to those "interests of the debtor in property" at the time of the filing of the petition, we view them as a definition of what is included in the estate, rather than as a limitation.[25]

Although this interpretation has an ipse dixit quality, it makes sense as a matter of first principle. The trustee can keep the machine after it is turned over only if the bank is not entitled to have the automatic stay lifted under §362(d). Hence, the only cases in which the issue is important are those in which the repossessed property is essential for an effective reorganization. If the bank were allowed to keep the collateral, the debtor would be forced to pay the bank all of what it is owed, even if the bank were undersecured. The bank, however, should not be entitled to have the unsecured portion of its claim paid in full. So long as the trustee ensures that the value of the bank's rights is adequately protected, the bank is not made worse off if the debtor gets the property back and the general creditors are made better off. Allowing the debtor to take the property back is not much different from curing a default on an executory contract.

---

[25] 462 U.S. 198, 203 (1983).

The Automatic Stay and Special Purpose Entities

The protections offered the secured creditor fall short of making the secured creditor indifferent to the commencement of a bankruptcy case. For this reason, investors have developed a number of devices that insulate them from the bankruptcy process. These often involve a special purpose entity ("SPE"). Investors put cash into a specially created entity, such as a limited liability company, and take a security interest in its assets. The entity then uses this money to "buy" assets, such as accounts receivable, from the debtor. So long as the transfer of assets to the SPE is treated as a "true sale," the debtor's bankruptcy has no effect on the SPE's investors. The SPE merely bought assets from the debtor. The debtor's Chapter 11 filing affects it no more than the Chapter 11 of a toaster-maker affects the consumers who buy their toasters before the filing of the petition.

Special purposes entities are bankruptcy remote in the simple cases. There is a true sale when the debtor sells an account receivable outright, and the entity that buys it has no obligation to remit money to the debtor even if the amount collected proves unexpectedly large and no right of recourse even if it proves unexpectedly small. The debtor's bankruptcy leaves the entity and its creditors utterly unaffected. The typical transaction, however, is much more complicated. Dozens of legal entities may be involved. The investors' confidence that they have indeed invested in a vehicle that is bankruptcy remote turns on whether, when the various transactions are collapsed together, the transfer does in fact have the attributes of a true sale. The easier it is to argue that the transaction falls short of being a fully consummated transfer between two distinct entities, the easier it is to raise doubts about when the investors are insulated from bankruptcy process.[26]

---

[26] See, e.g., In re LTV Steel Co., 274 Bankr. 278 (Bankr. N.D. Ohio 2001) (denying emergency relief from automatic stay for investors in a special purpose entity whose assets included, among other things, the

Nonbankruptcy law ultimately decides whether a true sale has taken place,[27] and recent state legislation attempts to make such sales easier.[28] In principle, bankruptcy should defer to state law. Several words of caution are in order, however. First, bankruptcy courts will apply the principle of *Chicago Board of Trade v. Johnson* and will look to the attributes of the transaction, not the label that a state court has applied. Moreover, as discussed in chapter 7, such transactions must still survive scrutiny of fraudulent conveyance law. A true sale statute can trump only the fraudulent conveyance law in that jurisdiction. Such a law cannot trump the fraudulent conveyance principles embedded in the Bankruptcy Code, nor those of other jurisdictions.

As a general rule, a debtor cannot waive the right to file for bankruptcy. This rule has been applied not only to individual debtors, for whom such a waiver would eliminate the fresh start, but also to corporate debtors.[29] Courts are sympathetic to more narrow limitations on the ability of a debtor to file, especially when they are part of a nonbankruptcy workout.[30] During a workout, for example, the debtor may accede to a drop-dead clause, in which it promises not to contest a creditor's motion to lift the automatic stay in the event of a bankruptcy filing. Courts, however, are apt to view efforts to limit the ability of a debtor to file a bankruptcy petition (such as requiring consent of independent directors whose sympathies lie with the creditors) with considerable suspicion.[31]

---

debtor's inventory (molten steel) still being processed on the debtor's factory floor).

[27] See Duke Energy Royal, LLC v. Pillowtex Corp. (In re Pillowtex, Inc.), 349 F.3d 711, 716 (3d Cir. 2003).

[28] See, e.g., Delaware Asset-Backed Securities Facilitation Act, 6 Del. C. §§2701A–2703A.

[29] See United States v. Royal Business Funds Corp., 724 F.2d 12 (2d Cir. 1983).

[30] See In re Colonial Ford, 24 Bankr. 1014 (Bankr. D. Utah 1982).

[31] See, e.g., In re Kingston Square Associates, 214 Bankr. 713 (Bankr. S.D.N.Y. 1997).

Chapter Ten

The Two Worlds of Chapter 11

More than 500,000 businesses shut their doors each year in the United States. Many more encounter financial distress, but only 10,000 of these file for Chapter 11. While the number of large corporations filing for Chapter 11 has increased in recent years, the total number is half what it was twenty years ago. Before we turn to the mechanics of corporate reorganization in the next chapter, we look first in this chapter at the types of corporations that file for Chapter 11 and the problems that await them. For much of this book, we have discussed the principles of bankruptcy more or less removed from the circumstances and characteristics of the typical debtor. To understand how Chapter 11 works in practice, it is useful to have a sense of what businesses end up there and why.

As it happens, Chapter 11 consists of two strikingly different worlds. The vast majority of Chapter 11 petitions are filed by small businesses. These cases comprise the entire docket of most bankruptcy judges. A very small number of Chapter 11 cases concern large corporations. These tend to be filed in Delaware, the Southern District of New York, and a handful of other jurisdictions. Most bankruptcy judges never see them. Because of their complexity and the size of their assets, these cases generate the vast majority of the legal work, and many bankruptcy lawyers see no other kind. We look at each type of case in turn.

Small Business Corporations in Chapter 11

As indicated above, the typical Chapter 11 case involves a small business corporation.[1] The assets are often worth less than $100,000.[2] The business employs only one or two people full-time other than the owner-manager. Imagine a computer consultant who happens to be doing business in corporate form. She employs no one besides herself, and she runs the business out of her home. The business assets consist of a telephone and a personal computer. In this case, the business has little connection with the corporate entity; the relationships belong to the individual. If as a customer you were happy with the consultant's work last year and wanted to use her services again, you would be indifferent to the existence of the corporation. You might reengage the consultant without ever knowing that she was doing business in corporate form or that the corporate form she is using this year was different from the one she used last year. The business's intangible assets reside in the consultant's expertise. Creditors have no way of reaching it.

A substantial number of the businesses in Chapter 11 are run by travel and insurance agents, lawyers, chiropractors, undertakers, livery drivers, and other self-employed individuals who require little more than a car, a desk, and a cell phone. Another substantial group are building contractors. The dry wall contractor, the plumber, the painter, and the electrician often work out of their home. Beyond a small office staff, they have no permanent employees. The people they hire are taken on only for particular jobs. The assets they need to do their work cost just a few thousand dollars.

In these cases, Chapter 11 is not so much about saving businesses as it is about allowing those who run their own busi-

---

[1] The description of the typical Chapter 11 case draws extensively on Edward Morrison's work. See Edward R. Morrison, Bankruptcy Decisionmaking: An Empirical Study of Continuation Bias in Small Business Bankruptcies, 49 J.L. & Econ. — (2006).

[2] The value of scheduled assets may be somewhat higher, but these valuations tend to be inflated.

nesses to sort out their finances. The owner-manager may have guaranteed a loan from an institutional lender or become personally liable for unpaid taxes. Both these obligations prevent the owner-manager from walking away from the old business before starting a new one. Chapter 11 buys time, even if the case is ultimately dismissed. The owner-manager gains two or three months during which he can preserve the status quo while identifying other options. More important, Chapter 11 creates an environment in which creditors—particularly the IRS and other tax authorities—are willing to stay their collection efforts.

The cost of providing this benefit falls largely upon trade creditors and small-time landlords. The filing of the petition cuts off trade creditors from the business's income stream, and the automatic stay prevents landlords from reentering the premises. And unlike tax authorities and institutional lenders, they lack personal recourse against the owner-manager, so their negotiating positions are weak. In the typical Chapter 11 case, general creditors are left empty-handed, as there is nothing left after the secured creditor and the tax collector are paid.

When we look at small business Chapter 11 cases, we see little that fits the conventional stereotype of a process that allows viable businesses to survive as stand-alone entities. The overwhelming majority are corporations that self-employed individuals create as a vehicle to run a business. Such individuals are, by nature, serial entrepreneurs. The founders of one-third of all small businesses have started other businesses in the past. Indeed starting a business, then closing it, and beginning another is no more a failure than accepting one job, leaving, and going to another. You might go to work for someone else after a business fails, but the longer you are in business for yourself, the less likely you will do this. Indeed, after you have been in business for yourself for more than ten years, you are unlikely to work for anyone else again—ever.

Serial entrepreneurship is the most persistent and most telling characteristic of small business bankruptcies. The benefits of Chapter 11 in these cases may seem modest, but the costs may be modest as well. Within a few months, capable bankruptcy judges sort out the debtors who will reorganize successfully and those who will not. Empirical evidence suggests that more than half the debtors who cannot reorganize successfully are identified and dismissed within three months of the filing of the petition; more than three-quarters are dismissed or converted within five months. Thus, under able judges, owners of small businesses in hopeless condition cannot use Chapter 11 to drag out the inevitable for very long. The Bankruptcy Code requires the debtor to propose a plan within three hundred days of the filing of the petition unless the debtor can show that, more likely than not, the court will confirm a plan within a reasonable time period. §1121(e). These deadlines should, however, have little effect on able judges. The only cases around after three hundred days should be the ones in which the debtor is likely to reorganize successfully.

These bankruptcy judges seem to rely on several rules of thumb:[3]

1. *The 13 O'Clock Rule.* When a clock strikes thirteen, you know both that the clock is broken and that you have to doubt anything it has told you before. Judges are likely to dismiss or convert if the debtor has misrepresented anything to the court or has violated a court order, particularly with respect to cash collateral. The court is responding both to the violation itself and the possibility that other misdeeds lie undiscovered.

2. *The Cash-Flow Rule.* The judge receives regular statements that show how much cash has come into the business and how much has gone out.[4] A business that remains cash-flow negative for more than a few months is not likely to make it.

---

[3] The use of such proxies (or "heuristics") is a standard part of expert decisionmaking. See Gerd Gigerenzer, Peter M. Todd, and the ABC Research Group, Simple Heuristics That Make Us Smart (1999).

[4] Section 308 requires small business debtors to provide extensive information. Some of it, such as reports of the debtor's "profitability," is not useful since such debtors lack audited financial statements that reflect profits in a meaningful way. But reports of cash and comparison of cash receipts with projected receipts are useful.

3. *The Two-Strikes-and-You're-Out Rule.* A debtor in bankruptcy must cut square corners. If it fails to file a schedule, misses a §341 meeting, or fails to pay a fee, the United States Trustee will move for conversion or dismissal. The judge will forgive a single misstep if the debtor's owner-manager quickly appears in court and is sufficiently repentant. But a second failure to follow the rules triggers a dismissal.

4. *The Meet-Your-Own-Goals Rule.* At the status conference and in its §308 reports, the debtor puts forward certain goals (such as increasing earnings or finding a new investor) by a particular date. If the goals are not met and major players oppose the debtor's effort to extend the deadline, the bankruptcy judge sees a red flag, a sign that the company is not on the path to reorganizing effectively.

5. *The Company-You-Keep Rule.* Bankruptcy judges may take their cue from the identity of the debtor's lawyer. When lawyers appear frequently before the same court, they develop reputations. Some may be more inclined to take on cases that have little merit.

Modern bankruptcy judges are triage officers. They have no desire to help debtors who are merely delaying the inevitable. Those who cannot successfully reorganize will remain under the radar screen for only a short period of time. A debtor can file a frivolous Chapter 11 petition, but the case will remain in the system only as long as it takes a creditor or the United States Trustee to find out about it, file a motion, properly notify the parties, and appear in court. In the absence of some emergency, this process takes several weeks, but it can take longer if the United States Trustee or the various creditors do nothing. Bankruptcy judges, like other judges, generally do not act sua sponte, but rather only when advocates call matters to their attention.

Large Corporate Reorganizations

As mentioned above, most of the assets (and most of the lawyers) can be found in the very largest cases. We now turn to describing this world. The dynamics of large Chapter 11 cases today are different from what they were only a few years ago. Traditionally, a large business in financial distress faced three conditions simultaneously: (1) It had substantial value as a going concern; (2) its investors could not sort out the financial distress through ordinary bargaining and instead required Chapter 11's collective forum; and (3) the business could not be readily sold in the market as a going concern. Today these conditions are rarely found in a financially distressed business, much less at the same time.

The bankruptcy of Global Crossing is emblematic of Chapter 11's past and its future. In December 2002, the bankruptcy court in Delaware confirmed Global Crossing's plan of reorganization. One of the largest corporations ever to go through Chapter 11, Global Crossing was formed in 1997 to close one of the last gaps in the Internet. The telecommunications cables connecting the continents were too small to accommodate the expected growth in Internet use outside of North America. In 1997, persons outside North America made up only one-fifth of all Internet users; by 2000, they accounted for almost half.

Wanting to seize this opportunity, Global Crossing laid a transatlantic cable within ten months and embarked on ambitious plans to create a global fiber network. It reached $1 billion in revenues within its first twenty months. Global Crossing continued to invest billions in creating the first network of fiber optic cable across the world's oceans. Global Crossing was to be a major player in the Digital Age, and its market capitalization soon exceeded that of General Motors.

Global Crossing's fall, however, was as swift as its rise. Competitors appeared. Internet traffic grew, but it doubled only every year, not every hundred days as some had predicted. Moreover, technological innovation allowed much more information to be carried over the same cable, resulting in massive overcapacity. Global Crossing's revenue barely paid its ongoing expenses. Its stock price collapsed as people quickly came to see that Global Crossing would never make back the billions it spent building its fiber optic network.

Fiber optic cable was to the 1990s what iron rails and wooden ties were to the 1880s; a promising technology in a heavily regulated environment can bring people together like nothing else. An entrepreneur bravely raises the enormous capital investment the technology requires, but demand falls far short of expectations. A visionary business that attracted capital from all over the world and that employs thousands cannot generate the funds needed to pay its creditors. Games are played with the business's finances to hide this reality for a time, but the truth is discovered eventually.

When this happens, we have to make the best of a bad situation. While we investigate the financial frauds and those who perpetrated them, we have to accept the fact that the railroad has been built and the fiber optic cable has been laid. We need to sort through the financial mess and ensure these assets are put to their best use. The equity receivership in the nineteenth century allowed investors to take control of the business, throw out bad managers, and agree on a new capital structure consistent with the less-than-expected revenue of the railroad going forward. Chapter 11 provides a similar forum today. From this perspective, Global Crossing is merely old wine in a new bottle. The technology is different, but the legal challenge is the same.

Closer examination, however, reveals fundamental differences between railroads and dot.com businesses such as Global Crossing. The railroads had to raise capital in bits and pieces. No single source of capital was large enough to build the entire project. Dozens of different types of bonds were secured by different parts of the road. Bondholders were scattered in New York, London, and Amsterdam. Creditors could not work together to hold a single foreclosure sale. Even if they could, no single buyer could muster the resources to bid.

Today creditors of insolvent businesses—even those as large as Global Crossing—no longer need a substitute for a market sale. Instead, Chapter 11 now serves as the forum where such sales are conducted. In the equity receivership, judges protected minority investors when valuations could not be set in the market. To carry out this task, they developed the absolute priority rule. In Chapter 11, the judge ensures that the sale is conducted in a way that brings the highest price. The emerging case law focuses on lock-up agreements and bust-up fees.

In the equity receivership, no actual sale could take place, but as Global Crossing illustrates, sales are now part of the warp and woof of Chapter 11 practice. In 2002, eight of the ten largest Chapter 11 cases relied on the bankruptcy court as a way of selling their assets to the highest bidder, whether piecemeal or as a going concern. Of the large, publicly traded corporations that now use Chapter 11, the assets of more than half were sold in Chapter 11 or were transferred to a new owner under the plan of reorganization.[5] In some cases, the sales are more or less completed before the fact, and Chapter 11 merely ensures that no one else will bid more. In other cases, the bankruptcy judge conducts an auction in open court.

If we take a snapshot of the business before and after Chapter 11, we would not be able to tell whether there has been a Chapter 11 or a traditional corporate-control transaction. The old shareholders are gone, as are the old managers and the old board; in addition, the business may be folded into another. New managers run a business whose operations have been streamlined and whose workforce has been reduced. The process itself resembles the takeover battles we see outside of bankruptcy. Corporate raiders square off against each other in a bidding war, while the board's independent directors pay careful heed to their *Revlon* duties to maximize the company's value, just as they would in a hostile takeover. Lawyers shuttle between their offices in New York and a courtroom in Wilmington. Chapter 11 has morphed into a branch of the law governing mergers and acquisitions.

Sometimes, the business assets are not for sale in Chapter 11. In these cases, the embers of the equity receivership still burn. Here again, however, the differences between the equity re-

---

[5] These conclusions are based on an examination of Chapter 11 cases in 2002, drawn from Lynn M. LoPucki's Bankruptcy Research Database.

ceivership and Chapter 11 are enormous. The railroads possessed primitive capital structures. When the Atchison, Topeka, and Santa Fe entered receivership, there were forty-three different types of bonds. Corporations today are set up with far simpler capital structures. Global Crossing's capital structure, for example, was designed so that it had to return repeatedly to capital markets. A bank group held much of the senior debt and was well positioned to monitor the business and negotiate with it as its condition deteriorated.

The elaborate committee structure of the equity receivership made it possible, if cumbersome, for investors to communicate with one another. The creditors' ability to control their debtor and negotiate with one another outside of Chapter 11 is now vastly greater than it was during the equity receivership—or even in Chapter 11 just twenty years ago. Often Chapter 11 is needed only to put in place a plan that the key players negotiated before the petition was filed. Of the large businesses whose assets are not sold in Chapter 11, half enter Chapter 11 with a prenegotiated plan. The judge usually confirms it within several months after only minor modifications.

One other striking contrast between businesses in Chapter 11 and the railroads reorganized in the nineteenth century has to do with the latter's manifest value as a going concern. The railroads generated substantial operating profits. Value would be lost if the railroad did not stay intact. The value of keeping the business intact is far less evident with businesses in Chapter 11 today. Global Crossing, for example, had to compete in a market in which one created networks through contract. So long as these contracting costs were low, Global's ability to offer direct connections between Tokyo and London was not necessarily worth much. A pulse of light can be transferred among multiple carriers much more easily than rail freight. A detour of thousands of miles is irrelevant. A route that is twice as long matters if one is conveying coal or wheat, but not if one is conveying information. The value of what is being preserved by keeping the business intact thus is much smaller than in the case of railroads.

The difference between the receivership and the large reorganizations today is even more apparent in other Chapter 11 cases. The bankruptcy is "prepackaged." The relevant classes of creditor agree on a plan of reorganization before the filing and appear before the bankruptcy judge with a plan in hand. Outside the telecommunications sector, businesses often lack large investments in infrastructure. Some are holding companies whose operating subsidiaries are not in bankruptcy. Here Chapter 11 provides a relatively cheap way to put a new capital structure in place, but the value being preserved is only that of the holding company.

In other large Chapter 11 cases, particularly those with neither a prenegotiated plan nor an asset sale, the corporation is a collection of discrete businesses, such as movie theaters, nursing homes, or hotels. What is at risk is the synergy gained from putting these different discrete businesses under one umbrella. This synergy itself, however, is often of recent vintage. The business itself was formed through the same highly leveraged acquisitions that precipitated the financial distress and the need to reorganize. Unlike a railroad, the synergy that these businesses possess is intangible and often quite small.

The disappearance of the traditional reorganization stems not from changes in the law but from changes in the economy that have been under way for a long time.[6] Few businesses today depend on specialized, long-lived assets. In a service-oriented economy, the assets walk out the door at 5 p.m. Today the costs of starting a business are those involved in creating and implementing a business plan. Millions are spent training staff, building a client base, and cementing relationships with suppliers. But these investments are fundamentally different from those made in building a railroad. The most salient characteristic of a railroad is low operating costs relative to the initial capital investment. Railroads of the nineteenth century generated at least enough revenue to cover their operating ex-

[6] See Douglas G. Baird and Robert K. Rasmussen, The End of Bankruptcy, 55 Stan. L. Rev. 751 (2002).

penses. Today, a new business venture may be unable to cover its expenses if the market provides an alternative way to make the same goods just a little bit cheaper.

Of all the large cases that have been concluded recently, the one most resembling the traditional Chapter 11 is that of Pillowtex, the manufacturer of Cannon and Royal Velvet towels and Fieldcrest sheets and pillows. Millions of dollars were spent building factories, hiring thousands of employees, and creating all the relationships that made Pillowtex's business work, but these assets lacked value in a world where towels, pillows, and sheets can be made under the same labels for less offshore. The Chapter 11 from which Pillowtex emerged in 2002 merely postponed the inevitable. It filed for Chapter 11 again in July 2003; this time its factories were closed and its remaining assets sold off piecemeal. The second bankruptcy was not so much the result of some failure of the first, but the natural consequence of a world in which there is increasingly less value associated with discrete business entities. The absence of going-concern value makes Chapter 11's traditional role increasingly irrelevant.

And there has been another change. Compared to creditors of distressed businesses in an earlier era, creditors today (ranging from banks and other financial institutions to universities, mutual funds, and hedge funds) increasingly tend to be professional investors willing to forgo a market sale in order to recapitalize the debtor through a stand-alone reorganization. The more sophisticated the investors and the more promptly they can reach agreement on a plan of reorganization, the less tolerant they will be of imperfections in the market for sale of the business as a going concern. The players in a large corporate reorganization, even those that most resemble the nineteenth-century railroad, no longer see a Hobson's choice between a sale in an illiquid market or a costly reorganization. Instead, they see the choice as one between selling the business to other investors in a developed, but not perfect, market or keeping it themselves in a proceeding that has become cheaper and easier to control over time.

Continuing the Business in Chapter 11

If a business in Chapter 11 is to survive as a going concern, it must continue to operate during the bankruptcy proceeding. In most Chapter 11 cases, no trustee is appointed, and the pre-bankruptcy management of the corporation remains in charge. In small Chapter 11 cases, that management is nearly always the controlling shareholder who has run the business throughout its life. Large Chapter 11 cases are a different matter altogether.

When a large business encounters financial distress, the lenders often bring about the appointment of a chief restructuring officer (CRO). With a sophisticated board of directors, the lenders may need only make it clear that they will look more kindly on future waivers of loan covenants if a CRO with whom they have worked is brought in. (By being oblique, they minimize the risk of lender-liability actions outside of bankruptcy and equitable subordination inside. For boards sensitive to Sarbanes-Oxley and potential shortfalls in directors and officers liability insurance, hints are usually sufficient.) Boards, of course, are nominally the ones who appoint the CRO, and creditors stop short of insisting on a particular individual. But only just short. Before WorldCom filed for bankruptcy, its creditors conditioned further financing in the bankruptcy case on the appointment of a CRO and gave the board freedom to choose anyone it pleased—so long as the person was one of three on a list the creditors provided.

The arrival of a CRO alters the terrain of corporate governance. The CRO is not a typical member of the management team. Unlike other corporate officers, the CRO reports directly to the board. The CRO is often expected to pass judgment on which members of the management team add value and which ones need to be replaced, including the CEO. Indeed, the Chapter 11 process may go forward only after the CRO has had a chance to straighten out the operational problems and the business has settled on a plan to straighten out its finances.

The radically different types of businesses entering bankruptcy require the bankruptcy judge to take into account the circumstances in each case. At the start of a large case, for example, many decisions are necessary. Provisions need to be made for handling the day-to-day running of the business. A number of first-day orders need to be entered to ensure the continued operation of the business. Some courts have promulgated rules that set out what orders they will approve and which ones require special scrutiny. Indeed, when lawyers choose where to file, they want to know in advance what sorts of first-day orders will be approved.

Over time, lawyers and judges have grown comfortable with the practices that have evolved in their courts. These practices remain largely unchecked until a district or appellate court is asked to square them with the Bankruptcy Code. A recent example concerns payments to prepetition general creditors at the start of the case. If the Chapter 11 petition is filed on Thursday, the workers owed paychecks on Friday are merely general creditors to the extent of their unpaid wages. To be sure, they are entitled to priority under §507, but nothing entitles them to be paid before anyone else, whether they have priority or not. Paying the workers, however, is routine in large cases. The debtor may argue that a number of other prepetition vendors should be given favorable treatment as well.

In many instances, the logic of honoring some prepetition claims is so compelling that no one objects even in contentious bankruptcies. In the Chapter 11 of Marvel Entertainment Group, for example, the business's largely teenage subscribers had paid their comic book subscriptions in advance and were therefore general creditors. Their subscriptions should have been put on hold, and they should await the plan of reorganization. In theory, they are supposed to participate in the process like any other creditor. The sheer silliness of making thousands of thirteen-year-olds parties to a Chapter 11 reorganization may have kept anyone from objecting, but in principle any comics sent to them amounted to paying a prepetition claim at 100 cents on the dollar.

More commonly, the debtor wants to pay a vendor whose goods are crucial to its continuing operations and who threatens to cut the debtor off if prepetition debt is not paid. The Bankruptcy Code does not provide an easy way to accommodate the vendor. Railroad reorganizations developed a "doctrine of necessity" that allowed for the payment of such vendors, but this doctrine was not used in other reorganizations before the adoption of the Bankruptcy Code.

For a time, too many bankruptcy judges seemed inclined to issue critical vendor orders without much inquiry. But this practice is changing in the wake of the Seventh Circuit's opinion in *Kmart*.[7] That case came to the appellate court with a particularly bad record. The debtor did virtually nothing before the bankruptcy to obtain the authority to pay prepetition vendors up to $200 million. (Indeed, when asked whether paying cash on delivery would be sufficient to obtain the supplies it needed postpetition, the CEO could do no better than say that doing this was not part of his business plan.) Judge Easterbrook was predictably unsympathetic: "A doctrine of necessity is just a fancy name for a power to depart from the Code."[8] He did suggest that payments to prepetition creditors to obtain postpetition services might be a permissible use of assets within the meaning of §363, but the debtor had to make a showing that such was the case.

In the wake of this decision, lawyers and judges are likely to become more careful. Workers will continue to be paid at the start of the case, but others will be paid only after the debtor shows that the payment leaves the general creditors better off than they would be if the payments were not made.[9] Here, as

---

[7] In re Kmart, 359 F.3d 866 (7th Cir. 2004).

[8] Id. at 871.

[9] A number of courts have used the test set out in In re CoServ, LLC, 273 Bankr. 487 (Bankr. N.D. Tex. 2002) ("The debtor must show three elements are present. First, it must be critical that the debtor deal with the claimant. Second, unless it deals with the claimant, the debtor risks the probability of harm, or, alternatively, loss of economic advantage to the estate or the debtor's going concern value, which is disproportionate to the amount of the claimant's prepetition claim. Third,

elsewhere, prebankruptcy planning makes life much easier. If a debtor's business depends on shipments from a particular vendor, the debtor ought to have a contractual right to those shipments. By entering into such a contract and then assuming it in bankruptcy, the debtor can ensure continued access to the goods.

The challenge of ensuring a stable workforce during the pendency of the bankruptcy case is another problem that calls for judges to be vigilant. When a business find itself in financial distress, the last thing it wants or needs is for its most valuable workers to go elsewhere. As businesses depend increasingly on human capital, they become more vulnerable to departures of key employees. At the same time, a business may be in financial distress precisely because its current managers are no good. Bankruptcy judges in large cases need to be skeptical of key employee retention programs ("KERPs"), as they can reward insiders despite their close association with the business's collapse. Bankruptcy judges also need to ensure that new managers can be recruited. The Bankruptcy Code contains several provisions aimed at this problem. Section 548(a)(1) makes voidable a transfer to an insider under an employment contract if the transfer was made outside the ordinary course of business for less than reasonably equivalent value.[10] Section 503(c) prohibits debtors from paying insiders to remain with the business unless a number of conditions are satisfied. Conditions include a showing that the person has a bona fide job offer from another employer and that the person provides services essential to the business. These recently enacted and undoubtedly well-intentioned provisions are likely to do more harm than good. Not only do they make recruiting managers to a financially distressed business more difficult, but they pro-

there is no practical or legal alternative by which the debtor can deal with the claimant other than by payment of the claim.").

[10] This 2005 addition does not require insolvency, which is peculiar as it makes a payment under an employment contract more suspect than a dividend or outright gift to the same person.

vide a number of very bad incentives. Bad managers should be fired, but the good ones should not be tempted to seek jobs elsewhere.

Third-party releases provide another example of how bankruptcy practice can be out of step with bankruptcy law as appellate courts interpret it. Professionals may insist that the plan release them from liability arising from their own negligence. Such a release seems unobjectionable if the likelihood of negligence is low and if it is needed to facilitate retention of qualified professionals.[11] But circuit courts will be reluctant to enforce other third-party releases.[12] Suppose a debtor seeks to sell a subsidiary free and clear of all claims even when the subsidiary itself has not filed for bankruptcy. In theory, the only asset of the estate is the debtor's equity interest in the subsidiary. Only this equity should be sold free and clear. Any sale should leave the rights of the creditors of the subsidiary unaffected. But the legal separation between corporate groups is not always respected. Even if such transactions would fail appellate scrutiny, they go forward anyway unless someone objects. In a world in which negotiations and side deals are common, objections may never arise.

The trustee (and by inference the debtor in possession) must maximize the value of the estate rather than promote the interests of any particular group.[13] Chapter 11 does not rely entirely on the debtor in possession to ensure this outcome. Creditors are given their own representative in reorganization proceedings through the creditors committee, whereas equity owners ordinarily have no such representative. Moreover, courts have

[11] United Artists Theatre Co. v. Walton, 315 F.3d 217 (3d Cir. 2003); In re Enron Corp., 2005 WL 1500875 (S.D.N.Y. 2005).

[12] See, e.g., Gillman v. Continental Airlines, 203 F.3d 203 (3d Cir. 2000).

[13] In re Central Ice Cream, 836 F.2d 1068 (7th Cir. 1987). This is consistent with nonbankruptcy law. See, e.g., Production Resources Group, LLC v. NCT Group, Inc., 863 A.2d 772, 790–92 (Chancery Del. 2004).

increasingly measured the performance of professionals in connection with fee requests by whether they have advanced the interests of the estate as a whole.[14]

The Bankruptcy Code puts in place oversight mechanisms to ensure that the managers are looking out for everyone's interests, not just their own. These procedures, embodied in §363, begin with the idea that many day-to-day business decisions are not controversial. The trustee (and hence the debtor in possession) has the general authority to use, sell, or lease property of the estate.[15] It would be crazy to require a retailer to go to court every time a customer came into the store to buy something. The debtor in possession has to be able to buy raw materials and sell finished products. If the debtor in possession cannot be relied on to do at least that, a trustee should be appointed. If a transaction falls outside the ordinary course of business, it is subject to judicial scrutiny. The trustee can act only after there has been notice and a hearing.[16]

In bankruptcy, courts must take care to ensure the absence of self-dealing and a process that is likely to "obtain the highest price or greatest overall benefit possible for the estate."[17] The diverse interests that require the bankruptcy proceeding in the first place also require the court to ensure that they have not colored the decision at hand. At the same time, the bankruptcy judge must take advantage of market mechanisms when available.[18] Hence, it should come as no surprise that bankruptcy courts are less likely to accept doctrines such as the business

[14] See Everett v. Perez, 30 F.3d 1209 (9th Cir. 1994).

[15] The trustee has this power only if the trustee has the authority to run the business, but such authority is presumed in Chapter 11 cases.

[16] Requiring notice and a hearing within the meaning of the Bankruptcy Code is not the same, of course, as requiring a hearing. See §102.

[17] Cello Bag Co. v. Champion International Corp., 99 Bankr. 124, 130 (Bankr. N.D. Ga. 1988).

[18] See Bank of America v. 203 North LaSalle Street Partnership, 526 U.S. 434 (1999).

judgment rule when the debtor's actions have circumvented the marketplace.[19]

Section 363 limits the debtor in possession's ability to make some sales in the ordinary course of business. If the money derived from such sales goes toward buying more inventory, the secured creditor has no cause to complain, but the cash might be used for something else. To protect a creditor with a security interest in inventory, we must be sure that proceeds from the sale of inventory do not go toward paying off other creditors or toward buying airplane tickets to Rio. Under §364(e), parties with a security interest in inventory can insist that their interest be adequately protected. The right to sell goods in the ordinary course of business does not free the trustee or the debtor in possession from this obligation. The court also may limit the ability to sell in the ordinary course as circumstances warrant.

When a business is in trouble, it may be hemorrhaging cash. The trustee may be paying off suppliers and making all sorts of other decisions that are irrevocable. A secured creditor may be left short if it is unable to do anything other than go to court and ask for adequate protection. For this reason, §363 limits the trustee's powers with respect to cash collateral. Even if the use of the cash collateral (cash, negotiable instruments, bank accounts, and other cash equivalents) is in the ordinary course, the trustee (and hence the debtor in possession) must go to court first and give the party with the security interest adequate protection.

Postpetition obligations must be paid before the general creditors receive anything. These are "administrative expenses," the "actual, necessary costs and expenses of preserving the estate." They are given priority over the unsecured claims of the debtor under §507(a)(1). Money spent to increase the value of the estate inures to the benefit of the general creditors. The rule is necessary to ensure that people do business with the debtor, but its reach is broader. It ensures, for exam-

---

[19] See, e.g., In re Bidermann Industries U.S.A., 203 Bankr. 547 (Bankr. S.D.N.Y. 1997).

ple, that those whose tort claims arise after the petition is filed are paid before the prepetition general creditors.[20] The risk of incurring tort liability is one of the necessary costs incident to taking time to sort out the debtor's affairs. We can ensure that those who benefit from the bankruptcy proceeding internalize this cost by giving postpetition tort claims priority over unsecured claims.

Over time, however, "administrative expenses" may cease being a category that captures the necessary expenses of Chapter 11 and instead become a repository for new provisions that ensure priority for some class of prepetition creditor. The 2005 amendments to the Bankruptcy Code, for example, included as an administrative expense the value of goods received by the debtor within twenty days of filing the case. This provision markedly increases the debtor's ability to engage in prebankruptcy planning and avoid the burdens of critical vendor orders. But why such prepetition creditors are treated as postpetition creditors is a mystery. Even if there were some reason for offering them priority among prepetition creditors, it is hard to see why they are more deserving of priority than unpaid workers (who enjoy a lower priority that is capped) or tort victims (who enjoy no priority at all, in bankruptcy or out).

One should not infer from this discussion that remaining assets are always sufficient to pay administrative expenses. Secured credit has become so pervasive that in many cases there are no unencumbered assets, so administrative expense priority is of little value. The trustee (and the debtor in possession) has the power under §506(c) to charge against the collateral the reasonable and necessary costs and expenses of preserving the property, but a third party has no right to reach such assets in the event that the trustee refuses to pay for them.[21] Postpetition lenders must ensure that the money is there and are well advised to reach an explicit agreement with the secured creditor

[20] Reading Co. v. Brown, 391 U.S. 471 (1968).

[21] See Hartford Underwriters Insurance Co. v. Union Planters Bank, 530 U.S. 1 (2000).

before extending credit themselves. Such "carve out" agreements are a standard part of first-day orders.

It might seem that secured creditors would be unwilling to give up some of their collateral when not compelled to do so. But often they are willing to reach deals with postpetition suppliers when the suppliers are engaging in transactions with the debtor that serve to maximize the value of the assets. Many Chapter 11 cases involving ongoing enterprises are in effect being run for the benefit of the secured creditor. The bankruptcy forum makes it easier for the secured creditor and the debtor in possession to work together to find a buyer of the assets because the buyer can be confident of obtaining assets free and clear in a sale under §363. As noted in our discussion of claims, successor liability under state law may limit the ability of the bankruptcy judge to give clean title, but buyers may be found when this risk is the only one they face.[22]

Distinguishing between the rights of pre- and postpetition creditors is difficult in the case of obligations that arise under environmental law. An obligation to clean up past pollution is a prepetition claim if the debtor committed the relevant acts and the environmental claimant was on notice of the environmental hazard before the petition was filed. Some courts have expanded the idea of a prepetition claim even further, requiring only that the acts were committed prepetition.[23] In the case of an individual, the question of when a claim arises is important because only prepetition claims are discharged. Section 727(b) provides that the discharge extends to debts that arose "before the date of the order for relief," and §301 provides that the commencement of a voluntary case "constitutes an order for relief."

---

[22] See, e.g., New National Gypsum Co. v. New National Gypsum Co. Settlement Trust, 219 F.3d 478 (5th Cir. 2000).

[23] Compare California Department of Health Services v. Jensen, 995 F.2d 925 (9th Cir. 1993), with United States v. The LTV Corp., 944 F.2d 997 (2d Cir. 1991).

In the case of a business that continues to operate in bankruptcy, the question of when the claim arises may not matter much. If the obligation gives rise to a prepetition claim, then the prepetition claim is discharged. But liability for the violation of environmental law arises from many sources. Even if a debtor can extinguish a prepetition claim, it may remain liable nevertheless. The toxic waste dump poses an ongoing hazard, and anyone who owns the dump at a particular moment may be liable to clean it up, even if they took no part in creating the hazard in the first place. Some courts are reluctant to force the trustee to clean up if there are no unencumbered assets to pay for the cleanup.[24] Nevertheless, if any current owner would be obliged to clean it up outside of bankruptcy, it would seem the trustee would have this obligation inside. The trustee must comply with applicable laws, and by virtue of owning the property, the trustee has a legal duty to clean it up. Under this view, the duty to clean up sites that pose a continuing hazard is an actual, necessary expense of preserving the estate within the meaning of §503(b).[25] The obligation arises independent of the debtor's prepetition conduct, so the discharge of any liability that arises from that conduct is irrelevant.

Some courts have suggested that the trustee can limit the estate's cleanup obligations by virtue of the ability to abandon property under §554.[26] This is wrong. Section 554 empowers the trustee to turn over collateral to secured creditors that is of no use to the estate. It does not give the trustee a license to do something that those running the business could not do outside of bankruptcy. The trustee should not be able, by invoking §554, to rid the estate of an obligation that arises from the

[24] See Borden, Inc. v. Wells Fargo Business Credit, 856 F.2d 12 (4th Cir. 1988).

[25] See United States v. The LTV Corp., 944 F.2d 997 (2d Cir. 1991).

[26] A case that tends to lead courts astray, not because of its holding but because of its use of balancing language in dictum, is Midlantic National Bank v. New Jersey Department of Environmental Protection, 474 U.S. 494 (1986).

debtor's postpetition ownership of the property. The debtor in possession, like the trustee, is obliged to obey applicable non-bankruptcy law, and this duty implicitly qualifies the powers that the debtor in possession enjoys under provisions such as §363. If you run over someone with a car, you do not escape liability by ridding yourself of the car. By the same measure, whatever obligations the trustee has—whether by virtue of prepetition torts of the debtor or postpetition ownership by the trustee—the abandonment of an asset should not change them.

Ownership brings with it benefits and burdens. The result in these environmental cases seems odd only because the benefits of ownership usually exceed the costs. But sometimes, what we own must be sold at a loss. Indeed, sometimes we have to pay someone to take the property off our hands, as "two desperate men" unhappily discovered in "The Ransom of Red Chief."

Creditor Control in Chapter 11

Debtor-in-possession financing (or an order approving the use of cash collateral) is so central to bankruptcy cases that senior lenders have been able to use it to exert substantial control over the dynamics of large reorganizations. To the extent that their interests do not correspond to those of the creditors as a whole, there is potential for abuse. The typical debtor-in-possession (dip) loan grants the lender virtually complete control over the reorganization process. The dip financing agreement has many financial covenants, and the violation of any of them gives the dip lender the ability to terminate the financing. The dip loan also limits the reach of bankruptcy's automatic stay. The dip lender in the Winn-Dixie bankruptcy insisted that it could seize any of its collateral upon default so long as it provided the debtor with five days' notice. The dip lender provides only limited degrees of freedom for the business while it remains in Chapter 11. One typical provision waives the debtor's right to seek to use the lender's cash collateral over the lender's objection, while another waives the debtor's right to seek a priming lien on the secured creditor's collateral. Moreover, the dip financing agreement may provide that the loan terminates if the debtor fails to arrange for a sale of some or all of its assets by a specific date.

The dip lender can control both how long the debtor takes to formulate a plan and the shape the plan ultimately takes. The credit agreement often provides that it is an event of default if a plan is not filed within a certain time period. Such a provision effectively puts the decision about the length of the exclusivity period in the hands of the dip lender rather than the court. The debtor's freedom to shape a plan of reorganization is limited as well. The financing agreement may include a promise not to file a plan or even a motion in the bankruptcy case without the lender's prior written consent. Provisions such as these effectively remove the debtor's power to cram down a plan over creditor dissent. Courts are just beginning to explore the limits of creditors to exercise control in this fashion.[27]

Dip loans can also mute the rights of shareholders.[28] Any change in control, defined to include a new majority of the board, is a default on the loan. Similarly, the dip lending agreement can provide that the replacement of a CRO is an event of default. Provisions can go further still. The dip financing agreement might give the dip lender a power of attorney entitling it to sell any of the debtor's assets in the case of a default. A creditor empowered to act *as the debtor* is not a creditor in the traditional sense at all.

To be sure, not all courts approve these provisions. Yet, by cobbling together provisions that a secured lender knows will pass judicial muster in the chosen venue (a choice over which the secured lender has considerable influence), the dip lender

[27] See Official Committee of Unsecured Creditors v. New World Pasta Co., 322 Bankr. 560 (M.D. Pa. 2005).

[28] In theory, shareholders still retain the right to replace the board of directors while the corporation is in bankruptcy. See In re Johns-Manville, 801 F.2d 60 (2d Cir. 1986); Official Bondholders Committee v. Chase Manhattan Bank (In re Marvel Entertainment Group, Inc.), 209 Bankr. 832 (D. Del. 1997).

can ensure that no major decision is made in a way that it finds objectionable. Cash collateral orders often contain similar provisions. The dip lender's agreement to allow the debtor to use cash collateral often includes an acknowledgement of the validity of the lender's lien, the promise that the debtor will not seek to charge the collateral under §506(c), the requirement that the debtor receive the lender's consent before granting any future postpetition liens, and payment of all of the lender's expenses.

Given the difficulty of obtaining another dip lender, the effect of these provisions (coupled with the dip lender's unwillingness to waive them) is to cede control of the Chapter 11 case. Creditors once had to demand the appointment of a trustee if they wanted to displace the management. Under modern Chapter 11 practice, however, they have no reason to ask the court to order the appointment of the trustee. Indeed, it is an event of default.

Going-Concern Sales

Section 363 authorizes the trustee or the debtor in possession to engage in transactions outside the ordinary course of business, provided creditors are given notice and a hearing. The nonbankruptcy principles likely to provide the best guidance here are those that operate when a corporation is "in play" outside of bankruptcy.[29] Under the *Revlon* doctrine, once a takeover becomes inevitable, the board of directors "has a duty to maximize the company's value at a sale." The board members become "auctioneers" with a duty to get the best price.[30]

In *Committee of Equity Security Holders v. Lionel Corporation*, the Second Circuit set out a standard for the sale of a major asset under §363.[31] One of Lionel's most important assets was its

[29] See Josef S. Athanas, Using Bankruptcy Law to Implement or Combat Hostile Takeovers of Targets in Chapter 11, 55 Bus. Law. 593 (2000).

[30] Revlon, Inc. v. MacAndrews & Forbes Holdings, 506 A.2d 173, 182 (Del. 1986).

[31] 722 F.2d 1063 (2d Cir. 1983).

82 percent ownership interest in Dale Electronics, a healthy, publicly traded corporation. The debtor in possession and the creditors committee wanted to sell the stock immediately under §363. The committee of equityholders wanted to postpone the sale. The Second Circuit found that the sale could go forward in the face of an objection only if a "good business reason" justified the sale. The court stopped the sale of Lionel's equity interest in Dale because the only justification that the debtor in possession offered was that the creditors committee wanted the sale. There is no business reason to sell such an asset outside of the plan of reorganization. The stock might go down in value, but it might rise as well. Either is equally likely.

Lionel has generated widespread approval,[32] but its holding has different consequences when those in control propose an all-asset sale. A going-concern sale is different from the sale of a share of publicly traded stock. The assets, by their nature, are not fungible. One can always point to *some* reason for a sale now rather than later. The judge is poorly positioned to reject the debtor in possession's assertion that the terms of the proposed sale are favorable after the debtor has given multiple potential buyers the chance to bid. Far from limiting the debtor's ability to sell the business as a going concern, *Lionel* has become the authority one cites to permit such a sale to go forward. The judge ensures that the process of finding a buyer is sensible and that the debtor is not trying to fix the terms of a reorganization plan at the same time, but the judge will not second-guess a process that evidences due care and reasonable business judgment.[33]

Breakup fees are a frequently litigated question in the context of going-concern sales. No buyer wants to become a "stalking horse," doing the due diligence and satisfying itself that the business is worth keeping intact as a going concern only to watch someone else enjoy the fruits of its research, make a

---

[32] See, e.g., Stephens Industries v. McClung, 789 F.2d 386 (6th Cir. 1986); In re Abbotts Dairies, 788 F.2d 143 (3d Cir. 1986).

[33] In re Global Crossing Ltd., 295 Bankr. 726 (Bankr. S.D.N.Y. 2003).

slightly higher bid, and walk away with the company. Outside of bankruptcy, the first bidder commonly insists on being paid a fixed amount if the corporation is ultimately sold to someone else. This breakup fee can have a chilling effect on the bidding, but it can also entice someone to make a solid bid that generates additional bids.

Many bankruptcy courts have not been as deferential to breakup fees as courts outside of bankruptcy.[34] Nevertheless, courts have been willing to approve them when their purpose and effect was to increase the sale price.[35] Bankruptcy judges should not be in the business of second-guessing market mechanisms, but they must be vigilant in ensuring that the mechanisms are working. In small markets, it is often not easy to tell the difference. Potential buyers may be insiders. Potential buyers may acquire major positions in a corporation's debt or equity to ensure themselves a place at the bargaining table. The mechanism that ignites bidding in one case can smother it in another. Here, as elsewhere, the court is charged with a high-wire act.

[34] See, e.g., Calpine Corp. v. O'Brien Environmental Energy, 181 F.3d 527, 535 (3d Cir. 1999); AgriProcessors, Inc. v. Fokkena (In re Tama Beef Packing, Inc.), 321 Bankr. 496, 498 (8th Cir. BAP 2005) (noting breakup fees in bankruptcy usually limited to 1 to 4 percent of purchase price).

[35] Official Committee of Subordinated Bondholders v. Integrated Resources, 147 Bankr. 650 (S.D.N.Y. 1992).

Chapter Eleven

Forming the Plan of Reorganization

Overview of the Reorganization Process

We now turn to the plan of reorganization and the reorganization process. The ideal sequence as envisioned by the drafters is as follows. A corporation that is unable to make its loan payments, but is worth keeping intact, files a Chapter 11 petition. The old managers continue to run the business. They may make some nonordinary course decisions after notice and a hearing, but they mostly stick to business as usual. The rest of the world continues to do business with the corporation the same way as before. Shortly after the petition is filed, the United States Trustee appoints a committee of creditors. This committee usually consists of the creditors with the seven largest unsecured claims who are willing to serve or the creditors who formed the committee that tried to do the nonbankruptcy workout. This committee may hire professionals to look into the debtor's affairs, and it provides a vehicle for negotiations between the debtor and the creditors.

While the debtor's business continues, the debtor tries to come up with a reorganization plan. Even when one or more groups of claimholders oppose a plan, the debtor may still be able to confirm it if the plan meets, in addition to all the usual tests, the special ones set out in §1129(b). The process of obtaining confirmation of a plan over the objection of a class is called *cramdown*. But cramdown requires outside valuations, and these are expensive and unreliable. Ideally you want a plan each class of claimholders can live with. Even if you could cram down a plan on the general creditors, you would prefer not to have to do so. General creditors typically will insist on receiving something. They will make a calculation of what they would receive in the event of liquidation. If those pickings are small enough, they may be willing to accept a small amount. The business may be in a high-tech industry, and much of its value may lie in projects that only the shareholder-manager knows how to finish. The representatives of the general creditors, however, must worry about their reputations in future negotiations with different debtors but the same lawyers. At some point they will draw a line. Many an old-time bankruptcy veteran can recall (now fondly) a particular creditor's lawyer in the garment trade who always stood on principle—and his principle was 50 cents on the dollar.

The Bankruptcy Code initially gives the debtor 120 days to file a plan of reorganization. The judge can extend the plan, but is likely to do so only if the debtor can show things are on track and that those in control are meeting the goals they set for themselves. For most small business corporations in Chapter 11, 120 days is enough time to see whether the business can survive. Large corporations need more time. Nevertheless, if the debtor does not propose a plan of reorganization within 18 months of the filing of the petition, other parties in interest have a chance to propose their own plan. See §1121(d)(2).

The plan divides the claims of the creditors into various classes and proposes a treatment for each class. After the debtor files the plan, the debtor must try to get the plan accepted. The debtor must write a *disclosure statement* and persuade the court to approve it. The purpose of the disclosure statement is to explain the plan to those who must vote on it. Once the disclosure statement is approved, the debtor may begin seeking acceptance of the plan from the various classes. The debtor may obtain approval in one of two ways. First, those whose claims are in a given class can approve the plan. A majority of the creditors holding claims in the class who vote must vote in favor of the plan, and their claims must have a value equal to at least two-thirds of the value of the claims of those who are voting. In the case of equity interests, the debtor simply needs two-thirds of the shares being voted. This is consistent with state corporate law in that the number of shareholders does not matter, just the number of shares. Second, the debtor can receive constructive approval from a class if that class is *unimpaired* within the meaning of §1124. Generally speaking, a class is unimpaired if it consists only of claims that the plan does not restructure. A creditor's claim, for example, is unimpaired if the original terms of the loan are reinstated (and all defaults are cured).

After the votes are received, the debtor can ask the court to approve the reorganization plan. The court must satisfy itself that the plan meets all the requirements of Chapter 11. Many are spelled out in §1129(a). The plan must, for example, pay off administrative expense claims in cash. §1129(a)(9)(a). This requirement may not be burdensome for a large corporation that has ready access to capital markets, and practices have emerged that make this requirement less rigid than it might first appear even for those that lack such access. Administrative creditors are free to scale back or modify their claims in a side deal. Their willingness to do so depends on their past and future relationship with the debtor. For example, among the largest administrative claims may be payments owed to debtor's counsel, and these are often structured initially with a schedule over time.

Nevertheless, §1129(a)(9)(a) sets a baseline that matters, particularly for smaller businesses. Among other things, they must find the cash to pay all vendors who shipped goods within 20 days of the filing of the petition. §503(b)(9). The success of some Chapter 11 reorganizations depends on the debtor's ability to bring a preference or fraudulent conveyance action. Failing that, the only source of new cash may be the old equityholder. For such small businesses, a reorganization may be possible only if the old equityholder has at least enough cash to pay administrative expenses. The longer the reorganization lasts, the greater this amount will be and the harder it will be for the debtor to confirm a reorganization plan, at least without extraordinarily patient accountants and lawyers.

Similarly, §1129(a)(9)(b) requires that a plan provide cash for specified prebankruptcy claims afforded high priority by §507(a)(3)–(7). These include, for example, specified obligations to employees and employee benefit plans. Immediate full payment is required for such claims if the class of claims has not accepted the plan. If the class has accepted the plan, an individual creditor cannot demand immediate payment, but may insist on full payment over time, including appropriate interest. This is the case even if the claim is not of a high enough priority to have warranted payment in full under Chapter 7.

Perhaps the most important of these requirements is the condition stated in §1129(a)(9)(c) that a plan provide for the deferred cash payment of those taxes afforded priority by §507(a)(8), including income, excise, and withholding taxes. These cash payments must be made within a six-year period and must have a value, as of the date of the plan, equal to the amount of taxes owing, whether or not the claim would have been paid in full under Chapter 7. These provisions are clear and give rise to few reported decisions. Nevertheless, tax claims may dominate the landscape of many debtor corporations. A debtor in bankruptcy may not have been earning enough before bankruptcy to become liable for significant corporate income tax, but even an unprofitable business owes or must withhold taxes related to the business's role as an employer. Small businesses often fail to meet these obligations when they encounter trouble, notwithstanding the risk of criminal liability to the businesses' managers. (Tax laws treat the failure to turn over taxes withheld from employees' paychecks much more seriously than a failure to pay the business's own taxes.) Negotiations over how these tax obligations will be paid are often the primary focus of Chapter 11 when the debtor is a small, family-run business.

Another requirement that is not often litigated but can affect the plan is in §1129(a)(10). Even if a plan meets the absolute priority rule, a court cannot confirm it unless at least one class of impaired claims approves the plan. A Chapter 11 plan is supposed to be a product of negotiations among the interested parties. To show that there were negotiations and at least some give and take, you must gain the approval of one class that has the right to reject. Although there is rarely a dispute about whether a class has accepted, there has been a great deal of litigation over whether the initial classification of claims was manipulated to create one class that would accept the plan. The greater the debtor's ability to divide claims into many separate classes, the more likely it is that one class will vote in favor of the plan.

A number of requirements in §1129(a) become focal points of plan negotiations. For example, §1129(a)(13) requires that the plan provide for the continued full payment of retiree benefits as modified under §1114. These obligations, as well as shortfalls in a corporation's pension plan, loom large in the Chapter 11 cases of large industrial corporations. At the time it entered Chapter 11, Bethlehem Steel had 11,500 active employees and 120,000 retiree benefits. Its pension plan was underfunded to the tune of $2.9 billion. Promised health and insurance benefits totaled $3.1 billion, and these were not funded at all. A plan of reorganization could not be confirmed without confronting these obligations, and they alone rendered the company insolvent. Put differently, these obligations could not be paid in full even if the obligations owed everyone else disappeared. As with so many other modern Chapter 11 reorganizations of large corporations, Bethlehem Steel's bankruptcy ended with a going-concern sale.

Section 1129(b) embodies the substantive component of the absolute priority rule. When a class (as opposed to a minority within a class) dissents and a class junior to it is receiving something under the plan, the court must ask whether the dissenting class is being paid in full. As reviewed below, determining whether a plan satisfies §1129(b) requires a valuation that uses marketplace benchmarks. By contrast, courts tend to use a less rigorous method when an objection is brought by an individual creditor. Under §1129(a)(7) the court must be satisfied that each individual creditor either consents to the plan or is getting as much as it would have received in a Chapter 7 liquidation. This is commonly called the *best-interests-of-creditors test*. When a business can be sold as a going concern, the value that might be realizable in Chapter 7 may be the same as the value of the business reorganized in Chapter 11. The less rigorous valuation methods, however, make §1129(a)(7) much easier to meet than §1129(b).

There is one other important requirement that is frequently the focus of litigation. The court must be satisfied that the corporation will not end up in a reorganization again. §1129(a)(11). This is commonly called the *feasibility test*. It is subjective, but the court can give it some hard edges by comparing the capital structure of the reorganized corporation with other corporations in the same industry. A reorganization plan that leaves a corporation too highly leveraged relative to other corporations in the same industry may not be feasible within the meaning of the Bankruptcy Code.

If the court confirms the plan, the plan is carried out according to its terms. Under §1141, confirmation of the plan discharges *all* debts (that arose prior to confirmation) except for (and insofar as) those debts that are dealt with in the plan. On its face, Chapter 11 permits the discharge of all corporate debts. Due process, however, mandates a minimum level of notice, and this ultimately places a check on the scope of the bankruptcy discharge in Chapter 11.[1] The discharge does not abrogate any obligations that arise after the plan is confirmed. Recall, for example, the debtor that owns property on which it (or someone else) had dumped toxic wastes before the filing of the bankruptcy petition. The environmental claims that arose before confirmation are discharged, but the discharge of these claims is not sufficient to insulate the debtor from cleanup obligations if it remains the owner of the property and incurs obligations in that capacity. Such a debtor remains liable for environmental cleanup obligations that arise by virtue of postbankruptcy ownership in the same way that someone to whom the debtor sold the property would be liable.[2]

---

[1] See Christopher v. Kendavis Holding Co., 249 F.3d 383 (5th Cir. 2001).

[2] See In re CMC Heartland Partners, 966 F.2d 1143 (7th Cir. 1992).

A number of rules in Chapter 11 treat small businesses in a way that is quicker and more streamlined. The court is required to confirm a plan that complies with the dictates of Chapter 11 within 45 days of the filing of the plan. §1129(e). The disclosure statement itself can be submitted on standard forms, and the court may conditionally approve it. The disclosure statement is subject to close scrutiny after the voting takes place at the same hearing in which the court decides whether to confirm the plan. §1125(f).

Chapter 11 is also available to individual debtors. The individual might be a lawyer or a doctor. She does not do business in corporate form, and her personal finances have become intertwined with those of her practice. If no trustee is appointed, it is the individual debtor, rather than the debtor in possession, who runs the business and proposes a plan. The rules for confirmation are the same. Unlike the corporate debtor, however, the individual maintains an identity separate from the productive assets she owns. Thus, an individual debtor under Chapter 11 commits only that future income promised by the plan. There are exceptions to discharge for certain obligations, such as child support. When a creditor objects, the debtor must commit her disposable income (as measured by §1325(b)(2)) to paying back creditors for five years. See §1129(a)(15). Creditors, however, may not insist on such plans, as the debtor can often convert to Chapter 7 and obtain an outright discharge. Individual debtors are not be subject to means testing under §707(b) as long as most of their obligations are business rather than consumer debts.

Classification

A plan of reorganization must sort the claims of the various creditors and the interests of the various equityholders into different classes. In the language of the Bankruptcy Code, creditors have claims and equityholders have interests. All claims or interests in a class must be treated the same unless the holder of a claim agrees to less favorable treatment. See §1123(a)(4). A plan cannot give one claim ten cents on the dollar and another five cents. Nor can it provide that some claims in a class be paid in cash and others with long-term promissory notes.

The Bankruptcy Code does not set out in detail how much freedom the debtor or any other plan proponent enjoys in the way in which claims are sorted into different classes. Section 1122(a) provides that only substantially similar claims or interests can occupy a single class. This provision requires at least that claims with different legal rights be classified separately. For this reason, each secured claim is typically in a class by itself. Two claims are not substantially similar if they are secured by different collateral, for example, nor are they substantially similar when they are secured by the same collateral if one claim enjoys priority over the other. Other determinations are harder to make. Consider, on one hand, a deficiency claim held by a secured creditor for the difference between the amount it is owed and the value of its collateral and, on the other hand, the claim of a trade creditor who looks forward to continuing business with the reorganized debtor. When these two claims are put in one class, the ability of one of them to invoke the absolute priority may turn on whether the other wants to as well.

The bankruptcy judge must decide whether a plan proponent can put different claims in the same class, must put them in separate classes, or can enjoy the freedom to do either. Section 1122(a) tells us that we can put together substantially similar claims "except as provided by subsection (b)." The latter subsection allows a plan to designate a separate class of unsecured claims below a plan-specified threshold if necessary for administrative convenience. The "except as provided by subsection (b)" language in §1122(a), therefore, suggests that except for administrative convenience claims, substantially similar claims *must* be put into the same class. Arguably, unsecured claims are, by their nature, substantially similar because their legal attributes under nonbankruptcy law are identical.[3]

---

[3] See Granada Wines, Inc. v. New England Teamsters & Trucking Industry Pension Fund, 748 F.2d 42, 46 (1st Cir. 1984).

Another way to read §1122(a) starts with the observation that substantially similar claims *may* be put in the same class but are not *required* to be.[4] But even then we still need to decide whether the claims are indeed substantially similar. Returning to our example of creditors with trade and deficiency claims, one could argue that the claims are substantially similar because both are unsecured claims and neither enjoys priority over the other. But one can also adopt a different view. Consider a real estate case involving a nonrecourse mortgage. If the debtor defaults outside of bankruptcy, the creditor can look only to the real property to satisfy the obligation. Even if the property proves to be worth much less than the amount of the loan, the creditor cannot go against the debtor's other assets for the deficiency. A different rule applies to the debtor in bankruptcy. As we discuss in greater detail below, §1111(b)(1) of the Bankruptcy Code permits an undersecured creditor with a nonrecourse loan to treat the loan as if it were recourse in Chapter 11 (but not in Chapter 7). Thus, in Chapter 11 a creditor holds both a secured claim equal to the value of the collateral and an unsecured claim for the balance of its loan.

One can argue that the legal rights of a real estate lender who holds an unsecured claim are not identical to those of a trade creditor. The real estate lender's unsecured claim is worthless in Chapter 7 and hence it receives no protection from the best-interests test, while the trade creditor does. The Seventh Circuit found that this and other differences kept the two from being substantially similar and hence mandated that they be placed in separate classes.[5] Other courts, however, have

[4] See, e.g., Barakat v. Life Insurance Co. of Virginia, 99 F.3d 1520 (9th Cir. 1996); Boston Post Road Ltd. Partnership v. FDIC, 21 F.3d 477 (2d Cir. 1994); Phoenix Mutual Life Insurance Co. v. Greystone III Joint Venture, 995 F.2d 1274 (5th Cir. 1991). For a useful summary of the case law, see In re Dow Corning Corp., 244 Bankr. 634 (Bankr. E.D. Mich. 1999).

[5] See In re Woodbrook Associates, 19 F.3d 312 (7th Cir. 1994).

found that these differences are not sufficient to mandate putting such claims in separate classes.

If those whose claims are in the same class have differing interests, one cannot be sure that the majority will in fact make a decision that is in the best interests of the group. The possibility of manipulation if unsecured claims could be placed in a class with secured claims is obvious. Secured creditors should be paid in full and general creditors only a few cents on the dollar. It makes no sense for those holding one kind of claim to be able to speak on behalf of those holding another. If they were classified together, dissent from one group or the other is likely to be suppressed. In the typical bankruptcy, their interests are adverse to each other. One can argue that the claim of a creditor who is also a shareholder should not be in the same class as the claim of someone who is simply a creditor. A shareholder-creditor's approval of the plan does not accurately reflect what is in the interest of creditors who are not shareholders.

Consider the question whether the claims of trade creditors can be put in the same class as the claim of a bank that has made an unsecured loan to a debtor. The bank may be anxious to cut its losses and may intend to have no future dealings with the debtor. By contrast, the trade creditors may look forward to future dealings. They have much more to gain from a successful reorganization and may be more inclined to vote in favor of a plan that gives creditors less and leaves the company better capitalized. The bank and the trade creditors have interests that differ radically, even though their legal rights—those of unsecured creditors—are the same. There are, however, no ready benchmarks by which to judge whether a creditor is *sufficiently* different to justify its claim being put in a separate class. It may be that the bank is not different enough from the trade creditors. The usual presumption is that creditors holding claims that have the same legal status should be placed in the same class. The claims of the trade creditors and the bank would ordinarily be grouped together.

Creating two or more classes increases the chance that the plan will have to meet the absolute priority rule. Only if a class dissents must a plan satisfy the absolute priority rule in order to be confirmed. Therefore, the smaller each class, the larger the role each dissenting creditor has. Forcing the debtor to put creditors into separate classes increases the chance that dissenters will be able to keep their class from approving a plan. In the face of the rejection of this class of creditors, the debtor has to show that, as to them, the absolute priority rule is satisfied. But this effect can be offset, as we have already noted. A court can confirm a plan only if one class of impaired claims approves the plan. Just as increasing the number of classes increases the chance that one of them will dissent, it may also increase the chance that one of them will approve.

Many of the classification cases arise when the debtor's only asset is a single parcel of real estate. In these cases, the court will ask whether the separate classification has been undertaken solely for the purpose of creating an impaired class that will vote in favor of the plan. As the court put it in *Greystone*, there is "one clear rule that emerges from the otherwise muddled caselaw on §1122 claims classification: thou shalt not classify similar claims differently in order to gerrymander an affirmative vote on a reorganization plan."[6] Separate classification is easier to justify outside of the single-asset real estate case.[7]

Section 1123(a)(4) provides that everyone in the same class be treated the same. The person proposing the plan cannot escape the absolute priority rule by being generous to a bare majority that holds two-thirds of the claims and giving short shrift to the claims of the rest. Similarly, the "unfair discrimination"

[6] Phoenix Mutual Life Insurance Co. v. Greystone III Joint Venture, 995 F.2d 1274, 1279 (5th Cir. 1991); Boston Post Road Ltd. Partnership v. FDIC, 21 F.3d 477 (2d Cir. 1994).

[7] See, e.g., In re Jersey City Medical Center, 817 F.2d 1055 (3d Cir. 1987) (separating claims of physicians, medical malpractice victims, employee benefit plan participants, and trade creditors); Teamsters National Freight Industry Negotiating Committee v. U.S. Truck Co., 800 F.2d 581 (6th Cir. 1986) (separating claims of collective bargaining unit members).

component of the absolute priority rule in §1129(b) protects creditors from the temptation the debtor may have to put creditors into different classes and treat some more favorably than the others. A plan cannot be confirmed if an objecting class can point to another class containing the same legal claims that the plan treats more favorably. The protections of §1129(b), however, may not go far enough toward ensuring that creditors put in different classes are treated equally. A debtor may be able to put creditors into separate classes and provide for complex payout schemes that are difficult to value. (One class might get one type of preferred stock and another might receive a convertible debenture.) The debtor might assert that creditors in each class received rights that gave them the equivalent of ten cents on the dollar for their claims, and disproving this assertion can be hard. Forcing creditors into the same class wherever possible (and hence forcing the same kind of payout to each under §1123(a)(4)) makes this problem disappear.

Forming the Plan of Reorganization

Negotiations are the lifeblood of a reorganization, but relying on negotiations makes sense only if the parties are well informed. Indeed, a predecessor to modern bankruptcy law—the Chandler Act—came into being in the 1930s in large part because Congress believed that the existing bargaining environment favored sophisticated insiders and professionals at the expense of outside investors.[8] Two reforms in the Bankruptcy Code improved the protections provided outsiders. The United States Trustee provides a voice for dispersed trade creditors in small cases. Equally important are the disclosure and solicitation rules in §1125. These twin reforms largely supplant the role that the Securities and Exchange Commission played—unsuccessfully—in old Chapter X.

Ordinary trade creditors and public investors are in no position to know the debtor's true financial condition. By requiring

---

[8] See, e.g., Max Lowenthal, The Investor Pays (1933); Thurman W. Arnold, The Folklore of Capitalism 258–59 (1937).

that they be provided with a disclosure statement before being asked to vote on a plan, the Bankruptcy Code helps them make sensible decisions. Investors need to have, in the words of the Bankruptcy Code, "information of a kind, and in sufficient detail, as far as is reasonably practical . . . to make an informed judgment about the plan," taking into account the ability of the typical holder of a particular class of claim or interest to acquire information from other sources.[9]

To this end, §1125 prohibits parties from soliciting acceptance or rejection of a plan before the court has approved the disclosure statement. A party cannot circulate a draft disclosure statement to all creditors, informed and uninformed alike, if the draft will have the effect of fixing in place the views of the less sophisticated. If the draft renders many small trade creditors incapable of later evaluating the approved disclosure statement on its own terms, circulating the draft is a solicitation within the meaning of §1125. The point of having a hearing at which the court approves a disclosure statement is lost if parties are free to act in a way that makes it irrelevant.

This understanding of solicitation is reflected in, among other things, Bankruptcy Rule 3017(a). It provides that a plan proponent mail the plan and the disclosure statement "only to the debtor, any trustee or committee . . . and any party in interest who requests in writing a copy of the statement or plan." Drafts of unapproved disclosure statements will not taint the judgment of sophisticated creditors actively involved in the case, but blanket distribution of the document might.

By the same measure, parties should not be able to solicit acceptance of their own plan under the pretext of soliciting a rejection of some other plan. It is one thing to point out deficiencies in the debtor's plan. But it is quite another to focus unsophisticated creditors' attention on another, unreviewed, plan and tell them that to vote in favor of it, they must first reject the plan before them. Solicitations must be directed only to the plan that is on the table.

[9] See 11 U.S.C. §1125(a).

These principles are not controversial. A creditor can freely discuss a draft plan of reorganization with the creditors committee and can consult with other professional investors without fear of violating §1125. A creditor can also urge others to vote against a plan on the ground that alternative courses of action provide them with a better pay-off.[10] But a competitor that has been in litigation with the debtor for many years should not think it has license to distribute a letter extolling the virtues of its own plan under the guise of soliciting rejection of the debtor's plan.[11]

A sensible interpretation of §1125 looks at whether the communication effectively preempts an unbiased reading of an approved disclosure statement. Distributing a draft plan and disclosure statement to lawyers who by training and inclination are attuned to the smallest changes in fine print is radically different from distributing a draft to tens of thousands of tort victims whose opinions, once formed, may be unlikely to change. Parties must be on their guard when communicating with investors as a whole, especially if these investors know little about bankruptcy in general and less about the case itself.

Before deciding whether to accept or reject a plan, a stakeholder will likely want some sense of the alternatives. Here again, discussing alternatives with a stakeholder is different from distributing a draft plan to the masses. A draft disclosure statement can be distributed to the creditors committee and institutional investors, but an unapproved disclosure statement cannot be broadly disseminated to tort victims. The former will be able to look later at the approved disclosure statement with clear eyes and the latter will not.

[10] See Century Glove v. First American Bank, 860 F.2d 94, 100 (3d Cir. 1988).

[11] See Colorado Mountain Express, Inc. v. Aspen Limousine Service, Inc., 198 Bankr. 341, 345, 348 (Bankr. D. Colo. 1996).

Nonbankruptcy law permits lock-up agreements.[12] Once a debtor files for bankruptcy, however, such agreements are permitted only if they were reached before the commencement of the bankruptcy case in a manner complying with applicable nonbankruptcy law. §1125(g). As mentioned above, one-on-one discussions with another stakeholder rarely pose a problem, even if the communication is a draft plan. Negotiations per se are similarly unproblematic. Nor is §1125 violated by obtaining informal assurances from a creditor to support a particular plan. But such informal assurances are sometimes not enough. The holder of a particular claim may be a bank today and a vulture investor tomorrow. Ensuring that you can rely next month on the support you garner this week by obtaining a writing that binds the party is useful. But obtaining a binding commitment to vote in a particular way is not "negotiating."

Some courts have found that obtaining binding postpetition agreements to support a plan of reorganization falls short of a solicitation within the meaning of §1125. In their view, "solicitation" refers only to the formal voting process itself.[13] Section 1125 does not affect settlements that parties reach, even when those settlements include stipulations that oblige a creditor to support a particular plan.[14] Such an interpretation is completely consistent with the spirit of §1125. The sophisticated professionals who are parties to these agreements are well informed and do not need the protections that a disclosure statement provides.

---

[12] Nonbankruptcy law, of course, does impose limits. For example, lock-ups are impermissible if they limit the ability of a corporation's directors to exercise their fiduciary duties at some later time. See Omnicare, Inc. v. NCS Healthcare, Inc., 818 A.2d 914 (Del. 2003). In bankruptcy, the general obligation of the directors to act in a way that maximizes the value of the estate entirely supplants this fiduciary duty.

[13] See, e.g., In re Kellogg Square Partnership, 160 Bankr. 336, 340 (Bankr. D. Minn. 1993).

[14] See, e.g., Trans World Airlines, Inc. v. Texaco Inc., 81 Bankr. 813 (Bankr. S.D.N.Y. 1988).

Other courts take a different view, especially when, because of *Century Glove*, lawyers try to shoehorn binding agreements into the category of "negotiation." When plausible, lawyers should argue that what they have is a settlement. This argument, however, will sometimes fail, especially when the binding agreement is not part of an overall settlement of many issues between the parties (as was the case in *Kellogg* and *Texaco*) but is merely a commitment to vote in a particular way.

Even if one does obtain a binding commitment to vote in a particular way, it cannot be relied upon in a contentious Chapter 11 case. A court interpreting §1125 can easily conclude that a disclosure statement must be approved before someone can be asked to make a binding commitment to vote in favor of a plan. The statute provides no safe harbor for negotiations or settlements. Such an interpretation of §1125 may run counter to some practices that have emerged in recent years and be inconsistent with sensible bankruptcy policy, but some courts, especially appellate courts, have little sympathy for interpretations that are out of step with what seems the plain language of the statute.

Once holders of claims and interests have the approved disclosure statement, interested parties are free to solicit claims and rejections. Those who oppose the debtor's plan are free to put forward their own narrative and offer their own conclusions, even if they differ dramatically from what is in the disclosure statement.[16] The Bankruptcy Code is not intended to force creditors to seek court approval of every communication they have with creditors.[17]

Some courts lament the difficulty of determining what communications are permissible. As the court put it in *Century Glove*, "[w]e find no principled, predictable difference between

---

[16] See In re Apex Oil, 111 Bankr. 245, 249 (Bankr. E.D. Mo. 1990).

[17] See Century Glove v. First American Bank, 860 F.2d 94, 100 (3d Cir. 1988).

negotiation and solicitation of future acceptances."[18] Such line-drawing problems, however, are easy to overstate. Creditors sanctioned for improper solicitation seldom argue that they were merely engaging in negotiations. You are not negotiating when you send a draft of a plan and a disclosure statement to the entire creditor body without a cover letter or even a return address.[19] Nor are you negotiating when you append a draft of your plan and disclosure statement to a pleading against the debtor's disclosure statement and then serve it on the entire creditor body.[20]

Century Glove, a case in which the court found in favor of a creditor who circulated a draft plan, bears little resemblance to the cases in which courts have frowned on the practice. In *Century Glove*, a lawyer for one of the creditors telephoned several lawyers representing other creditors. He told them that, while there was no plan other than the debtor's "on the table," he had drafted an alternative that he had shown to the creditors committee. These lawyers then asked to see the plan. The lawyer sent a copy of the plan, marked as "draft," and asked for comments. The court in *Century Glove* found that the right to file a plan was a modest one and did not give the debtor the right "to have its plan *considered* exclusively."[21]

Although conduct of the sort seen in *Century Glove* is rarely, if ever, sanctioned, courts have interpreted §1125 in ways that make the conduct suspect nevertheless. They have found that the debtor does have the right to have its plan considered independent of other plans. Putting competing plans before voters during the exclusivity period undercuts the debtor's rights under §1121. One court, for example, found that "§1121 provides the debtor with the exclusive right to propose a plan of

[18] Id. at 101.

[19] In re Rook Broadcasting, 154 Bankr. 970 (Bankr. D. Idaho 1993).

[20] See, e.g., In re Clamp-All Corp., 233 Bankr. 198 (Bankr. D. Mass. 1999).

[21] 860 F.2d at 101 (emphasis in original).

reorganization"[22] thus creditors should not be allowed to put forward their own plan until after the debtor's is rejected. If one takes this point of view, the problem of putting forward a draft plan has nothing to do with the solicitation process under §1125 but rather with the nature of the exclusivity period. The ability of each creditor to compare its plan with the debtor's in the course of soliciting a rejection is in tension with giving the debtor the right to have its plan evaluated on its own.

Century Glove expressed the fear that parties who were merely negotiating would run afoul of §1125. In practice, the opposite is often the case. Angry and disappointed litigants are the ones who tend to be sanctioned under §1125. The solicitation takes place because the negotiations have broken down. From the judge's perspective, their efforts are improper solicitations because the parties *failed to negotiate* or at least failed to negotiate within the norms of Chapter 11. In any event, litigants who fight and lose a battle with the judge in open court should be cautious about refighting that battle in the documents they distribute during solicitation and voting.[23] Bankruptcy judges, like all judges, take a dim view of litigants who are insubordinate.

The hearing on the disclosure statement is an important event and provides an opportunity to resolve many issues. These include whether exclusivity should be lifted to allow a creditor to propose its own plan. The information in the disclosure statement itself, however, may not be as useful as one might expect. Section 1125(b) explicitly states that "[t]he court may approve a disclosure statement without a valuation of the debtor or an appraisal of the debtor's assets." A creditor that

---

[22] 233 Bankr. at 207. Section 1121, of course, uses the word "file," not "propose."

[23] In *Aspen*, the creditor in question wrote a letter to all creditors complaining that it "had been disadvantaged by the Judge's decision," promised that it intended to "pursue every legal remedy available to forestall the . . . Plan," and declared to one and all, "We are not going away!" See 198 Bankr. at 345.

has to vote on a plan should want to know at least whether it is being treated better than it would be under a liquidation. That seems to require some sort of valuation. In addition, if one is receiving stock, it may not be possible to know the value of what one is receiving under a plan without taking account of how much the debtor's assets are worth.

Sections 1124 and 1126(f) take the right to vote away from classes of claims or interests when they are not being compromised in the reorganization. To use the language of the Bankruptcy Code, such claims are not "impaired." If a class of claims receives the same set of rights in the reorganization that it had before the reorganization, those who hold such claims have nothing to complain about. §1124(1). A loan is unimpaired if the debtor is willing to continue to make the same payments and accept the same terms. A loan may also be deemed unimpaired under §1124 even if the loan is in default. Section 1124 confronts a problem we encountered before in the context of executory contracts. Just as a debtor may breach an executory contract on the eve of bankruptcy only because it has too little incentive to watch out for the interests of others, a debtor may also allow a favorable loan to go into default. Like §365, §1124 overcomes this problem by allowing past defaults to be cured and the original loan reinstated. Just as the trustee can keep an executory contract in place by curing defaults and assuming its obligations, the trustee can reinstate a loan. The principal difference is that this power to assume a loan that is in default exists only when the corporation is being reorganized in Chapter 11, while an executory contract can be assumed in Chapter 7 as well.

Making a creditor unimpaired is one way of avoiding a cramdown. The trustee (or, more likely, the debtor in possession) will favor reinstatement when it allows the corporation to enjoy the benefits of a below-market loan from a fully secured creditor. Assume a bank has lent $1 million on a long-term basis at an interest rate that is now substantially below the market rate. The debtor, however, is now in default. Unless the debtor takes advantage of §1124, the default accelerates the loan and makes the entire $1 million in principal due and owing. Under §502, the bank has a claim for $1 million. The best-interests-of-creditors test would entitle the bank to a bundle of rights with a present value of $1 million. Section 1124(2), however, allows the bank's claim to be "de-accelerated." The terms of its contract are reinstated, and the bank is deemed unimpaired. The bank is deemed to have accepted the plan, and hence the bank cannot invoke the best-interests-of-creditors test, let alone the absolute priority rule, even though the present value of the stream of payments the bank will now get is significantly less than $1 million. As in this example, continuing a below-market loan makes the most sense when the loan is oversecured. The oversecured creditor is entitled to interest under §506(b) and therefore will be paid in full in any event. There is no cost associated with taking advantage of the loan's favorable terms.

As noted, creditors with unimpaired claims are deemed to have accepted the plan, and no solicitation of them is required. §1126(f). The reorganization plan is not affecting these creditors, thus their approval of the plan is irrelevant. By similar reasoning, a class that receives nothing under the plan is deemed to have rejected it. §1126(g). There is no reason to ask whether the plan gives them enough. (Rejection, of course, brings the absolute priority rule into play.)

For classes that do vote, approval is determined by §1126. That provision requires positive votes by those who hold two-thirds in amount and a majority by number of the allowed claims duly voted in a class. In the case of equity interests, actual approval requires positive votes by those who hold two-thirds in amount of the shares duly voted. Whether a claim or interest is duly voted depends on §1126(e), which allows the court to disqualify votes not procured and exercised in good faith.

In *Young v. Higbee Company*, the Supreme Court suggested that bad faith could be attributed to those "whose selfish purpose was to obstruct a fair and feasible reorganization in the hope that someone would pay them more than the ratable equivalent of their proportionate part of the bankrupt assets."[24] This definition reflects a problem that arose under prior law. Under the 1898 Act, the absolute priority rule could be invoked by single creditors, and some bought claims in bankruptcy merely to hold up the reorganization unless they were paid more than others holding the same securities. Courts have also found bad faith when a company purchased a claim for the purpose of blocking an action against it, or where creditors associated with a competing business were voting to advance the interests of their businesses at the expense of the debtor's. Similarly, if old equityholders or those close to them buy claims in order to promote or block a plan because of the way it treats their equity interests, courts have found bad faith as well.[25]

In recent cases, the problem is much more likely to arise when an outsider enters and seeks to gain control of a class in order to put its own reorganization plan in place. Imagine that a debtor proposes a reorganization plan within the exclusivity period and solicits acceptance of the plan. In the meantime, a prebankruptcy creditor, or an outsider, purchases claims at a discount. The purchaser hopes to gain complete control of the debtor and substitute its own plan for the debtor's plan. The purchaser also hopes to substitute its management for current management. Like any other corporate acquirer, the purchaser hopes ultimately to profit from its acquisitions. One might argue that this anticipated profit is not a legitimate creditor's attempt to protect its rights as a creditor but instead advances a different, and illegitimate, interest. This was the court's view, for example, in *In re Allegheny International*.[26] In that case the court found that a would-be acquirer acted in bad faith under §1126(e) and decided not to permit the acquirer to vote its purchased claims.

[24] 324 U.S. 204, 211 (1945).

[25] For a discussion, see Figter, Ltd. v. Teachers Insurance & Annuity Association, 118 F.3d 635 (9th Cir. 1997).

[26] 118 Bankr. 282, 289–90 (Bankr. W.D. Pa. 1990)

Under one view, those who buy up claims of businesses in Chapter 11 disrupt the bargaining process that is at the core of Chapter 11. It is hard to gain acceptance of a reorganization plan if the owners of the claims shift constantly. But one can take a more generous view of these "vulture" investors, as they are sometimes called. They assemble dispersed claims and thus mitigate the problem that makes bankruptcy necessary in the first place. The negotiation and conflict inherent in the reorganization process would vanish or greatly diminish if a single entity owned all or most of the claims against a debtor. A sole or majority owner of claims has a strong incentive to maximize the value of the debtor's assets. Moreover, the other creditors are protected in bankruptcy by the best-interests test of §1129(a)(7). Finally, by creating a market for claims in distressed businesses, these investors create competition for the claims. This competition may increase the amount that pre-bankruptcy creditors can realize on their claims if they are not able to wait until the conclusion of the case. While the structured negotiation inherent in the reorganization process may be desirable when markets do not function properly, one might well argue that the process itself should not keep a market from coming into being. From this perspective, the prospect of profiting by trading in claims should not without more be considered an illicit ulterior motive and should not constitute lack of good faith or disqualify votes of purchased claims.

Confirmation of the Plan

After the vote on the plan, the court must decide whether to confirm the plan. The court must satisfy itself that a plan meets the requirements of Chapter 11, particularly §1129. Section 1129(a)(1) requires a court to review a plan to make sure it complies with "the applicable provisions of this title." Thus, the court is supposed to review things such as classification sua sponte. Two of the more important items the court reviews are the substantive standards for confirmation—the best-interests-of-creditors test and the absolute priority rule. As we have noted, §1129(a)(7) requires that for a plan to be confirmed, either every member of every class must have accepted it or each member that voted against it must receive at least the liquidation value of its claim. Given the costs of asserting its rights under §1129(a)(7), a creditor may be better off consenting to a plan, even if the creditor would have done better in Chapter 7. Moreover, as we have already observed, the valuation procedures under §1129(a)(7) are not rigorous. Section 1129(a)(7) requires us to posit the counterfactual world in which a corporation that properly belongs in Chapter 11 finds itself in Chapter 7 under the control of a trustee, and courts tend to assume that any liquidation that takes place in Chapter 7 involves the piecemeal sale of corporate assets. Finally, bankruptcy judges may use different and less careful valuation procedures than under §1129(b). More casual valuations can work against the creditors' interests, especially if the judge believes that finding in favor of a dissenter will undermine the corporation's prospects for a successful reorganization.

Assume that §1129(a)(7) is satisfied (perhaps because we can avoid rigorous valuations). The plan still has to satisfy the absolute priority rule if a class rejects a plan. Section 1129(a)(8) prevents the plan from being confirmed unless the plan meets the tests set out in §1129(b). Section 1129(b)(2) provides that each class must be paid in full before a class junior to it can get anything. During the era of the equity receiverships, the absolute priority rule was a right that each creditor enjoyed. Under the Bankruptcy Code, however, it applies only to dissenting classes. Section 1129(b)(2) contains three different glosses on the rule, and the one to be applied depends on the nature of the claim or interest of the class on whom the plan is being crammed down. Section 1129(b)(2)(a) deals with the issue of secured claims, §1129(b)(2)(b) with unsecured claims, and §1129(b)(2)(c) with interests. (As noted, the difference between "claim" and "interest" is the difference between debt and equity.) The basic point is this: either the claimants in the senior class must get the full amount of their claims as of the effective date of the plan—a present value concept—or junior classes must get nothing. Junior classes can receive something on account of their former rights against the corporation only if one of two conditions is met: (1) the senior classes, by class-wide vote, consent to their participation; or (2) the senior classes receive payment i`n full.

Junior classes, however, have the right to invoke the procedures of Chapter 11 (and particularly the valuation procedures) in every case. This right can dramatically alter the positions of junior parties from what they would be if the business were sold for cash and the cash parceled out according to nonbankruptcy priorities. Senior creditors may prefer a plan that does not fully compensate them rather than incur the costs of the procedures to which the junior parties would be entitled if they opposed the plan. So long as a class approves the plan, of course, it no longer matters whether the dictates of the absolute priority rule are being met. The court under §1129(a)(11) must be confident that the business will not need to be reorganized again. This requirement is usually called the *feasibility test*. The court, however, must rely on the record before her. Like any other legal rule in a system committed to an adversary process, this requirement has bite only to the extent that those objecting to plan confirmation present the necessary evidence.

The §1111(b) Election

Understanding the rights of a secured creditor under §1129(b) requires a close examination of the special rights the secured creditor is given under §1111(b). Nonrecourse claims are made recourse, and a secured creditor can waive its unsecured claim and have its entire claim treated as secured. Much is unknown about the consequences of making the §1111(b) election, but identifying what is at stake is not difficult. Consider a bank that lends a debtor $1 million. The loan is secured by Blackacre. The loan is nonrecourse. Outside of bankruptcy, the bank can look only to Blackacre for satisfaction of its claim. If Blackacre sells at a foreclosure sale for only $600,000, the bank is out of luck on the remaining $400,000. What would happen in bankruptcy if §1111(b) did not exist? The bankruptcy judge would put a value on the bank's claim. If the judge valued it at $600,000, the bank could be crammed down with a package of rights having a present value of $600,000. The bank would have no unsecured claim because of the nonrecourse nature of the loan. The $400,000 deficiency would simply disappear. Congress introduced the §1111(b) election because it thought that a bankruptcy judge should not be able to eliminate the bank's deficiency with the stroke of a valuation pen.

The problem that Congress addressed in §1111(b) gained wide attention after *Great National Life Insurance Company v. Pine Gate Associates*, a decision under the old 1898 Act.[27] In that case, a nonrecourse secured creditor unsuccessfully objected to a plan in which its collateral would be appraised and the creditor would be paid the appraised value. The secured creditor wanted either to be paid in full or to have the property surrendered to it. If the appraisal was done correctly, of course, the secured creditor would have been paid as much as it would have received if it sold the property, but the secured creditor may have feared that the appraisal would not be done correctly. Because its claim was nonrecourse, it had no unsecured claim for any deficiency and hence no vote in the reorganization. Section 1111(b) responds to this situation—known as the *Pine Gate* problem—first by saying that all loans, whether or not they are recourse outside of bankruptcy, are recourse in Chapter 11. Thus, the bank mentioned in our example above will (unless it elects differently) have a $400,000 unsecured deficiency claim. By holding this claim, the bank can vote with the unsecured creditors.

Section 1111(b) also gives the secured creditor an *election*. If the election is made, the creditor is deemed to have a secured claim for the entire amount of the debt, irrespective of the collateral's value. Thus, in the above example, the bank would have a secured claim of $1 million, not $600,000. The bank does not, however, receive a stream of payments worth $1 million.

[27] 2 B.C.D. 1478 (Bankr. N.D. Ga. 1976).

Under §1129(b)(2)(a)(i)(II) the bank would be given a stream of payments with a *present value* of $600,000. (The section provides that the stream of payments must equal "the value of such holder's interest in the estate's interest in such property." The court has valued the property at $600,000.) In this respect, the bank is treated no better or worse than if it had not made the election. By making the election, the bank gives up its deficiency claim of $400,000, and in return it receives the right to a stream of payments with a face amount equal to $1 million. Moreover, the stream of payments is secured by a *lien* of $1 million instead of $600,000. In many cases, the term of the loan is long enough that a note can have a present value of $600,000 and still have a stream of payments over $1 million. In such a case, the §1111(b) election benefits a secured creditor only if the court undervalued the property *and* there is likely to be either a default in the near future or a sale that would accelerate the $1 million obligation.

Implementing the Absolute Priority Rule

The Supreme Court set out the contours of the absolute priority rule in *Bank of America v. 203 North LaSalle Street Partnership*.[28] In that case a group of real estate investors acquired fifteen floors of an office building in downtown Chicago and obtained a nonrecourse mortgage from a bank. Real estate values dropped in the early 1990s, and the partners sought to restructure the bank's loan in Chapter 11. The partnership offered a plan that, in its view, left the bank with more than it would receive through a state law foreclosure yet allowed the prebankruptcy investors in the partnership to remain as owners and enjoy significant tax benefits. When the bank turned down the partnership's plan, the bankruptcy court had to decide whether the plan could be confirmed over the bank's objection. The precise legal issue can be set out simply. To the extent that it was owed more than its collateral was worth, the bank held an un-

---

[28] 526 U.S. 434 (1999).

secured deficiency claim in addition to its secured claim. The Seventh Circuit had already decided that the bank's §1111(b) deficiency had to be put in a class by itself.[29] Hence, when the bank voted against the plan, a class of unsecured claims necessarily voted against it as well. Section 1129(b)(2) of the Bankruptcy Code provides that when a class of unsecured claims dissents from a reorganization plan and is not being paid in full, a plan is fair and equitable only if, among other things, "the holder of any [junior] interest . . . will not receive or retain under the plan on account of such junior . . . interest any property."

In writing for the Court, Justice Souter found that this language required adherence to "absolute priority." Under a regime of absolute priority, old equity cannot receive any "property" if a dissenting class was not being paid in full. A plan that gives old equity the exclusive right to acquire the new equity gives them property within the meaning of §1129(b). As Justice Thomas recognized in his concurring opinion, the plan, in substance, gave the old equityholders the exclusive right to the equity of the reorganized entity. Such an exclusive right was a stock option, something ordinarily regarded as property and thus property within the meaning of the statute. Hence, equity could not participate without the process being opened up.

If old equity could participate at all, it had to contribute an infusion of new capital. Moreover, old equity could not be given any breaks. Old equity had to pay top dollar for the new interest. As we have noted elsewhere, *LaSalle* requires that bankruptcy judges implement the Bankruptcy Code in a way that ensures—by the use of market-based and other mechanisms—that the value of nonbankruptcy rights is preserved. In practice, bankruptcy judges now lift exclusivity when the debtor files a plan in which old equity contributes new value in return for a share of the reorganized corporation. Often the senior lender is a bank that has a security interest in all of the debtor's assets, and lifting exclusivity allows the bank to file its

---

[29] See In re Woodbrook Associates, 19 F.3d 312 (7th Cir 1994).

own plan. The bank's plan might propose a sale of the assets to the highest bidder. Because it has the senior security interest, the bank is entitled to the proceeds of the sale up to the amount of its claim. Hence, the bank can effortlessly offer a cash bid equal to its claim as any money it pays in will be returned instantly. As a matter of practice, at such sales the bank is allowed to *credit bid*. It can bid the amount of its claim without having to produce the cash that would come back to it anyway.

When multiple plans on the table satisfy §1129, the Bankruptcy Code charges the bankruptcy judge with choosing a plan after considering "the preferences of creditors and equity security holders." This provision is not helpful, as such preferences will likely go in opposite directions in cases of any moment. *LaSalle* itself also gives no guidance for the judge to follow in choosing among multiple plans. An interesting situation arises when a corporation has a future as a going concern only if its current owner-manager remains in place. A senior creditor typically will be owed more than the assets are worth, but if the senior creditor and the owner-manager could have reached a deal, the corporation would not be in Chapter 11. In many cases, the problem turns on valuation issues. The plan promises a package of rights that is hard to value. If the external market tests *LaSalle* requires are ignored, there is a built-in bias even when judges give accurate valuations. A judge in reviewing the plan might give an unbiased estimate of the value of the assets, but the debtor would systematically benefit as it loses nothing if the judge sets the value too high and profits if the value is set too low.[30] A serious conceptual issue exists, however, even if there is no dispute about valuations.

Consider the following case. There is a dinner theater in the suburbs of a large city. Its manager is the sole shareholder. He had only a modest career in Hollywood, but his gregarious good nature allowed him to develop many contacts with famous entertainers. He is able to persuade many of them to ap-

---

[30] See Kham & Nate's Shoes No. 2 v. First Bank, 908 F.2d 1351, 1360 (7th Cir. 1990).

pear at the dinner theater, but construction cost overruns and lackluster ticket sales lead the dinner theater to file under Chapter 11. Bank has a security interest in all of the dinner theater's assets, both tangible and intangible. It is owed $10 million. A number of trade creditors are owed a total of $4 million. During the reorganization, the dinner theater's assets are appraised at between $5 and $6 million. The dinner theater has no long-term contract with the manager, and he has made it clear that he will continue to run the dinner theater only if he owns the equity.

The manager proposes a reorganization plan. He has found an investor who is willing to invest $6 million cash in the business. The manager will put up $2 million of his own money, also in cash. Under the plan, the bank will receive a one-time cash payment of $7 million. The remaining $1 million will be reinvested in the business. The general creditors will receive a $1 million note, secured by all of the dinner theater's assets. The investor will take an unsecured $6 million note, and the manager will retain the equity. In most plans, of course, we would not find an outside investor willing to put up cash. To focus on the conceptual problem, however, we want to eliminate the disputes that arise whenever payment takes a form other than cash.

The bank objects to the confirmation of this plan. It asks the judge to lift exclusivity and allow it to propose a plan in which the property is auctioned off. Because it is the most senior creditor, the bank will receive the proceeds of the auction. Hence, the bank can either make a cash bid equal to its secured claim or—in what amounts to the same thing—credit bid the amount of its claim. The bank is not in fact putting $10 million on the line even though it is ostensibly making a cash bid. Any amount it bids in excess of the manager's bid and less than its claim will give it control of the assets without requiring it to make any additional contribution to the venture. An auction of the assets under these circumstances is no different from lifting the stay and allowing the bank to repossess.

The bank's behavior seems hard to explain. The manager is bringing something of value to the party. Old equity in *LaSalle* had tax benefits they wanted to preserve. For this reason, they were willing to give the bank any amount greater than it could hope to realize upon foreclosure. Similarly, in this case, the manager values the assets more than anyone else. (He is willing to pay $8 million in cash for them when no one else is willing to pay more than $6 million.) In many Chapter 11 cases, the debtor's plan on its face appears to give more to the creditors than a liquidating plan but its valuations are soft. Here, as in *LaSalle*, they are not. Indeed, after *LaSalle*, someone in the manager's position has to be able to show a willingness to pay top dollar. At a minimum, there has to be something that he is bringing to the party that makes him willing to pay more for the assets, whether it is contacts in show business or, as in *LaSalle*, tax benefits that only old equity could enjoy.

There are several possible explanations for the bank's behavior. First, the bank might want the ability to insist on its own right to take control of the property so it can strike a better deal with the old investors. The manager was willing to pay $2 million over the liquidation value to keep the dinner theater. If the bank can insist on the ability to liquidate, it might get the manager to pay even more. Similarly, in *LaSalle*, old equity offered $4.1 million over the value of the property because they were getting $20 million in tax benefits. The bank might have thought that by being hard-nosed it could get more. Alternatively, the bank may want to establish its reputation as a tough negotiator in future cases. Financial institutions are repeat players in bankruptcy and will be negotiating with the same lawyers and professionals in other cases. There is also the possibility that the bank (or its employees) are not negotiating rationally. Under our assumptions, for whatever reason, the bank and the manager have been unable to reach a deal even though agreement would be in their mutual self-interest.

We can approach this problem two different ways. One way is to note that outside of bankruptcy, few think it appropriate for a court to force a deal on large financial institutions and entrepreneurs on the ground that it is in their own self-interest. Given the lenders' ability to obtain blanket security interests, many reorganizations involve, for practical purposes, only two parties. Two sophisticated professionals have been unable to reach agreement, even though a mutually beneficial bargain between them seems possible. Such a situation may be a poor candidate for judicial intervention. Modern Chapter 11 cases are not like the nineteenth-century railroad reorganizations with dozens of different types of secured creditors. Two parties will sometimes fail to reach a deal with each other, through either avarice, stupidity, or miscalculation, but courts are likely to make matters worse rather than better if they intervene, whether inside or outside of bankruptcy.

We might take a different approach. A judge who confirms the dinner theater's plan makes not only the manager but also the general creditors better off than they would be under the bank's plan. The added value is coming not at the expense of the bank, but because of an asset (the manager's connections and expertise) in which the bank has no security interest. Under this view, it is emphatically the mission of bankruptcy law to bring about value-enhancing restructurings when multiple people have claims against assets. This debate over the fundamental purpose of bankruptcy remains unresolved.

A problem of a different sort arises when a senior creditor reaches a separate deal with an equityholder or someone else junior to a class that is not being paid in full. The senior creditor may find it useful to make peace with such a person, especially if the person might challenge the validity of its security interest or otherwise delay the bankruptcy process. There are two ways of characterizing such a transaction. According to one view, the secured creditor is entirely free to allocate its share of the reorganized entity as it pleases, just as it can with any other asset it owns.[31] "Carve outs" are, after all, a regular part of bankruptcy practice. Under the opposite view, a reor-

---

[31] Official Unsecured Creditors Committee v. Stern (In re SPM Manufacturing Co.), 984 F.2d 1305 (1st Cir. 1993).

ganization plan that, in form, includes equityholders while bypassing general creditors violates the absolute priority rule. Indeed, it is precisely the transaction struck down in *Boyd*.[32]

In understanding this problem, as with any other that lacks an easy answer, we must return to first principles, but in doing this, we should understand both bankruptcy law and its limits. Legal rules cannot cure nonlegal problems. Legal rules cannot make the imprudent wise and the unlucky fortunate. Nor can they insulate a poorly run business from the realities of the marketplace. The goals of bankruptcy are necessarily modest. Honest but unfortunate individuals should be given a fresh start. Corporations that have value as going concerns should be able to acquire a new capital structure, and those that cannot survive should be able to wrap up their affairs expeditiously. Bankruptcy law cannot work miracles, and more harm than good comes from seeking that which cannot be had. We should, in our efforts to make the bankruptcy system work, recall what my late colleague and mentor Walter Blum often observed: in law, 95 percent is perfection.

[32] See In re Armstrong World Industries, Inc., 320 Bankr. 523 (D. Del. 2005).

Table of Cases

Table of Statutes

Index